# EASY, ECO~~~
## ALWAYS DELICIOUS!

That's why everyone, especially the busy cook, loves a good chicken dinner. And now making that dinner extra-special is no mystery. FAMILY CIRCLE GREAT CHICKEN RECIPES shows you how to

- Buy the best chicken for your family and your budget
- Cut and bone a whole chicken at home
- Cook ahead for a hungry crowd
- Get dinner on the table in under an hour
- Carve a roaster neatly and quickly
- Make dieting delightful with low-calorie chicken
- Enhance your cooking with a touch of wine
- Serve up supper with a foreign flair
- And much, much more!

# Family Circle
# Great Chicken Recipes

Edited by Nancy A. Hecht

*All recipes tested in the*
*Family Circle's Kitchens*

BALLANTINE BOOKS • NEW YORK

With acknowledgments to National Broiler Council.

Library of Congress Catalog Card Number: 72-77161

ISBN 0-345-25943-2

This edition published by arrangement with
The Family Circle, Inc., an Iowa Corporation

Manufactured in the United States of America

First Ballantine Books Edition: February 1978
Second Printing: December 1979

First Canadian Printing: March 1978

# Contents

# In Answer to Every Request

We've all been there: In the meat department standing on one foot and then the other trying to decide what to have for dinner tonight, tomorrow and next Saturday when company's due. When pressed for time, we occasionally end up buying the most convenient but expensive meats.

That's the great thing about chicken. It's convenient but it's also economical, nutritious, low in calories and delicate in flavor. It can be prepared any way you like, is good hot or cold, for a large crowd or for one. And it's a natural for make-ahead dinners and inspired leftovers. In other words, chicken answers every request for enjoyable, practical meals.

The following recipes and cooking suggestions, all carefully tested by Family Circle's Food Staff, are dedicated to you and to the idea that food doesn't have to be expensive to be good.

# Chapter 1

# Supermarket Guidelines

The variety is incredible. Chicken is prepared for market in over 30 different ready-to-cook ways. It's economical, nutritious, easy-to-digest and can be prepared by every known cooking method.

How you buy chicken will naturally depend on your budget and family preferences. Whole chicken, of all the varieties available, is the least expensive. Cut-up chicken and chicken in parts may cost slightly more but will save you time in the kitchen. Parts such as chicken breasts are also more, but if your family prefers white meat this is a sensible way to buy. However you buy, you can be assured of a good buy. Chicken is lower in cost per pound of edible cooked meat than any other leading type of meat. It's government inspected for healthiness under the U.S.D.A.'s Wholesome Poultry Inspection Act and is marked accordingly for your protection.

## Before You Buy

Before you buy chicken, consider how you plan to use it. Do you want a special company dish, meat for soup, a roast, enough for a large gang? There are five age categories and general sizes of chicken to choose from and each is ideally suited for preparing numerous ways.

*Rock Cornish:* The smallest, youngest member of the chicken family, suitable for roasting, especially with a nice stuffing. May also be baked, broiled or fried. It usually weighs 1½ pounds or less; many people serve an individual bird to each person.

*Broiler-Fryer:* The all-purpose chicken, a young meaty bird about 9 weeks old that weighs 1½ to 3½ pounds. Don't be deceived by its name. A broiler-fryer can be cooked by any method—roasted, barbecued, broiled, sautéed, fried, etc. And it's available whole, halved, quartered, cut up in serving-size pieces, or in specific parts such as breast, thighs, drumsticks or wings.

*Roaster:* A little older and larger than the broiler-fryer, the roaster weighs 3½ to 5 pounds, is about 12 weeks old, and has tender meat.

*Capon:* A larger bird, weighing about 4 to 7 pounds, with a fine flavor and a good amount of white meat. This young, plump chicken is most often roasted.

*Broiler Hen or Stewing Chicken:* A plump, meaty laying hen, about 1½ years old, 3½ to 7 pounds in weight, that makes an excellent soup and does well in dishes that call for leisurely simmering, stewing or braising. Provides ample tender meat for dishes made with "cooked chicken" such as chicken pies, stews, salads or casseroles.

All five types of chicken come packaged in a large variety of ways; see pages 8 and 9 for a look at some of the more familiar.

## Packaging:

There's a pack for every cooking purpose. Here are some of the choices.

*Whole chicken* consists of over 50 percent meat. When you buy a 2-pound chicken, you can expect at least 1 pound of meat.

*Chicken halves and quarters* come packaged in 1½- to 2½-pound weights. One serving is one half or one quarter.

*Packaged chicken pieces* include the drumstick, thighs, breasts and wings. One serving is ½ breast, a thigh, drumstick or several smaller pieces.

*Breasts* have the greatest amount of meat to the piece. One serving is ½ breast.

*Thighs and drumsticks* are delicious dark meat in convenient form.

*Wings* are great party fare. Allow 2 for each serving.
*Chicken livers* are delicious and reasonable. Allow
¼ pound per serving.

## New Chicken Products

In addition to the more familiar types of packaging,
considerable work is being done in developing new
products with chicken. Such items as chicken frankfurters, chicken bologna, chicken sticks, smoked
chicken and chicken loaf are more and more finding
their way into supermarkets, along with such convenience products as chicken nuggets, party packs of
wings, chicken and chips (a chicken and potato combination), and pouch pack chicken fricassee. Frozen
whole chickens and parts are increasing in popularity,
too, as are boneless breasts and thighs.

## How Much Will You Need?

*For frying or roasting* allow ¾ to 1 pound per
serving.
*For broiling or barbecuing* allow ½ chicken or 1
pound per serving.
*For stewing* allow ½ pound to 1 pound per serving.
*Note:* A 3-pound bird yields 4 servings; a 2-pound
bird yields 2 servings.

## Fresh Chicken

Fresh chicken is best for same-day or next-day
cooking.
When you get home from the supermarket, remove
the store wrapping. Rewrap in wax paper, foil or transparent wrap and place chicken in the meat compartment or the coldest shelf of your refrigerator. Store
giblets separately and cook within 24 hours.
To freeze fresh chicken, again remove the store
wrapping, discard the backing board or tray and rinse

the chicken in cold running water. Pat dry, then wrap in transparent wrap, foil or freezer paper and place in your freezer. It will keep up to 12 months.

Note: Never freeze an uncooked chicken if you've stuffed it. The stuffing will sour.

## Frozen Chicken

Hard-frozen chicken may go right from your shopping cart into your freezer without rewrapping. However, do not allow it to thaw at all. If it has thawed in the store or in getting it home, cook it promptly and then freeze it, if you wish. Never refreeze thawed, uncooked chicken. If you are making a stew, chicken can go right into the pot from the freezer. If you're using it for fried, broiled, barbecued or roasted dishes, thaw it first. It will cook more evenly that way.

*To defrost:* Take chicken out of the freezer a day or two ahead and put it in the refrigerator. Don't unwrap it, because the skin tends to dry and toughen when exposed to air. To defrost chicken faster, place it (still wrapped) under cold running water.

## Cooked Chicken

Keep chicken that has been cooked for no more than 2 or 3 days in the coldest part of your refrigerator. Always refrigerate broth or gravy in separate containers, and remove any stuffing from stuffed birds; store separately, too.

*To freeze cooked chicken:* Wrap in transparent freezer wrap or aluminum foil, label with the amount and date. Use within 4 months.

ROASTING TIMETABLE FOR BROILER-FRYERS AND YOUNG ROASTING CHICKENS

After preparing chicken for roasting, roast according to the following timetable. If broiler-fryer is stuffed, increase the total roasting time by 15 minutes. To test for doneness, drumstick meat should feel soft when pressed between fingers, and leg should twist easily out of thigh joint.

| WEIGHT | TEMP | TIME PER POUND | TOTAL TIME |
|---|---|---|---|
| 1½ lb | 400° | 40 min | 1 hour |
| 2 lb | 400° | 35 min | 1 hour, 10 min |
| 2½ lb | 375° | 30 min | 1 hour, 15 min |
| 3 lb | 375° | 30 min | 1 hour, 30 min |
| 3½ lb | 375° | 30 min | 1 hour, 45 min |
| 4 lb | 375° | 30 min | 2 hours |
| 4½ lb | 375° | 30 min | 2 hours, 15 min |
| 5 lb | 375° | 30 min | 2 hours, 30 min |

# How to Cut and Bone a Chicken

1. Place chicken breast side up. Using a sharp knife, make lengthwise slit through skin and flesh from neck to cavity. Turn bird over and repeat cut.

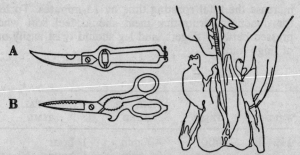

2. Using poultry shears (A) or kitchen shears (B), cut right through bones (ribs). Cutting to one side of breastbone is easier than cutting through it.

3. Turn chicken over. Cut through bones, cutting to one side of the backbone. You may remove backbone. A small bird is cut this way for serving.

4. For quartering chicken, continue using shears. Cut across half the bird, following the natural division just below the rib cage and the breastbone.

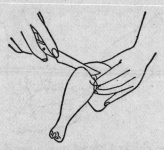

5. Thigh may be left attached to leg for broiling; but for frying, bend leg joint. Cut through joint with a sharp knife, separating leg from the thigh.

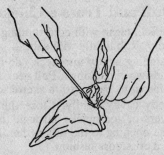

6. To separate wing from the breast, bend joint. Cut through joint with a sharp knife. The chicken will now be in eight pieces and ready for frying.

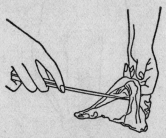

7. If your recipe calls for skinned chicken breasts, use a sharp, small paring knife to start, then slip fingers between skin and flesh and peel skin.

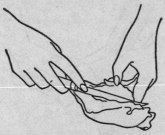

8. To bone chicken breast, use a small paring knife. Cut meat away from rib bones with quick little strokes, feeling your way along with your fingers.

## How to Stuff and Truss a Chicken

First rinse chicken clean with cold running water inside and out. Pat dry. Rub lightly with salt.

1. Spoon stuffing lightly into neck (do not pack, for stuffing expands when cooking). Pull neck skin over the opening and fasten to back with a skewer or toothpick.

2. Stuff body cavity lightly. Close the opening by running skewers or toothpicks through the skin from one side of the opening to the other; then lace securely with string in a crisscross fashion.

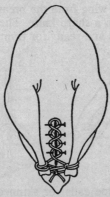

3. Loop the same string around the drumstick ends and tie them together, then fasten them to the tailpiece.

4. Fold wings up and over the back; this will help brace the chicken in the roasting pan.

Brush chicken lightly with melted butter or margarine and place, breast up, in a roasting pan.

*Or, if barbecuing on a spit:*

Press wings close to breast and run a string around under the chicken to completely encircle it, securing the wings snugly against the breast. The chicken should be tied so it makes a compact bundle.

## How to Carve a Chicken

1. Use a sharp, thin-bladed knife and long-tined fork. Remove all trussing equipment from the chicken —skewers, toothpicks, cord or thread. Then, place the

chicken breast-up on a serving platter or carving board in front of you. The legs should be toward your right. Grasp end of legs nearest you and bend it down toward the platter while you cut through thigh joint to separate whole leg from body. Separate drumstick and thigh by cutting through joint.

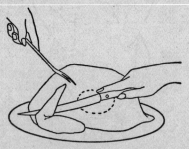

2. Stick fork into breast near breastbone and cut off wing close to body. Slanting knife inward slightly may make it easier to hit the joint.

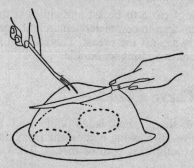

3. Slice white meat starting at tip of breastbone and cutting down toward wing joint. Repeat with other side of chicken, turning platter if necessary.

## Chapter 2

# Menu Ideas

Put these menus into action the very next time you have guests for dinner. They're designed to put you at ease during important entertaining moments and they illustrate chicken's ability to blend with seasonings, side dishes and other courses. Try the menus and then create your own to go with all our chicken recipes.

### EASYGOING BUFFET

*Pineapple Juice*
*Cheese Bread*
*\* Chicken a la Orange*
*\* Chive Risotto          Creamed Peas*
*Salad Bowl*
*Raspberry Sherbet*
*Coffee*

# CHICKEN A LA ORANGE

*Bake at 350° for 1 hour.*
*Makes 8 servings.*

8 boneless chicken breasts (about 10 ounces each)
⅓ cup flour
1½ teaspoons salt
1 teaspoon garlic powder
½ teaspoon paprika
⅓ cup sliced almonds
5 tablespoons butter or margarine

1 can (6 ounces) frozen concentrated orange juice
1½ cups water
1 teaspoon leaf rosemary, crumbled
¼ teaspoon leaf thyme, crumbled
2 tablespoons cornstarch
Chive Risotto

1. Coat chicken with a mixture of flour, 1 teaspoon salt, garlic powder and paprika.
2. Sauté almonds in butter or margarine until golden in a large frying pan; remove from pan. Brown chicken breasts in drippings in same pan; place in a single layer in a baking pan, 13x9x2. Pour all drippings from pan.
3. Stir orange-juice concentrate, water, rosemary, thyme and ½ teaspoon salt into pan. Heat to boiling; pour over chicken; cover.
4. Bake in moderate oven (350°) 1 hour, or until chicken is tender. Remove to another pan; keep warm. Reheat liquid in baking pan to boiling; thicken with cornstarch.
5. Spoon Chive Risotto onto a large serving platter; arrange chicken over rice; sprinkle with almonds. Serve sauce separately to spoon over chicken.

# CHIVE RISOTTO

Sauté 2½ cups packaged enriched precooked rice in 3 tablespoons butter or margarine, stirring constantly, until golden in a large frying pan. Drain liquid from 2 cans (3 or 4 ounces each) chopped mushrooms into a 4-cup measure; add water to make 2½ cups. Stir into rice with mushrooms, 3 envelopes instant chicken broth and ¼ cup cut chives. Heat to boiling; cover; remove from heat. Let stand 10 minutes. Makes 8 servings.

## HOLIDAY SPECIAL

*Bouillon Soup*
*\* Cornish Hens Indienne*
*\* Parsley Rice*     *Buttered Carrots*
*Salad*
*Cloverleaf Rolls*

## CORNISH HENS INDIENNE

*Roast at 375° for 1 hour and 20 minutes.*
*Makes 6 servings.*

| | |
|---|---|
| 6 frozen Rock Cornish game hens ( about 1 pound each), thawed | 1 tablespoon flour |
| | 1 tablespoon sugar |
| | 2 teaspoons curry powder |
| Salt | |
| ¼ teaspoon pepper | 2 teaspoons instant chicken bouillon |
| ¼ teaspoon leaf thyme, crumbled | |
| | 1 cup apricot nectar |
| ½ cup (1 stick) butter or margarine, melted | 1 tablespoon lemon juice |
| 4 slices bacon, diced | Parsley Rice |
| 1 medium-size onion, chopped (½ cup) | Buttered carrots |

1. Remove giblets from body cavities of hens and save to simmer for soup. Rinse hens inside and out; pat dry with paper toweling.

2. Mix 1 teaspoon salt with pepper and thyme in a cup; sprinkle ¼ teaspoonful inside each hen; tie legs together. Place hens, breast side up, in a jellyroll pan. Brush with part of the melted butter or margarine.

3. Roast in moderate oven (375°), brushing once or twice with remaining melted butter or margarine and

drippings in pan, 1 hour. Cut away strings with scissors; spoon all drippings from pan.

4. While hens roast, sauté bacon until almost crisp in a medium-size saucepan; remove with a slotted spoon and drain on paper toweling. Stir onion into drippings; sauté until soft.

5. Blend in flour, sugar, curry powder, chicken bouillon and ½ teaspoon salt; cook, stirring constantly, until bubbly. Stir in apricot nectar and lemon juice. Heat, stirring contantly, to boiling; simmer 5 minutes, or until mixture thickens slightly; spoon about half over hens.

6. Roast 10 minutes; spoon remaining curry mixture over top to make a thick coating. Continue roasting 10 minutes, or until hens are tender and richly glazed.

7. Spread rice on a large deep serving platter; arrange hens on top. Spoon carrots at each end.


## PARSLEY RICE

Combine 1 cup uncooked rice, 2 tablespoons butter or margarine, 2 teaspoons instant chicken bouillon and 2¼ cups boiling water in a 6-cup baking dish; cover. Bake along with hens in moderate oven (375°) 1 hour, or until rice is tender and liquid is absorbed. Fluff rice with a fork; stir in ¼ cup chopped parsley. Makes 6 servings.


### SUNDAY, SUNDAY

*Deviled Eggs*
*\* Parisian Chicken Roasts*
*Fried Apple Slices*
*Potatoes and Peas in Cream*
*Green Beans*
*Salad*
*Crescent Rolls*

# PARISIAN CHICKEN ROASTS

*Roast at 400° for 1 hour and 15 minutes.*
*Makes 6 servings.*

| | |
|---|---|
| 3 broiler-fryers (about 2½ pounds each) | 1 teaspoon salt |
| ¾ cup (1½ sticks) butter or margarine | ¼ teaspoon pepper |
| | ⅔ cup lemon marmalade |

1. Remove giblets from body cavities of chickens; save to simmer for soup. Rinse chickens inside and out; pat dry. Tie legs together. Place, breast side up, on a rack in a roasting pan.

2. Melt butter or margarine in a small saucepan; stir in salt and pepper; brush part over chickens.

3. Roast in hot oven (400°), brushing once with more butter mixture, 45 minutes.

4. While chickens cook, stir lemon marmalade into remaining butter mixture; heat slowly, stirring constantly, until marmalade melts. Brush half over chickens.

5. Roast 15 minutes; brush with remaining marmalade mixture. Roast 15 minutes longer, or until chickens are tender and richly glazed.

6. Place on a large serving platter; cut away strings. Overlap fried apple slices around edge of platter. Carve chickens into serving-size pieces.

## Chapter 3

# Appetizers, Pâtés and Dips

Some like them hot, some like them cold. Regardless of the preference, we're sure you'll agree appetizers are one of the biggest assets a hostess can have. They allow you time to visit with guests before disappearing into the kitchen for last-minute dinner preparations, and they help stimulate appetites for that glorious meal you've been working on.

Since chicken is easy to prepare and has the ability to blend well with so many foods and seasonings, it becomes an extremely good choice for the appetizer tray. Our recipes show how to combine it with eggs, mushrooms, ham, shrimp, cheese, sour cream and just about all the herbs and spices you can think of.

The combinations range from finger chicken served with sauces to molds and chafing dish specials. All add up to a delightful way to begin an evening.

## FINGER DRUMSTICKS

*Pick-me-ups, garnished with lemon slices and served hot from a chafing dish.*

*Bake at 400° for 1 hour and 10 minutes.*
*Makes 12 servings.*

| | |
|---|---|
| 3 pounds small chicken wings (about 15) | ½ teaspoon ground ginger |
| ½ cup sugar | ¼ teaspoon pepper |
| 3 tablespoons cornstarch | ¾ cup water |
| 1 teaspoon salt | ⅓ cup lemon juice |
| | ¼ cup soy sauce |

16

1. Singe chicken wings, if needed. Cut off tips and discard. Divide each wing in half by cutting through joint with a sharp knife. Place in a single layer on broiler pan rack.

2. Bake in hot oven (400°), turning once, 30 minutes.

3. Mix sugar, cornstarch, salt, ginger and pepper in a small saucepan; stir in water, lemon juice and soy sauce. Cook, stirring constantly, until mixture thickens and boils 3 minutes. Brush part over chicken wings.

4. Continue baking, turning and brushing several times with remaining lemon mixture, 40 minutes, or until richly glazed.

5. When ready to serve, place in a chafing dish or keep-hot server. Frame with a ring of thin lemon slices, if you wish. Serve hot.


# GOLDEN CHICKEN NUGGETS

*These make-aheads will disappear fast at your next get-together.*

*Bake at 400° for 10 minutes.*
*Makes 4 to 5 dozen nuggets.*

| | |
|---|---|
| 4 whole chicken breasts | 1 teaspoon salt |
| ½ cup unseasoned fine dry bread crumbs | 1 teaspoon dried leaf thyme |
| ¼ cup grated Parmesan cheese | 1 teaspoon dried leaf basil |
| 2 teaspoons monosodium glutamate | ½ cup butter or margarine, melted |

1. Bone chicken breasts; remove skin. Cut each breast half into 6 to 8 nuggets, about 1½ inches square.

2. Combine bread crumbs, cheese, monosodium glutamate, salt and herbs.

3. Dip chicken nuggets in melted butter, then in crumb mixture. Place in single layer on foil-lined baking sheets. Bake in hot oven (400°) 10 minutes. Chill until ready to use.

# CHICKEN AND SHRIMPS MARENGO

*For favorite guests—here's a festive appetizer, served in a chafing dish, warmer or scallop shells.*

*Makes 8 servings.*

| | |
|---|---|
| 1 **chicken breast** (about 12 ounces) | 1 **can** (2¼ **ounces**) **deviled ham** |
| 4 **tablespoons vegetable oil** | 1 **can** (8 **ounces**) **stewed tomatoes** |
| ½ **teaspoon monosodium glutamate** | 1 **can** (3 or 4 **ounces**) **whole mushrooms** |
| 1 **large onion, chopped** (1 cup) | 1 **teaspoon Worcestershire sauce** |
| 1 **clove garlic, minced** | 1 **pound fresh shrimps, shelled and deveined** |
| 2 **tablespoons flour** | **Chopped parsley** |

1. Pull skin from chicken breast; cut meat from bones in two large pieces, then cut into 1-inch pieces.

2. Brown in 2 tablespoons of the vegetable oil in a medium-size frying pan; sprinkle with monosodium glutamate; cover. Cook slowly 15 minutes, or until tender.

3. While chicken cooks, sauté onion and garlic until soft in remaining 2 tablespoons vegetable oil in a second medium-size frying pan; blend in flour; cook, stirring constantly, until bubbly.

4. Blend in deviled ham, then stir in tomatoes, mushrooms and their liquid, and Worcestershire sauce. Cook, stirring constantly, until mixture thickens and boils 1 minute; remove chicken from its frying pan with a slotted spoon and stir into sauce.

5. Stir shrimps into chicken drippings in frying pan; cook slowly, turning once, 10 minutes, or until tender. Stir into sauce mixture.

6. Spoon into scallop shells, a chafing dish or a keep-hot server; sprinkle with chopped parsley. Serve with small triangles of crisp toast, if you wish.

# PÂTÉ CONTINENTAL

*It's a lot of work and must be made well ahead, but the result is a beautiful pâté loaf to grace a party table.*

*Bake at 350° for 1½ hours.*
*Makes 8 servings.*

| | |
|---|---|
| 1 pound beef liver | 2 eggs, beaten |
| ½ pound chicken livers | ¼ teaspoon ground allspice |
| 1 medium-size onion, chopped (½ cup) | ¼ teaspoon leaf thyme, crumbled |
| 2 tablespoons butter or margarine | 5 slices bacon |
| ¼ cup water | Beef Aspic |
| 1 envelope instant chicken broth OR 1 chicken bouillon cube | 1 hard-cooked egg, shelled |

1. Snip out any large tubelike membranes from beef liver; cut into chunks. Halve chicken livers; snip out veiny parts or skin.

2. Put both meats through a food chopper, using a fine blade; place in a medium-size bowl.

3. Sauté onion in butter or margarine until soft in a small frying pan; stir in water and chicken broth or bouillon cube; heat to boiling, crushing bouillon cube, if used, with a spoon; stir into liver mixture with eggs, allspice and thyme.

4. Place 3 slices of the bacon in a loaf pan, 5x3x2; spoon in liver mixture; top with remaining bacon. Cover pan tightly with foil.

5. Set in baking pan on oven shelf; pour boiling water into pan to depth of about 1 inch.

6. Bake in moderate oven (350°) 1½ hours, or until loaf starts to pull away from sides of pan; remove from pan of water; take off foil. Cool loaf, then chill overnight.

7. Make Beef Aspic.

8. Peel bacon from top of loaf; loosen loaf around edges with a knife; invert onto a plate; peel off remaining bacon. Wash pan and dry well.

9. Pour ¼ cup of the aspic into loaf pan; place in a pan of ice and water to speed setting; chill just until sticky-firm.

10. While layer chills, halve hard-cooked egg lengthwise, cutting just through the white. Slice yolk carefully; cut white into 8 or 10 tiny flower shapes with a truffle cutter.

11. Arrange two of the yolk slices and white cutouts in a pretty pattern on sticky-firm aspic in pan; carefully pour in another ½ cup aspic; let set until sticky-firm.

12. Place pâté loaf over aspic layer in pan; pour in enough of the remaining aspic to fill pan to rim. Remove from ice and water; chill in refrigerator at least 4 hours, or until aspic is firm. Pour remaining aspic into a pan, 8x8x2; chill.

13. Just before serving, run a sharp-tip thin-blade knife around top of loaf, then dip pan *very quickly* in and out of hot water. Cover pan with a chilled serving plate; turn upside down; gently lift off pan.

14. Cut remaining aspic layer into tiny cubes; spoon around pâté loaf. Garnish with radish flowers and snips of radish leaves.

To make radish flowers, trim large radishes. Holding each, tip end up, cut lengthwise into 10 or 12 sections, not quite to stem. Place in ice and water until "petals" open up.

## BEEF ASPIC

Soften 1 envelope unflavored gelatin in ¾ cup cold water in a small saucepan; heat, stirring constantly, just until gelatin dissolves; remove from heat. Stir in 1 can condensed beef consommé and 2 tablespoons lemon juice. Cool.

## ORANGE CHICKEN D'OEUVRE

*A glamorous appetizer served with a zesty orange sauce.*

*Bake at 400° for 15 minutes.*
*Makes 6 appetizer servings (24 to 30 balls).*

| | |
|---|---|
| 2 cups ground cooked chicken | 1 teaspoon minced onion |
| ½ cup fine soft bread crumbs | 1 egg |
| 1 teaspoon salt | 1 tablespoon chicken broth |
| ¼ teaspoon pepper | |

1. Combine all ingredients in medium bowl. Form into balls ¾ to 1 inch in diameter.
2. Place on greased baking sheet. Bake in hot oven (400°) for 15 minutes.
3. Place in small chafing dish; add Orange Sauce and keep warm; serve with cocktail picks. Or serve on cocktail picks, with Orange Sauce as a dip.

## ORANGE SAUCE

| | |
|---|---|
| ½ cup currant jelly | 1 tablespoon chopped dill OR 1 teaspoon dried dill weed |
| ½ teaspoon minced onion | |
| ¼ teaspoon red-pepper sauce | 1½ cups orange juice |
| ¾ teaspoon salt | 2 tablespoons corn-starch |
| ½ teaspoon dry mustard | 2 tablespoons cold water |
| ¼ teaspoon ginger | |

1. In small saucepan heat currant jelly, onion, red-pepper sauce, salt, dry mustard, ginger, dill and orange juice until boiling.
2. Blend cornstarch with cold water and stir into mixture in saucepan. Cook until thickened, stirring constantly.

# CHICKEN CANAPÉS

*Flavory salad is heaped into tiny pastry shells and topped with a miniature tomato slice.*

*Makes 5 dozen, or about 25 servings.*

Canapé Shells
1 can (6 ounces) chopped broiled mushrooms
2 cans (5 to 6 ounces each) boned chicken, very finely chopped OR 2 cups very finely chopped cooked chicken
½ cup very finely diced celery
⅔ cup dairy sour cream
1 teaspoon grated onion
½ teaspoon curry powder
½ teaspoon salt
Cherry tomatoes, sliced
Parsley

1. Make, bake and cool Canapé Shells.
2. Drain and chop mushrooms very fine. Combine with chicken and celery in a bowl.
3. Mix sour cream, onion, curry powder and salt in a 1-cup measure; spoon over chicken mixture; toss well to mix; chill.
4. Just before serving, spoon into Canapé Shells, using 1 rounded teaspoonful for each. Garnish with a slice of cherry tomato and a sprig of parsley.

## CANAPÉ SHELLS

Prepare 1 package pie crust mix, following label directions, or make pastry from your own favorite two-crust recipe. Roll out, half at a time to a 12-inch round on lightly floured pastry cloth or board; cut into small rounds with a 1¾-inch scalloped cutter. Fit into tiny muffin-pan cups; prick shells with a fork. Reroll and cut out all trimmings. Bake in hot oven (425°) 7 minutes, or until delicately golden. Remove from cups; cool completely on wire racks. Makes about 5 dozen.

MAKE-AHEAD NOTE: Canapé Shells may be made a day ahead, if you like, then stacked and stored in a container with a tight-fitting cover. For 100 servings, make 3 times the recipe. For variety, fill with your favorite seafood or ham salad.

## CHICKEN TANGO DIP

*The secret ingredient (instant coffee) makes this a delicious, mellow dip.*

*Makes 2 cups.*

1 can (5 ounces) chicken spread
1 cup (8-ounce carton) dairy sour cream
¼ cup mayonnaise or salad dressing
¼ cup finely chopped walnuts
2 teaspoons instant coffee
¼ teaspoon salt
Dash of pepper
1 teaspoon lemon juice

1. Combine all ingredients in a medium-size bowl; stir lightly until well blended. Chill several hours to season.
2. Spoon into small bowls; sprinkle with paprika, if you wish. Serve with crisp green-pepper squares, carrot sticks, potato chips, pretzels or your favorite crackers.

# CHICKEN-SESAME BITES

*Your guests will think you're a genius because most of the preparation for these appetizers is done ahead of time.*

*Makes about 4 dozen appetizers.*

| | |
|---|---|
| 2 whole chicken breasts | 1 tablespoon sugar |
| 3 tablespoons lemon juice | 1 tablespoon sherry |
| 2 tablespoons soy sauce | ¼ cup butter or margarine |
| | Toasted sesame seeds |

1. Bone chicken breasts; remove skin. Cut meat in 1-inch pieces; place in shallow dish.
2. Combine lemon juice, soy sauce, sugar and sherry; pour over chicken, let stand ½ hour or more.
3. Sauté chicken in butter 5 minutes. Dip in sesame seeds. Serve with wooden picks.

# CHICKEN ROLLS

*A first-rate first course, or party fare: Crisp gingery rolls of white meat and ham.*

*Makes 6 servings (3 rolls each).*

| | |
|---|---|
| 1 whole chicken breast (about 12 ounces) | ¼ cup milk |
| 2 slices boiled ham, each cut into 9 pieces | ½ cup sifted regular flour |
| 18 small thin strips crystallized ginger | ½ teaspoon salt |
| 1 egg | ½ teaspoon sugar |
| | Shortening or vegetable oil for frying |

1. Pull skin from chicken breast; halve breast and cut meat in 1 piece from bone, then cut each half into 9 even pieces. Place, 2 or 3 at a time, between waxed paper and pound very thin with mallet or rolling pin until about 2 inches wide.

2. Top each with a piece of ham and ginger; roll up. Place, seam side down, in a single layer on a large platter; cover; chill.

3. When ready to cook, beat egg with milk in a medium-size bowl; beat in flour, salt and sugar until smooth. (Batter will be medium-thin.)

4. Melt enough shortening or pour in enough vegetable oil to make a 4-inch depth in an electric deep-fat fryer or large saucepan; heat to 380°.

5. Dip chicken rolls, 2 at a time, into batter; hold over bowl to let excess drip back.

6. Fry in hot shortening, turning once, 3 minutes, or until golden; lift out with a slotted spoon; drain on paper toweling. Serve hot with dips of prepared horseradish-mustard and Plum Sauce (see chapter on SAUCES).

MAKE-AHEAD TIP: Rolls may be fried several hours ahead and chilled. To reheat, arrange, not touching, in a shallow baking pan and heat in very hot oven (450°) 10 minutes.

## CHICKEN LIVER BROIL

*Serve as an appetizer or as a main dish.*

*Makes 6 to 8 appetizer servings.*

| | |
|---|---|
| 1 pound chicken livers | 2 tablespoons |
| ¼ cup bottled chili sauce | Worcestershire sauce |
| 2 tablespoons vegetable oil | 1 teaspoon monosodium glutamate |

1. Halve livers; snip out any veiny parts.

2. Mix remainder of ingredients in large bowl. Add livers and toss; let stand an hour.

3. Remove livers from marinade; thread onto long skewers; place on rack in broiler pan. Broil, 5 to 6 inches from the heat, turning several times, 5 minutes.

4. While livers cook, heat marinade to boiling in small saucepan. Remove livers from skewers and arrange on a serving plate; serve sauce in a small bowl as a dip.

# PÂTÉ MIMOSA

*A pearly chicken-flavored mold.*

*Makes 12 servings.*

| | |
|---|---|
| 1 envelope unflavored gelatin | 1 teaspoon prepared horseradish |
| 1 envelope instant chicken broth | 1 teaspoon salt |
| 1½ cups water | ⅛ teaspoon cayenne pepper |
| ½ cup mayonnaise or salad dressing | 6 slices crisp bacon, crumbled |
| 2 teaspoons cider vinegar | 4 hard-cooked eggs, shelled and sieved |
| 1 teaspoon grated onion | |

1. Combine gelatin, chicken broth and water in a small saucepan; heat, stirring constantly, until gelatin dissolves.

2. Beat in mayonnaise or salad dressing, vinegar, onion, horseradish, salt and cayenne pepper. Pour into a shallow pan; chill in freezer 20 minutes, or until firm at edges.

3. Spoon into a bowl; beat until fluffy. Fold in bacon and eggs; spoon into a 3-cup mold. Chill until firm.

4. Unmold onto a serving plate. Garnish with sieved hard-cooked egg yolk.

# PÂTÉ-CHEESE MOLD

*Stuffed olives crown a pretty double-molded spread of meat and cheese.*

*Makes 25 servings.*

## MEAT LAYER

1 envelope unflavored gelatin

1 envelope instant chicken broth OR 1 chicken bouillon cube

1 cup water

1 tablespoon lemon juice

3 large stuffed green olives, sliced

½ pound bologna

¼ cup mayonnaise or salad dressing

¼ cup sweet mustard relish (from a 9-ounce jar)

## CHEESE LAYER

1 envelope unflavored gelatin

¼ cup water

2 wedges (1⅓ ounces each) Camembert cheese

¼ pound blue cheese

¼ teaspoon curry powder

1 egg, separated

1 cup (8-ounce carton) dairy sour cream

Green food coloring

1. Make meat layer: Soften gelatin with chicken broth or bouillon cube in water in a small saucepan. Heat, stirring constantly and crushing cube, if using, with a spoon, just until gelatin dissolves. Measure ¼ cup into a 6-cup mold; stir in lemon juice. (Keep remaining gelatin mixture at room temperature.)

2. Set mold in a pan of ice and water to speed setting; chill just until syrupy-thick. Arrange stuffed olive slices in gelatin to make a pretty pattern. Chill until sticky-firm.

3. While mold chills, remove skin from bologna; put meat through a food chopper, using a fine blade. Mix with remaining gelatin mixture, mayonnaise or

salad dressing and relish in a medium-size bowl; spoon over sticky-firm olive layer in mold. Continue chilling in same pan of ice and water until sticky-firm while making cheese layer.

4. Make cheese layer: Soften gelatin in water in a small saucepan; heat slowly just until gelatin dissolves.

5. Beat Camembert and blue cheeses until well-blended in a medium-size bowl; beat in curry powder, egg yolk and the dissolved gelatin.

6. Beat egg white until it stands in firm peaks in a small bowl. Fold into cheese mixture, then fold in sour cream. Tint mixture light green with a drop or two of food coloring.

7. Spoon over sticky-firm meat layer in mold; cover with waxed paper, foil or transparent wrap. Chill in refrigerator several hours, or until firm. (Overnight is best.)

8. When ready to unmold, run a sharp-tip, thin-blade knife around top of mold, then dip mold *very quickly* in and out of a pan of hot water. Cover mold with a serving plate; turn upside down; gently lift off mold. Surround with your choice of crisp crackers.

## PÂTÉ MAISON

*Prepare the chicken livers, add the seasonings and cream and you're ready to bring out the appetizer tray.*

*Makes 1⅓ cups Pâté.*

| | |
|---|---|
| ¼ cup butter or margarine | ¼ teaspoon each dry mustard, freshly ground black pepper and powdered thyme |
| 1 pound chicken livers | |
| ½ cup finely chopped onion | |
| 1 teaspoon salt | ⅛ teaspoon mace |
| | ¼ cup cream |

1. Heat butter in skillet. Add chicken livers and onion; cook over medium heat, stirring frequently, for 5 to 8 minutes or until livers are done and onion is tender but not brown.

2. Force livers with onion through strainer or food

mill. Blend in seasonings and cream. Turn into serving container or mold. Serve with thinly sliced French bread, crackers or toast rounds.

# HAM AND CHICKEN PINWHEELS

*These pretty little appetizers, with their fresh parsley edging, are sliced dainty-thin just before serving.*

*Makes about 5 dozen.*

1 can (4½ ounces) deviled ham
1 teaspoon prepared mustard
2½ teaspoons grated onion
Dash liquid red-pepper seasoning
1 can (4¾ ounces) chicken spread
½ teaspoon anchovy paste
½ teaspoon Worcestershire sauce

1 loaf unsliced bread (white or whole wheat)
1 cup (2 sticks) butter or margarine, softened
5 ripe olives, chopped
1 whole pimiento, chopped
3 cups finely chopped parsley (about 2 large bunches)

1. Combine ham, mustard, teaspoon of the grated onion and red-pepper seasoning in a small bowl.

2. Combine chicken spread, anchovy paste, the remaining grated onion and Worcestershire in a second small bowl.

3. Trim crusts from top and sides of unsliced loaf, leaving bottom crust intact. Cut lengthwise into eight ¼-inch-thick slices; cover with dampened paper toweling to prevent drying.

4. Roll bread slices lightly with rolling pin. Spread with softened butter or margarine. Spread deviled-ham filling on 4 slices and chicken filling on remaining 4 slices.

5. Taking 1 slice of deviled ham at a time, sprinkle chopped olives along the near long edge and roll up tightly, jelly-roll fashion. Spread outer surface with

butter or margarine and roll in chopped parsley. Wrap tightly in plastic wrap, twisting ends well.

6. Repeat with remaining deviled-ham slices and chopped olives. Sprinkle chopped pimiento on chicken slices and repeat rolling, coating and wrapping.

7. Do-ahead note: Place wrapped rolls in foil or plastic boxes; cover firmly; label and freeze.

8. Party day: Slice each frozen roll into 8 thin sandwiches with a sharp knife. Arrange on serving plates (they will thaw quickly).

NOTE: If you do not wish to freeze sandwiches, they should be chilled for at least 8 hours in plastic wrap before slicing.

If unsliced bread is not available, sandwiches may be prepared using sliced bread. Trim the crusts from 2 slices of bread; roll lightly. Place slices side by side; butter joining edges. Press edges together; proceed as above, rolling from long edge so joining is in the center of roll.

## CORN-CRISPED DRUMSTICKS

*They look like fried chicken, but these drumsticks are actually baked . . . with no messy clean-up.*

*Bake at 350° for 1 hour.*
*Makes 8 servings.*

| | |
|---|---|
| 2 cups packaged corn flake crumbs | ¼ teaspoon pepper |
| | 16 drumsticks |
| 2 teaspoons mono- sodium glutamate | ¾ cup evaporated milk |
| 2 teaspoons salt | |

1. Combine corn flake crumbs with monosodium glutamate, salt and pepper in shallow dish.

2. Line 2 shallow baking sheets or pans with aluminum foil.

3. Dip drumsticks in evaporated milk, then roll immediately in seasoned corn flake crumbs. Place the drumsticks in foil-lined pans; do not crowd.

4. Bake in moderate oven (350°) 1 hour, or until tender. At the end of ½ hour, exchange place of pans on the shelves; continue to bake. No need to cover or turn chicken while cooking. Serve with Deviled Dunking Sauce.

## DEVILED DUNKING SAUCE

Combine ⅓ cup prepared mustard, ⅓ cup pickle relish, 1 can (8 ounces) tomato sauce, 1 tablespoon horseradish, 1 tablespoon of Worcestershire sauce and ⅛ teaspoon cayenne; mix thoroughly. Makes 1⅔ cups sauce.

## Chapter 4

# Soups for Every Season

Memories are made of moments that surpass the ordinary. The child better remembers cold winter days that included hot, homemade soup for lunch than days that were just cold. The adult thinks back with more pleasure to evenings that offered a hearty broth in front of the fire than an evening just in front of the fire.

Soup sets the mood for relaxed, enjoyable moments; when it includes chicken, the moments become truly memorable. As our recipes prove, hot or cold, creamy or clear, thin or hearty, chicken soup is easy and fun to make. You can start from scratch or use canned soup as a base. Whatever your choice, make some soup now. The day will be worth remembering.

## BASIC CHICKEN BROTH

*It is well worthwhile to make homemade chicken broth. This recipe gives you enough broth and meat to make 2 soups and even extra meat for a salad or casserole, if you wish.*

*Makes 12 cups.*

| | |
|---|---|
| 2 broiler-fryers, 3 to 3½ pounds each | 2 stalks celery |
| Chicken giblets | 2 celery tops |
| 2 medium carrots, pared | 3 sprigs parsley |
| 1 large parsnip, pared | 1 leek, washed well |
| 1 large onion, chopped (1 cup) | Water |
| | 2 tablespoons salt |
| | 12 peppercorns |

1. Combine chicken, chicken giblets, carrots, pars-

nip, onion and celery in a large kettle; tie celery tops, parsley and leek together with a string; add to kettle. Add enough cold water to cover chicken and vegetables, about 12 cups.

2. Heat slowly to boil; skim; add salt and peppercorns; reduce heat. Simmer very slowly 1 to 1½ hours, or until meat falls off the bones. Remove meat and vegetables from broth, discard the bundle of greens.

3. Strain broth through cheesecloth into a large bowl. (There should be about 12 cups.) Use this delicious broth in the following soup recipes or in any of our recipes calling for chicken broth.

4. When cool enough to handle, remove and discard skin and bones from chicken; cut meat into bite-size pieces; use as called for in following recipes, or use in salads, casseroles, etc. To store in refrigerator, up to 3 to 4 days, keep in covered container. To freeze, pack in small portions, 1, or 2 cups, in plastic bags or freezer containers, to use as needed.

5. To store in refrigerator, up to 4 days, leave fat layer on surface of broth until ready to use, then lift fat off and discard, or use in other cooking. To freeze, transfer broth to freezer containers, allowing space on top for expansion. Freeze until ready to use (3 to 4 months maximum).

# CHICKEN SOUP WITH DUMPLINGS

*A creamy-thick soup with tender little chicken balls and vegetables to munch.*

*Makes 6 servings.*

## CHICKEN DUMPLINGS

1 cup diced cooked chicken (from Basic Chicken Broth)
1 cooked chicken liver
1 egg
⅓ cup flour
¼ cup milk
1 teaspoon salt
Dash of pepper
Dash of nutmeg
1 tablespoon chopped parsley
1 cup water
6 cups Basic Chicken Broth

SOUP

¼ cup chopped green onion

¼ cup chicken fat, butter or margarine

¼ cup flour

1 package (10 ounces) frozen mixed vegetables

½ teaspoon salt

1½ cups diced cooked chicken (from Basic Chicken Broth)

1. Combine chicken, liver, egg, flour, milk, salt, pepper and nutmeg in blender; blend at high speed until smooth. Turn into small bowl, stir in parsley; cover.

2. Bring water and 1 cup of the CHICKEN BROTH to boiling in large saucepan. Shape chicken mixture, one-half at a time, into ¾-inch balls with a teaspoon. Drop one by one into boiling broth. Simmer gently, uncovered, 8 to 10 minutes; remove with a slotted spoon; keep warm. Repeat with second half.

3. Sauté onion in chicken fat, or butter or margarine in kettle or Dutch oven, until soft but not brown, 3 to 4 minutes; stir in flour; gradually add remaining chicken broth; stirring constantly; bring to boil; add vegetables and salt: cover. Cook 10 minutes, or until vegetables are tender.

4. Add chicken dumplings, cooking broth and chicken: heat 5 minutes. Ladle into soup bowls; serve with crusty bread.

# CHICKEN IN THE POT

*Eat this country-style soup with your spoon plus a knife and fork.*

*Makes 6 servings.*

1 broiler-fryer (3 pounds)

1 pound small new potatoes, washed

4 carrots, pared and diced

2 turnips, pared and diced

2 stalks celery with tops, diced

1 leek, trimmed and washed well

1 tablespoon salt

2 sprigs of parsley

6 peppercorns

1 bay leaf

5 to 6 cups water

1. Cut chicken into serving-size pieces: 2 legs, 2 thighs and 2 wings. Cut each side of breast crosswise into 3 pieces. Layer chicken, potatoes, carrots, turnips, celery and leek in a 3-quart flameproof casserole or Dutch oven; sprinkle salt between layers. Add water almost to cover.

2. Tie tops from celery, parsley, peppercorns and bay leaf in a piece of cheesecloth. Push under liquid.

3. Bring to boiling; reduce heat; cover. Simmer 45 minutes to 1 hour, or until meat and vegetables are tender. Discard herb bag.

4. Ladle into soup bowls, spooning 2 pieces of chicken into each bowl. Serve with crusty bread.


## CHICKEN-LEMON SOUP

*Here's a cool and tangy opener for a warm-weather supper.*

*Makes 4 to 6 servings.*

| | |
|---|---|
| 1 envelope chicken-noodle soup mix | 4 teaspoons lemon juice |
| 1 cup thinly sliced celery | 2 hard-cooked eggs, finely diced |

1. Prepare soup mix, following label directions; cook 5 minutes; add celery and cook 2 minutes longer.

2. Remove from heat; stir in lemon juice; pour into bowl; cover; chill.

3. Serve in cups or small bowls, with diced hard-cooked eggs sprinkled over.

## CHUNKY CHICKEN-BEEF SOUP

*An entire broiler-fryer and plenty of beef go into this made-from-scratch soup*

*Makes 8 servings.*

1½ pounds chuck beefsteak, cut into ½-inch cubes
1 large onion, chopped (1 cup)
1 broiler-fryer (about 2½ to 3 pounds), quartered
1 cup chopped celery
2 teaspoons salt
1 teaspoon seasoned salt
½ teaspoon pepper
½ teaspoon leaf rosemary, crumbled
½ teaspoon leaf thyme, crumbled
1 bay leaf
10 cups water
2 cups uncooked medium noodles

1. Brown beef in its own fat in a kettle or Dutch oven; stir in onion and sauté lightly.
2. Add chicken, celery, salt, seasoned salt, pepper, rosemary, thyme, bay leaf and water to kettle; heat to boiling; cover. Simmer 1 hour, or until chicken is tender; remove from kettle. Continue cooking beef 20 minutes, or until tender; remove bay leaf.
3. While beef finishes cooking, pull skin from chicken and take meat from bones; cut meat into cubes. Return to kettle; heat to boiling.
4. Stir in noodles. Cook 10 minutes, or until noodles are tender.
5. Ladle into soup plates. Sprinkle with chopped parsley and serve with your favorite crisp crackers, if you wish.

## *What Is Broth?*

Broth is a stock or clear soup made of water in which meat, fowl or fish and vegetables have been simmered. It's used as a base for soups, sauces and gravies, as the liquid for cooking vegetables, rice, noodles or pasta and as a baste for roasted poultry as it cooks.

Broth is also referred to as stock, bouillon and consommé.

## CHICKEN AND HAM BURGOO

*A meal to come home for: Robust stew, perfect for an after-the-game or after-skating crowd of hungry dynamos.*

*Makes 12 servings.*

1 roasting chicken (about 3 pounds)
4 smoked ham hocks (about 1 pound each)
Water
3 teaspoons salt
½ teaspoon cayenne pepper
2 cups diced pared potatoes
2 cups diced pared carrots
2 large onions, chopped (2 cups)
1 package (10 ounces) frozen Fordhook lima beans

2 cups shredded cabbage
2 cups fresh corn kernels
2 cups thinly sliced celery
2 cups diced tomatoes
1 package (10 ounces) frozen whole okra
2 tablespoons Worcestershire sauce
1 cup diced green pepper
½ cup chopped parsley

1. Combine chicken and ham hocks in a kettle or roasting pan; add just enough water to cover. Heat to boiling; cover. Simmer 1½ hours, or until chicken is tender; remove from kettle. Continue cooking ham hocks 1 hour, or until tender; remove from kettle.

2. Let broth stand until fat rises to top, then skim off. Measure broth and return 12 cups to kettle. Stir

in salt, cayenne, potatoes, carrots, onions and lima beans. Heat to boiling; simmer 15 minutes.

3. While vegetables cook, remove skin from chicken and ham hocks; take meat from bones, discarding fat; dice meat.

4. Stir cabbage, corn, celery, tomatoes, okra and Worcestershire sauce into kettle; simmer 15 minutes, or until all vegetables are crisply tender. Stir in green pepper, parsley and diced meats; heat just to boiling.

5. Ladle into soup plates or bowls. Serve with corn bread or crusty hard rolls, if you wish.

## CHOWDER DIAMOND HEAD

*Ginger, pineapple and coconut make this an enchanting South Seas soup.*

*Makes 6 servings.*

| | |
|---|---|
| 1 cup sliced celery | 1⅓ cups water |
| 1 small onion, chopped (¼ cup) | 1⅓ cups milk |
| 2 tablespoons butter or margarine | 1 can (5 ounces) boned chicken, diced |
| ½ teaspoon ground ginger | 1 can (about 9 ounces) pineapple tidbits, drained |
| 2 cans condensed cream of chicken soup | Shredded coconut |

1. Sauté celery and onion in butter or margarine until soft in a large heavy saucepan or Dutch oven; add ginger, blending thoroughly.

2. Stir in soup, water and milk. Add chicken and pineapple. Heat, stirring frequently, until bubbly-hot.

3. Ladle into soup bowls. Sprinkle with coconut. Serve with hot buttered rolls, if you wish.

# CHICKEN CHOWDER

*Canned soups are just the beginning!*

*Makes 6 servings.*

3 cups water
1 can or 1 envelope
  chicken noodle soup
  mix
1 can or 1 envelope
  cream of mushroom
  soup mix
½ cup sliced pared
  carrots

¼ cup sliced celery
¼ cup chopped green
  pepper
1 can (5 or 6 ounces)
  boned chicken, diced
3 cups light or table
  cream

1. Heat water to boiling in a large saucepan; stir in soup mixes until blended, then carrots, celery and green pepper.
2. Heat to boiling; simmer 10 minutes.
3. Stir in chicken and cream; heat very slowly just until bubbly.
4. Ladle into heated soup plates or bowls. Serve with your favorite crisp crackers.

# CHICKEN-CORN CHOWDER

*Canned chicken soup, canned corn, canned milk—by the time the kids wash up, soup's on!*

*Makes 6 servings.*

1 medium-size onion,
  chopped (½ cup)
2 tablespoons butter
  or margarine
2 cans condensed
  chicken noodle soup
1 soup can water

1 can (about 1 pound)
  cream-style corn
1 small can evaporated
  milk (⅔ cup)
¼ teaspoon pepper
2 tablespoons chopped
  parsley

1. Sauté onion in butter or margarine just until soft in medium-size saucepan.

2. Stir in remaining ingredients, except parsley. Heat just to boiling.

3. Pour into heated soup bowls or mugs; sprinkle with parsley.

## CUCUMBER-CHICKEN CUP

*Float a spoonful of sour cream on top.*

*Makes 6 servings.*

| | |
|---|---|
| 2 cans condensed chicken broth | ⅓ cup dairy sour cream |
| 2 soup cans of water | Dillweed |
| 1 large cucumber, pared and shredded | |

1. Combine chicken broth and water in a medium-size saucepan; heat to boiling. Stir in cucumber and salt to taste, if needed. Heat again until bubbly.

2. Ladle into soup cups or small bowls. Float a spoonful of sour cream on each; sprinkle dillweed over cream. Serve with small wheat crackers, if you wish.

## Basic Broth Soup Cookery

A savory, richly flavored stock is essential for good soup. It can be the base for cream soups, stews, chowders and appetizer soups. Whenever your soup recipe calls for stock, use canned broth if you don't plan to make one from scratch.

# COLD CURRIED CHICKEN SOUP

*This is one of the most delicious of all iced soups.*

*Makes 6 servings.*

3 tart apples, pared, cored and sliced (apples must be tart)
1 large onion, peeled and sliced
1 tablespoon butter or margarine
2 teaspoons curry powder
Salt to taste

Freshly ground pepper to taste
3 drops red-pepper seasoning
3 cups chicken consommé or broth
1 cup dry white wine
1 cup light cream
¼ to ½ cup very finely diced cooked chicken
Paprika

1. Cook apples and onion in butter or margarine over low heat, stirring often, until soft. Do not let them brown.
2. Stir in curry powder and cook 3 minutes longer. Add salt, pepper, red-pepper seasoning, chicken consommé or broth and wine. Simmer, covered, 10 minutes, stirring frequently.
3. Puree in blender or press through a fine sieve. Chill thoroughly.
4. Just before serving, stir in cream and chicken; sprinkle with paprika. Serve icy cold.


# HOT SENEGALESE SOUP

*This creamy soup is an exotic but very easy version of an honored specialty.*

*Makes 8 servings.*

2 cans condensed cream of chicken soup
3 cups milk

½ teaspoon curry powder
2 tablespoons toasted coconut

1. Combine soup, milk and curry powder in medium-size saucepan; heat just until bubbly-hot, then beat with rotary beater until creamy smooth.
2. Pour into 8 small bowls or cups, dividing evenly; sprinkle with coconut.

## CHICKEN N' VEGETABLES

*An easy-to-make soup that's ready to serve in about 30 minutes.*

*Makes 6 hearty servings.*

1 medium-size onion, chopped
2 medium-size potatoes, peeled and chopped
1 can (1 pound) whole kernel corn, drained
1 package (10 ounces) frozen lima beans, cooked and drained
2 cans (13¾ ounces each) chicken broth
1 can (1 pt. 10 oz.) tomato juice
1 cup cooked chicken
1½ teaspoons salt
¼ teaspoon pepper
1 tablespoon butter or margarine
1 tablespoon Worcestershire sauce

Combine all ingredients in a large kettle or Dutch oven; simmer about 30 minutes or until vegetables are done.

# COMPANY SOUP

*Garnish this tasty soup with bacon, scallions and cucumbers.*

*Makes 4 to 6 servings.*

3 cans (13¾ ounces
each) chicken broth
¼ cup dry white wine
(optional)
1½ teaspoons salt
⅛ teaspoon pepper
1 teaspoon leaf tarra-
gon, crumbled
1½ cups cooked
chicken, chopped

1 package (10 ounces)
frozen green peas,
cooked and drained
1 can (7½ ounces)
water chestnuts,
sliced
⅓ cup sliced ripe
olives
Chopped cooked bacon
Diced hard-boiled
chopped scallions
Cucumber slices

Combine soup ingredients in a large kettle or Dutch
oven; cook over a low flame for 15 minutes. Serve with
garnishes (bacon, scallions and cucumber slices) in
individual bowls or on one serving tray.

# MULLIGATAWNY SOUP

*A classic soup with origins in India, is richly flavored
with exotic curry.*

*Makes 6 servings.*

3 medium carrots,
   pared and sliced
2 stalks of celery,
   sliced
6 cups Basic Chicken
   Broth (see page 32)
3 cups cooked diced
   chicken (from Basic
   Chicken Broth)
1 large onion, chopped
   (1 cup)
4 tablespoons (½
   stick) butter or
   margarine

1 apple, pared, quar-
   tered, cored and
   chopped
5 teaspoons curry
   powder
1 teaspoon salt
¼ cup flour
1 tablespoon lemon
   juice
2 cups hot cooked rice
¼ cup chopped
   parsley
6 lemon slices
   (optional)

1. Cook carrots and celery in 1 cup broth in a
medium-size saucepan 20 minutes, or until tender. Add
chicken; heat just until hot; cover; keep warm.

2. Sauté onion until soft in butter or margarine in
Dutch oven; stir in apple, curry powder and salt; sauté
5 minutes longer, or until apple is soft; add flour.
Gradually stir in remaining chicken broth; heat to boiling, stirring constantly; reduce heat; cover; simmer 15
minutes.

3. Add vegetables and chicken with the broth they
were cooked in; bring just to boiling. Stir in lemon
juice.

4. Ladle into soup plates or bowls; pass hot cooked
rice and chopped parsley and lemon slices, if you wish,
for each to add his own garnish. Good with crusty
French bread.

# CHILLED CHICKEN CREAM

*Celery seeds give canned cream soup an exceptional flavor.*

*Makes 6 servings.*

1 can condensed cream of chicken soup
1 cup light or table cream
½ cup milk
1 teaspoon lemon juice
½ teaspoon celery seeds

1. Combine all ingredients in an electric-blender container; cover. Blend 1 minute, or until creamy smooth. (Or beat slightly longer with an electric beater.) Chill.
2. Pour into mugs or cups. Garnish each with a celery-stick stirrer and serve with tiny croutons to sprinkle over, or a dash of paprika, if you wish.

# CHICKEN QUEBEC

*Serve this spoon-up main dish in soup plates to enjoy with thick slices of crusty bread.*

*Makes 6 servings.*

1 stewing chicken, cut into serving-size pieces
6 slices back bacon
1 medium-size onion, chopped (½ cup)
1 teaspoon salt
3 or 4 peppercorns
6 cups water
1 package (8 ounces) elbow macaroni
1 tablespoon parsley flakes

1. Trim fat from chicken; melt fat in large heavy kettle or Dutch oven. Brown chicken, a few serving-size pieces at a time; drain on paper toweling.
2. Fry bacon lightly in same kettle; remove and set aside; pour off all fat. Return browned chicken and bacon to kettle; add onion, salt, peppercorns and water.

3. Cover tightly; heat to boiling, then simmer 2 hours, or until chicken is tender. (If much fat has cooked out, remove the kettle from heat; let stand 5 to 10 minutes; then skim off all fat.)

4. Reheat to boiling; stir in macaroni and parsley flakes. (Add 1 cup water, if needed.) Cook, uncovered, stirring occasionally, 15 to 20 minutes, or until macaroni is tender. Season to taste with salt, if needed.

NOTE: If little new potatoes are in season, use in place of macaroni. Leave jackets on and cook in stew, covered, until tender.

## BRUNSWICK CHOWDER

*Chicken, canned soup and vegetables add up to this satisfying meal in a bowl.*

*Makes 8 servings.*

| | |
|---|---|
| 1 **broiler-fryer (about 2¼ pounds), quartered** | 2 **packages (10 ounces each) frozen Fordhook lima beans** |
| 5 **teaspoons seasoned salt** | 2 **cans condensed tomato-rice soup** |
| **Water** | 2 **cups thinly sliced celery** |
| 1 **large onion, chopped (1 cup)** | 2 **cans (1 pound each) cream-style corn** |
| 2 **tablespoons butter or margarine** | |

1. Combine chicken, 3 teaspoons of the salt and 4 cups water in a kettle; cover. Simmer 45 minutes, or until chicken is tender. Take meat from bones; dice. Strain broth into a 4-cup measure; add water, if needed, to make 4 cups.

2. Sauté onion in butter or margarine until soft in same kettle; add lima beans, soup, two soup cans of water and celery; cover. Simmer 15 minutes, or until

beans are tender. Stir in chicken, broth, corn and remaining 2 teaspoons seasoned salt.

3. Heat slowly just to boiling. Ladle into heated soup bowls.


# COLD SENEGALESE SOUP

*Midsummer's dream: A cold and simple gourmet dish.*

*Makes 6 servings.*

| | |
|---|---|
| 1 can condensed cream of chicken soup | 1 tablespoon lemon juice |
| 1 tall can evaporated milk | 1 teaspoon curry powder |

1. Combine all ingredients in large bowl; beat (or blend in an electric blender) until creamy-smooth; chill.

2. Serve in cups or bowls. If you like, sprinkle with chopped toasted almonds or flaked coconut.

*Chapter 5*

# Chicken in a Hurry

To the casual observer, a table set with delightfully prepared food means one thing: Dinner is going to be great. Unfortunately the chef of the house often views this scene with a sigh of relief. Hours of kitchen time have gone into making dinner happen.

Happily, you don't have to be in the martyr's seat when it comes to chicken dinner. It's naturally easy to prepare and when joined with recipes specifically designed to save you time, it adds up to a meal everyone will enjoy.

Our short-time recipes include make-ahead dishes that are especially practical for working wives; and those in the Fast and Simple section are geared for new cooks and mothers-on-the-go.

Since some of the recipes can be prepared well ahead of time, they're also great for a day when you've been out just enjoying yourself.

# Fast and Simple

## CHICKEN CREOLE

*This recipe will have dinner on the table in half an hour.*

*Makes 4 servings.*

1 broiler-fryer, cut in serving-size pieces

2 teaspoons salt, divided

½ teaspoon paprika

2 tablespoons butter or margarine

1 medium onion, sliced

1 medium green pepper, cut in strips

½ cup chopped celery

1 can (1 pound) tomatoes

½ teaspoon dried leaf thyme

1 can (3 or 4 ounces) mushrooms

1. Sprinkle chicken pieces with 1 teaspoon salt and paprika. Melt butter in large skillet; add chicken and brown on all sides.

2. Add onion, green pepper, celery, tomatoes, remaining 1 teaspoon salt and thyme.

3. Bring to a boil, reduce heat, cover and simmer 20 minutes. Add mushrooms and liquid. Simmer 5 to 10 minutes longer.

## QUICK CACCIATORE

*An easy way to make the Italian favorite.*

*Makes 4 servings.*

1 medium-size onion, chopped (½ cup)

3 tablespoons salad oil

1 broiler-fryer (about 3 pounds) cut in serving-size pieces

½ teaspoon salt

⅛ teaspoon pepper

1 clove garlic, minced

1 can (about 1 pound) tomatoes

1 tablespoon vinegar

½ teaspoon rosemary

½ teaspoon sugar

1. Sauté onion in 1 tablespoon salad oil in large frying pan about 5 minutes; remove and save for Step 3.

2. Sprinkle chicken with salt and pepper; brown in same frying pan with remaining 2 tablespoons oil and garlic.

3. Return onion to pan; add remaining ingredients; cover tightly. Simmer 40 minutes, or until chicken is tender.

# CHICKEN-TOMATO SKILLET

*The chicken pieces are browned and cooked with fresh rosy tomatoes and dill.*

*Makes 4 servings.*

| | |
|---|---|
| 1 broiler-fryer, cut in serving-size pieces | ½ cup chopped celery with leaves |
| 1½ teaspoons salt, divided | 4 medium tomatoes, peeled and chopped |
| ¼ teaspoon pepper | ¼ cup snipped fresh dill or 1 tablespoon dried dill weed |
| 2 tablespoons butter or margarine | |
| ¼ cup chopped onion | Grated Parmesan cheese |

1. Sprinkle chicken with 1 teaspoon of the salt and pepper. Heat butter in a large skillet. Add chicken and brown on all sides. Remove from skillet.

2. Add onion and celery; cook until tender. Add tomatoes and dill; sprinkle with remaining ½ teaspoon salt. Add chicken; spoon some of the tomato mixture over chicken.

3. Cover; simmer 30 minutes, until chicken is tender. Serve sprinkled light with grated Parmesan cheese.

# CHICKEN BAKED WITH BARBECUE SAUCE

*Whip the sauce together in no time, spoon it over chicken, pop the dish in the oven, and forget it while it cooks to savory tenderness.*

*Bake at 400° about 1 hour.*
*Makes 6 servings.*

| | |
|---|---|
| 2 broiler-fryers (about 2 pounds each), cut in serving-size pieces | Butter or margarine Barbecue Sauce |

1. Wash chicken pieces; pat dry; remove skin if you wish.
2. Arrange chicken pieces in a single layer in a well-buttered large shallow baking pan.
3. Spoon Barbecue Sauce over chicken so pieces are well coated. (If you have any leftover sauce, it will keep in a covered jar in the refrigerator.)
4. Bake, uncovered, in hot oven (400°) about 1 hour, or until chicken is tender.

## BARBECUE SAUCE

*Makes 2½ cups.*

| | |
|---|---|
| 2 cans (8 ounces each) tomato sauce | ¼ cup soy sauce |
| 1 medium-size onion, chopped (½ cup) | 2 tablespoons sugar |
| 1 clove garlic, minced | 1 teaspoon dry mustard |
| | ⅛ teaspoon cayenne |

Mix all ingredients in a medium-size bowl.

## MEDITERRANEAN CHICKEN

*A savory skillet dish that's quickly prepared.*

*Makes 4 servings.*

| | |
|---|---|
| 1 broiler-fryer, quartered | 1 medium eggplant, pared and cubed |
| 1½ teaspoons salt, divided | 2 medium tomatoes, peeled and chopped |
| ¼ teaspoon pepper | ¼ teaspoon each, dried leaf basil, thyme and oregano |
| 3 tablespoons butter or margarine | ¼ cup grated Parmesan or Romano cheese |
| 1 medium onion, chopped | |
| ½ cup chicken broth | |

1. Sprinkle chicken with 1 teaspoon salt and pepper. Heat butter in a large skillet; add chicken and brown on both sides. Remove from skillet.

2. Add onion and cook until tender. Add broth, scraping brown particles from bottom of skillet. Add eggplant and tomatoes; sprinkle with herbs and remaining ½ teaspoon salt. Add chicken; spoon some of the vegetable mixture over chicken.

3. Cover; simmer 30 minutes, until chicken is tender. Serve sprinkled with grated Parmesan or Romano cheese.

# CHINESE CHICKEN WITH RICE

*When you've got less than 30 minutes to prepare dinner, this is the dish to choose.*

*Makes 6 servings.*

3 boneless chicken breasts (chicken cutlets), weighing about 1¾ pounds
½ pound mushrooms
1 can (5 ounces) bamboo shoots
3 green onions
1 small stalk celery
1 small sweet red pepper OR 1 can or jar (4 ounces) pimientos
4 tablespoons vegetable oil

¼ cup dry sherry
2 tablespoons soy sauce
2 tablespoons cornstarch
1 cup chicken broth (from an about-14-ounce can)
2 cups precooked rice (from a 14-ounce package)
Boiling water
Salt

1. Pull skin from chicken breasts; slice meat thin. Trim mushrooms and slice. Drain bamboo shoots and slice, if needed; trim green onions and celery; slice both thin. Halve red pepper, seed, and dice. (If using pimientos, drain and cut into strips.)

2. Sauté chicken quickly in vegetable oil in a large frying pan 3 minutes, or until chicken turns white.

3. Stir in mushrooms, bamboo shoots, green onions, celery and red pepper; sauté 2 minutes. Stir in sherry and soy sauce; cover. Cook 2 minutes, or until vegetables are crisply tender.

4. Blend cornstarch into chicken broth until smooth in a small bowl; stir into frying pan. Cook, stirring constantly, until sauce thickens and boils for 3 minutes.

5. While chicken mixture cooks, prepare rice with boiling water and salt, following label directions. Spoon around edge on a large serving platter; spoon chicken

mixture on top. Garnish with a half mushroom and serve with additional soy sauce, if you wish.

# CHICKEN CORDON BLEU

*A party aristocrat, and easy to make in spite of its fancy French name.*

Bake at 400° for 40 minutes.
Makes 4 servings.

2 whole chicken breasts (about 12 ounces each)

4 thin slices boiled ham, about 3 inches square

2 triangles (1 ounce each) process Gruyere cheese, sliced

4 tablespoons (½ stick) butter or margarine

½ cup fine dry bread crumbs

½ teaspoon salt

⅛ teaspoon paprika

1. Halve chicken breasts; remove skin, if you wish, then cut meat in one piece from bones. Pull each half breast open in the middle to make a deep pocket.
2. Fold ham around cheese slices, dividing evenly; tuck one into each pocket.
3. Melt butter or margarine in a pie plate; mix bread crumbs, salt and paprika in a second pie plate.
4. Roll stuffed chicken breasts first in butter or margarine, then in crumb mixture to coat well. Place in a single layer in buttered baking dish.
5. Bake in hot oven (400°) 40 minutes, or until chicken is golden brown.

# SPANISH RICE CHICKEN BAKE

*A packaged mix is your short cut to a fine Castilian dish.*

*Bake at 350° for 1 hour.*
*Makes 8 servings.*

2 broiler-fryers (about 3 pounds each), quartered
¼ cup flour
¼ cup salad oil
1½ cups raw rice
3 cups water

1 envelope Spanish rice seasoning mix
1 large green pepper, cut in 8 rings
1 cup sliced stuffed green olives

1. Shake chicken with flour in a paper bag to coat well. Brown, a few pieces at a time, in salad oil in large frying pan; drain on paper toweling.
2. Place rice in a 10-cup shallow baking dish; arrange browned chicken on top.
3. Stir water into chicken drippings in frying pan; blend in Spanish rice seasoning mix; heat to boiling. Pour over chicken and rice; cover.
4. Bake in moderate oven (350°) 30 minutes; uncover and lay green pepper rings and sliced olives on top. Cover and bake 30 minutes longer, or until chicken and rice are tender, and liquid is absorbed.

## Make-Aheads

### CHICKEN TETRAZZINI

*This excellent chicken-spaghetti-cheese dish is an all-time party favorite—especially with hostesses, who can make it ahead of time.*

*Bake at 450° for 20 minutes.*
*Makes 6 servings.*

1 package (8 ounces) thin spaghetti
1 small onion, chopped (¼ cup)
2 tablespoons butter or margarine
2 tablespoons flour
1 envelope instant chicken broth OR 1 chicken bouillon cube
1 teaspoon salt
1 teaspoon dry mustard

½ teaspoon pepper
1 large can evaporated milk
1 can (3 or 4 ounces) sliced mushrooms
2 pimientos, diced
3 cups diced cooked chicken
1 cup (¼ pound) grated sharp Cheddar cheese
¼ cup grated Parmesan cheese

1. Cook spaghetti, following label directions; drain; place in buttered 8-cup shallow baking dish.
2. While spaghetti cooks, sauté onion in butter or margarine until soft in large saucepan. Remove from heat; blend in flour, instant broth or bouillon cube, salt, dry mustard and pepper. Slowly stir in evaporated milk, then liquid from mushrooms plus water to make 1½ cups. Cook, stirring constantly, until sauce thickens and boils 1 minute; stir in mushrooms and pimientos.
3. Mix 2 cups sauce with drained spaghetti in baking dish, making a well in center to hold the chicken mixture.
4. Combine chicken with remaining sauce; spoon into dish with spaghetti; sprinkle cheese on top.

5. Bake in hot oven (450°) 20 minutes, or until bubbly and golden. (If made ahead, cover lightly, cool, then chill until 30 minutes before baking. If put into oven cold, allow an additional 15 to 20 minutes' baking time.)

# AHEAD OF TIME CHICKEN CASSEROLE

*This meal-in-one dish understands a busy household and caters to its cook.*

*Bake at 350° for 1 hour.*
*Makes 4 servings.*

| | |
|---|---|
| 1 cup creamed cottage cheese | ¼ cup sliced pitted ripe olives |
| 1½ cups sour cream | 3 cups spinach or |
| 6 tablespoons grated Parmesan cheese | regular medium egg noodles, cooked |
| 1½ teaspoons salt | 2½ cups cooked cut-up chicken (from Simmered Chicken) |
| ¼ teaspoon red-pepper sauce | |

1. In large bowl mix cottage cheese, sour cream, 4 tablespoons Parmesan cheese, salt and red-pepper sauce. Stir in olives, noodles and chicken.

2. Turn into a greased 2-quart casserole. Sprinkle with remaining 2 tablespoons Parmesan cheese. Cover and refrigerate.

3. One hour before serving, place in moderate oven (350°); bake, covered, for 35 minutes. Uncover and bake 25 minutes more.

## Freezer Tip

**Slightly undercook dishes which must be cooked again. Those that require an hour of reheating can be undercooked by 30 minutes.**

## SIMMERED CHICKEN

*Makes about 2½ cups diced cooked chicken.*

1 broiler-fryer (about
  3 pounds), whole or
  cut in serving-size
  pieces
2 cups water
1 small onion, sliced

2 celery tops
2 bay leaves
1 teaspoon mono-
  sodium glutamate
1 teaspoon salt
¼ teaspoon pepper

1. Put chicken in kettle; add water and remaining
ingredients. Bring to a boil, cover tightly. Reduce heat
and simmer 1 hour.
2. Remove from heat; strain broth. Refrigerate
chicken and broth. When chicken is cool, remove meat
from bones; dice.

## QUICK CHICKEN CASSEROLE

*Built-in cream sauce makes this easy-do casserole a
dinner winner.*

*Bake at 375° for 15 minutes.*
*Makes 4 servings.*

2 packages (10 ounces
  each) frozen corn,
  carrots and pearl
  onions with cream
  sauce
2 cans (5 ounces each)
  boned chicken

¼ cup chopped
  parsley
1 package refrigerated
  butterflake dinner
  rolls
Sesame seeds

1. Cook vegetables in a large saucepan, following
label directions; drain. Dice chicken and add to saucepan with chopped parsley. Stir; pour into a 6-cup
baking dish.

2. Separate rolls to make 24 even pieces. Arrange, buttery-side up, on top of hot mixture; sprinkle with sesame seeds.

3. Bake in moderate oven (375°) 15 minutes, or until biscuits are golden.

## CHICKEN WITH MUSHROOMS AND SOUR CREAM

*A little mixing makes it all happen.*

*Makes 4 servings.*

2 whole chicken breasts
3 tablespoons butter or margarine
2 tablespoons finely chopped scallions
½ teaspoon salt
1 can (10½ ounces) condensed cream of mushroom soup

1 can (3 or 4 ounces) sliced mushrooms
¼ cup water
½ cup dairy sour cream
Hot cooked rice

1. Bone chicken breasts; remove skin. Cut each breast half into 10 or 12 strips. Assemble remaining ingredients.

2. Melt butter or margarine in a large skillet over high heat. Add chicken and scallions; sprinkle with salt. Cook 6 minutes.

3. Add undiluted mushroom soup, sliced mushrooms with liquid and water. Heat to boiling, stirring until mixture is smooth. Reduce heat; blend in sour cream. Do not boil. Serve over hot cooked rice.

## CHICKEN IN ORANGE SAUCE

*This luscious dish can be made the day before.*

*Makes 4 servings.*

| | |
|---|---|
| 1 broiler-fryer, cut in serving-size pieces | ½ teaspoon ground ginger |
| ½ cup (1 stick) butter or margarine | ⅛ teaspoon pepper |
| ¼ cup flour | 1½ cups orange juice |
| 2 tablespoons brown sugar | ½ cup water |
| 1 teaspoon salt | 2 oranges, pared and sectioned |

1. Wash chicken pieces; pat dry. Brown slowly in butter or margarine in large frying pan; remove from pan; set aside.

2. Blend flour, brown sugar, salt, ginger and pepper into drippings in pan; cook, stirring all the time, just until mixture bubbles. Stir in orange juice and water slowly; continue cooking and stirring until sauce thickens; boil 1 minute; remove from heat.

3. Return chicken to pan; cool. Cover and chill (this much can be done the day before).

4. About 45 minutes before serving time, reheat chicken and sauce just to boiling, then simmer, covered, 30 minutes. Lay orange sections around chicken; continue cooking 15 minutes longer, or until chicken is tender. Serve with fluffy hot rice.

# CHICKEN AND HAM SEVILLE

*Slices of chicken and stuffed rolls of ham bake with a spicy fruit glaze.*

*Bake at 350° about 1 hour.*
*Makes 12 servings.*

6 whole chicken breasts, split
1 bottle (8 ounces) Italian salad dressing
2 tablespoons minced onion
1 cup diced celery
4 tablespoons (½ stick) butter or margarine
1¼ cups water
1 can (6 ounces) frozen concentrated orange juice
1 package (8 ounces) ready-mix bread stuffing (4 cups)
¼ cup chopped celery leaves
12 large slices boiled ham, cut not more than ⅛-inch thick (about 2 pounds)
½ cup orange marmalade
2 teaspoons ground ginger

1. Remove skin and snip off small rib bones from chicken breasts. Arrange in a single layer in large shallow baking pan, 13x9x2; pour salad dressing over; turn to coat all sides; cover lightly; let stand at room temperature, turning occasionally, 2 to 3 hours, or overnight in refrigerator.
2. Sauté onion and celery in butter or margarine 2 to 3 minutes in medium-size frying pan. Stir in water and ¼ cup orange juice; heat to boiling. Pour over stuffing and celery leaves in a bowl; stir to moisten.
3. Spoon a scant ½ cup stuffing into each slice of ham; roll up; fasten with a wooden pick if needed; place, folded side down, in single layer in greased large baking pan; cover lightly. (This much can be done a day ahead and kept chilled.)
4. About 1 hour before serving, take chicken and ham rolls from refrigerator. Drain marinade off chicken

into a small bowl; stir in saved concentrated orange juice, marmalade and ginger. Brush over meats.

5. Place chicken, uncovered, in moderate oven (350°). Bake, basting often with marmalade mixture, about 1 hour, or until tender.

6. Bake ham, uncovered, in some oven, also basting with marmalade mixture, about 40 minutes, or until heated and glazed.

7. Arrange meats in separate piles on a heated platter; garnish with watercress and preserved kumquats stuck with fancy picks, if you wish.

## CHICKEN AND PINEAPPLE CASSEROLE

*The chicken is glazed with a gleaming fruit sauce.*

*Bake at 375° for 1 hour and 5 minutes.*
*Makes 8 servings.*

| | |
|---|---|
| 2 broiler-fryers, quartered | 3 tablespoons cornstarch |
| 2 tablespoons salt, divided | ¼ cup lemon juice |
| 1 tablespoon melted butter or margarine | ½ teaspoon dry mustard |
| 1 can (1 pound, 4 ounces) sliced pineapple in syrup | ½ teaspoon ginger |
| | 2 teaspoons instant minced onion |
| 2 cans (1 pound, 1 ounce each) yams in syrup | ½ cup currant jelly |
| | 8 maraschino cherries with stems |

1. Sprinkle chicken quarters with 1½ teaspoons salt. Place skin side up in shallow 3-quart casserole. Brush with melted butter or margarine. Bake in moderate oven (375°) for 45 minutes.

2. While chicken is baking, prepare sauce. Drain syrup from pineapple and yams into saucepan. Add

cornstarch, lemon juice, remaining ½ teaspoon salt, dry mustard, ginger and instant minced onion. Stir until cornstarch is well blended. Add currant jelly. Cook, stirring constantly, until mixture thickens and comes to a boil. Remove from heat.

3. When chicken has baked for 45 minutes, remove from oven. Add drained pineapple slices and yams. Pour sauce over all. Return to oven and bake 20 minutes longer, until chicken is tender. Serve garnished with maraschino cherries.

## CORN-FLAKE CHICKEN

*You can give this chicken its corn-flake coating ahead of time and refrigerate it, oven-ready, till you're ready.*

Bake at 425° about 45 minutes.
Makes 4 servings, 2 pieces each.

| | |
|---|---|
| 1 broiler-fryer (about 3 pounds), cut into 8 serving-size pieces | 1 teaspoon salt |
| ½ cup buttermilk | 1 teaspoon poultry seasoning |
| ½ cup packaged corn-flake crumbs | 4 tablespoons (½ stick) melted butter or margarine |
| ½ cup flour | |

1. Remove chicken skin, if you wish; then dip chicken pieces in buttermilk in shallow pan; coat with mixture of corn-flake crumbs, flour, salt and poultry seasoning combined in second shallow pan; arrange chicken pieces in single layer in well-buttered baking pan; pour melted butter or margarine over. (This much may be done ahead.)

2. Bake in hot oven (425°) 45 minutes, or until tender.

# KING MIDAS CHICKEN

*An obliging casserole that minds itself in the oven.*

*Bake at 350° for 1¼ hours.*
*Makes 4 servings.*

1 broiler-fryer, cut in
serving-size pieces
1 teaspoon salt
1 can (8¼ ounces)
crushed pineapple in
syrup

¼ cup prepared
mustard
½ cup chopped
chutney
½ cup coarsely
chopped pecans

1. Sprinkle chicken pieces on both sides with salt. Place skin side up in single layer in shallow 2-quart casserole.
2. Mix together pineapple and remaining ingredients; spoon over chicken. Bake uncovered in moderate oven (350°) for 1 hour and 15 minutes.

*Chapter 6*

# Chicken: Baked, Broiled and Roasted

When chicken takes to the oven, the result is delightful—whether it's baked or broiled to a tender golden-brown or roasted whole with its own stuffing.

Oven chicken is also easy. Once you've finished the basic preparations and the chicken is popped in the oven, your work is done (except for a peek now and then or a quick basting with a buttery sauce).

If it's stuffed, the flavor possibilities are almost endless. For instance, the stuffing recipes in this chapter range from a simple bread-crumb mixture to an elaborate blending of fruits and nuts.

Added to your own repertoire of recipes, they'll guarantee mouth-watering diversity for many meals to come. Just remember to suit the stuffing to the rest of your menu and to follow the roasting timetable, stuffing and trussing directions outlined in Chapter 1.

# Baked Chicken

## CREAMY BAKED CHICKEN

*Two cream soups make the rich gravy; one also adds flavor to fluffy corn biscuits on top.*

*Bake at 350° about 1 hour, then at 450° about 15 minutes.*
*Makes 4 servings.*

| | |
|---|---|
| 1 broiler-fryer (2½ to 3½ pounds), cut in serving-size pieces | ½ teaspoon ground ginger |
| 1 can condensed cream-of-mushroom soup | 1 cup biscuit mix |
| 1 can condensed cream-of-chicken soup | ¼ cup yellow corn-meal |
| ½ cup plus 3 table-spoons milk | ½ tablespoon finely chopped crystallized ginger |

1. Cut away small bones from chicken breasts; remove all skin if you prefer chicken cooked without it.

2. Arrange chicken pieces in buttered 12-cup casserole; combine the cream-of-mushroom soup, ½ can (½ cup plus 2 tablespoons) cream-of-chicken soup (save the rest for Step 4), ½ cup milk and ground ginger in small bowl; mix well; pour over chicken pieces in casserole; cover.

3. Bake in moderate oven (350°) 30 minutes; remove cover; stir to mix sauce and juices from chicken; cover again; bake 30 minutes longer, or until chicken is tender. Reset oven to hot (450°).

4. Combine biscuit mix, cornmeal and crystallized ginger in small bowl; mix 3 tablespoons milk with saved chicken soup; stir into biscuit mixture, mixing lightly.

5. Remove casserole from oven; uncover casserole and drop dough by spoonfuls to make 8 mounds in a ring on top of chicken.

6. Bake in hot oven (450°) about 15 minutes longer, or until biscuits are puffed and golden-brown.

### Herb Idea

For oven chicken: Mix a pinch of marjoram into melted butter or margarine for coating the chicken before you put it in the oven, or when you baste while cooking.

## CURRY GLAZED CHICKEN

*The happy blend of curry and marmalade makes this a special-occasion dish.*

*Bake at 400° for 1 hour.*
*Makes 8 servings.*

2 broiler-fryers, quartered
6 tablespoons (¾ stick) butter or margarine
1 large onion, chopped (1 cup)
8 slices raw bacon, finely diced
2 tablespoons flour
1 tablespoon curry powder
1 can condensed beef broth
¼ cup marmalade (ginger or orange)
2 tablespoons catsup
2 tablespoons lemon juice

1. Wash chicken quarters; pat dry; remove skin, if you wish.
2. Melt butter or margarine in a large shallow baking pan. Dip chicken in butter to coat both sides; then arrange, meaty side up, in a single layer in same pan.
3. Bake in hot oven (400°) 20 minutes, or until starting to turn golden.
4. While chicken bakes, combine remaining ingredients in a medium-size saucepan; heat, stirring constantly, to boiling, then simmer, stirring often, 15

minutes, or until thick. Spoon about half over chicken to make a thick coating.

5. Continue baking 20 minutes; spoon on rest of glaze. Bake 20 minutes longer, or until chicken is tender and richly glazed.

## SMOTHERED CHICKEN

*Baked in liquid under cover, chicken makes its own delicious gravy.*

*Bake at 350° for 1 hour.*
*Makes 6 servings.*

| | |
|---|---|
| 3 broiler-fryers (about 2 pounds each), split | 6 tablespoons (¾ stick) butter or margarine |
| ⅔ cup flour | 1 medium-size onion, chopped (½ cup) |
| 2 teaspoons salt | 2½ cups water |
| ¼ teaspoon pepper | |

1. Wash chicken halves; pat dry. Shake with mixture of ⅓ cup flour, 1½ teaspoons salt and pepper in a paper bag to coat evenly.

2. Brown pieces, several at a time, in butter or margarine in a large frying pan; place in a single layer in a roasting pan.

3. Sauté onion until soft in drippings in frying pan; stir in 1½ cups of the water and remaining ½ teaspoon salt. Heat, stirring constantly, to boiling; pour over chicken; cover.

4. Bake in moderate oven (350°) for 1 hour or until chicken is tender. Remove to a heated serving platter and keep warm in slow oven while making gravy.

5. Blend remaining ⅓ cup flour and 1 cup water until smooth in a 2-cup measure. Heat liquid in roasting pan to boiling; slowly stir in flour mixture. Cook, stirring constantly, until gravy thickens and boils 1 minute. Darken with a few drops bottled gravy coloring, if you wish. Serve separately to spoon over chicken.

# CHICKEN CORIANDER

*This unusual chicken dish has a delightfully spicy flavor.*

*Bake at 350° for 1 hour.*
*Makes 6 servings.*

3 chicken breasts (about 12 ounces each)
4 tablespoons (½ stick) butter or margarine
1 small onion, grated
1 tablespoon coriander
1½ teaspoons salt
½ teaspoon chili powder
1 tablespoon lemon juice
Pan Gravy

1. Halve chicken breasts; remove skin, if you wish; then cut meat in one piece from bones.
2. Melt butter or margarine in a shallow baking pan; stir in seasonings.
3. Roll chicken in mixture to coat well, then arrange in a single layer in same pan. Bake in moderate oven (350°) 30 minutes; turn.
4. Continue baking, basting several times with buttery liquid in pan, 30 minutes longer, or until chicken is tender. Serve with Pan Gravy (for recipe, turn to chapter on GRAVIES).

# ONION DIP CHICKEN

*Sharp onion-soup mix gives this crumb-coated chicken a zesty flavor.*

*Bake at 350° for 1 hour.*
*Makes 8 servings.*

2 broiler-fryers (about 2 pounds each), cut up
1 envelope (1⅜ ounces) onion-soup mix
1 cup soft bread crumbs (2 slices)
1 teaspoon salt
⅛ teaspoon pepper

1. Remove skin from chicken, if you wish; cut away small bones from breast pieces.
2. Combine soup mix, bread crumbs, salt and pepper in a paper bag. Shake chicken pieces, a few at a time, in mixture to coat well. Place, not touching, in a single layer in a buttered large shallow baking pan.
3. Bake in moderate oven (350°) 1 hour, or until chicken is tender and richly browned.

## CHICKEN DIABLE

*The flavor secret: Honey, mustard and curry powder, an oddly delectable blend.*

*Bake at 375° for 1 hour.*
*Makes 4 servings.*

1 **broiler-fryer (about 3 pounds), cut up**
4 **tablespoons (½ stick) butter or margarine**
½ **cup honey**
¼ **cup prepared mustard**
1 **teaspoon salt**
1 **teaspoon curry powder**

1. Wash chicken pieces; pat dry; remove skin, if you wish.
2. Melt the butter or margarine in a shallow baking pan; stir in remaining ingredients. Roll chicken in butter mixture to coat both sides; then arrange, meaty side up, in a single layer in same pan.
3. Bake in moderate oven (375°) 1 hour, or until chicken is tender and richly glazed.

# BAKED CHICKEN ORIENTALE

*This chicken has a rich honey-and-soy glaze, at once sweet and sour.*

*Bake at 350° for 1 hour.*
*Makes 4 servings.*

| | |
|---|---|
| 1 broiler-fryer (about 3 pounds), cut in serving-size pieces | 8 tablespoons (1 stick) butter or margarine |
| ½ cup flour | ¼ cup honey |
| 1 teaspoon salt | ¼ cup lemon juice |
| ¼ teaspoon pepper | 1 tablespoon soy sauce |

1. Wash chicken pieces; drain. Shake in mixture of flour, salt and pepper in paper bag to coat well.
2. Melt 4 tablespoons of the butter or margarine in a baking dish, 13x9x2; roll the chicken pieces, one at a time, in melted butter to coat all over. Place, skin side down, in single layer in baking dish.
3. Place baking dish in moderate oven (350°); make for 30 minutes.
4. Melt remaining 4 tablespoons butter or margarine in small saucepan; stir in honey, lemon juice and soy sauce until well mixed.
5. Turn chicken; pour honey mixture over. Bake, basting several times with syrup and drippings in pan, 30 minutes longer, or until tender and richly glazed.


# SAN FERNANDO PEPPER CHICKEN

*Seasoned pepper—a spunky blend—flavors this Southwest chicken dish.*

*Bake at 350° for 1 hour.*
*Makes 6 servings.*

| | |
|---|---|
| ½ cup (1 stick) butter or margarine | 1½ tablespoons seasoned pepper |
| 2 broiler-fryers (about 2 pounds each), cut in serving-size pieces | 2 teaspoons salt |
| | Savory Mushroom Gravy |

1. Melt butter or margarine in large shallow baking pan. Roll chicken pieces one at a time in butter to coat well; then arrange, skin side down, in single layer in pan.

2. Combine seasoned pepper and salt in a small cup; sprinkle half evenly over the chicken.

3. Bake in moderate oven (350°) 30 minutes; turn; sprinkle remaining seasoning mixture over. Bake 30 minutes longer, or until chicken is tender and lightly browned.

4. Arrange on heated serving platter; keep warm in a slow oven while making gravy. Serve gravy in separate bowl to spoon over chicken.

## SAVORY MUSHROOM GRAVY

Pour off all chicken drippings from pan; return ¼ cupful. Stir in 1 can condensed cream-of-mushroom soup mix. Blend in ½ cup water. Cook slowly, stirring constantly, 8 to 10 minutes, until thickened. Makes 2 cups.

## BAKED LEMON CHICKEN

*Lemon baste is the secret ingredient here.*

*Bake at 375° for 1 hour.*
*Makes 4 servings.*

1 broiler-fryer (about 2½ pounds)
½ cup flour
1¼ teaspoons salt
1 teaspoon leaf tarragon, crumbled
½ cup (1 stick) butter or margarine
⅓ cup lemon juice
1 tablespoon instant minced onion
1 clove of garlic, mashed
⅛ teaspoon pepper

1. Cut broiler-fryer into serving-size pieces.

2. Combine flour, 1 teaspoon of the salt and tarragon in a plastic bag. Shake chicken in flour to coat; tap off excess.

3. Melt butter or margarine in a 13x9x2-inch baking pan. Coat chicken on all sides in melted butter or margarine, then turn the pieces skin-side up.

4. Bake in moderate oven (375°), brushing often with pan drippings, 30 minutes.

5. Meanwhile, make Lemon Baste: Mix lemon juice, instant minced onion, garlic, remaining ¼ teaspoon salt and pepper in a small bowl. Brush chicken pieces with part of the Lemon Baste.

6. Bake, brushing occasionally with remaining Lemon Baste, 30 minutes longer, or until chicken is tender.

# POTATO-FLAKE CHICKEN

*Mashed potato flakes make the coating for oven-crisped chicken.*

*Bake at 350° for 1½ hours.*
*Makes 6 servings.*

⅔ cup evaporated milk (from a tall can)
1 teaspoon salt
1 teaspoon mixed Italian herbs
⅛ teaspoon pepper

1 envelope (1½ cups) instant mashed potato flakes
2 broiler-fryers (about 2 pounds each), cut up
Quick Cream Gravy

1. Pour evaporated milk into a pie plate; stir in salt, Italian herbs and pepper. Empty mashed potato flakes into a second pie plate.

2. Dip chicken pieces into evaporated milk mixture, then into potato flakes to coat well. Place in single layer on ungreased cooky sheet.

3. Bake in moderate oven (350°) 1½ hours, or until tender and golden brown.

4. Serve with Quick Cream Gravy (for recipe, turn to chapter on GRAVIES).

# BUTTER BAKED WINGS AND DRUMSTICKS

*Finger food with a poultry seasoning flavor.*

*Bake at 375° for 45–60 minutes.*
*Makes 12 servings.*

| | |
|---|---|
| 12 drumsticks (3 pounds) | 2 cups saltine cracker crumbs |
| 12 wings (2 pounds) | 1 teaspoon poultry seasoning |
| 2 teaspoons salt | |
| ¼ teaspoon pepper | 1 cup (2 sticks) butter, melted |

1. Sprinkle chicken with the salt and pepper. Combine crumbs and poultry seasoning. Dip chicken in butter, then roll in crumbs to coat well.
2. Place on two foil-lined 15½x10½x1-inch baking pans. Drizzle remaining butter over chicken. Bake in moderate oven (375°) 45 to 60 minutes, until tender.

# RUBY CHICKEN

*A freezer-to-oven chicken with a tangy fruit sauce.*

*Bake at 350° for 2 hours.*
*Makes 12 servings, or 6 servings for 2 meals.*

| | |
|---|---|
| 3 broiler-fryers (2½ pounds each), quartered | 1½ teaspoons ground ginger |
| 1 tablespoon salt | 1 tablespoon grated orange rind |
| ¼ cup vegetable oil | 2 cups orange juice |
| 3 medium-size onions, chopped (1½ cups) | 3 tablespoons lemon juice |
| 1½ teaspoons ground cinnamon | 2 cans (1 pound each) whole-berry cranberry sauce |

1. Sprinkle chicken pieces with salt. Brown chicken on one side in hot oil, using two skillets; turn, add onions; brown on second side.

2. Sprinkle on the cinnamon and ginger. Add orange rind and juice and lemon juice. Cover; simmer 20 minutes. Add cranberry sauce. Simmer, covered, 15 minutes longer, or until almost tender. Cool quickly.

3. Line two 10-cup freezer-to-table baking dishes with heavy foil. Remove chicken to foil-lined dishes.

4. Measure cooking liquid and thicken, if you wish. Allow 1 tablespoon of flour mixed with 2 tablespoons water for each cup of liquid. Bring to boil, cook 3 minutes, cool, pour over chicken.

5. Freeze chicken and sauce. When frozen, remove foil-wrapped food from baking dishes; return to freezer.

6. To serve: Remove foil, place food in same baking dish. Heat, covered, in moderate oven (350°), turning pieces once, 2 hours, or until bubbly-hot.

## PINEAPPLE-STUFFED CHICKEN BREASTS

*An elegant chicken served with a sweet-sour sauce.*

Bake at 350° for 40–45 minutes.
Makes 8 servings.

| | |
|---|---|
| 8 whole small chicken breasts, boned | ½ cup chopped celery |
| 1¼ teaspoons salt, divided | ¼ cup chopped onion |
| 1 can (8¼ ounces) crushed pineapple | ½ teaspoon dried leaf tarragon |
| 6 tablespoons butter or margarine, divided | ½ cup fine dry bread crumbs |
| ½ cup chopped green pepper | 1 tablespoon chopped pimiento |
| | Sweet-Sour Pineapple Sauce |

1. Place boned chicken breasts skin side down on board. Sprinkle with ¾ teaspoon salt.

2. Drain pineapple and reserve the syrup for Sweet-Sour Pineapple Sauce.

3. Heat 4 tablespoons butter or margarine in skillet; add green pepper, celery, onion and remaining ½ teaspoon salt. Cook until vegetables are tender. Remove from heat; add tarragon, bread crumbs, pimiento and drained pineapple; mix well.

4. Place about ¼ cup stuffing mixture in center of each chicken breast; fold the sides over and fasten with skewers or string.

5. Heat remaining 2 tablespoons butter in large skillet. Add chicken breasts, four at a time, and brown lightly on all sides. Remove to shallow baking pan. Bake in 350° oven 40 to 45 minutes, until tender. Serve with Sweet-Sour Pineapple Sauce.

## SWEET-SOUR PINEAPPLE SAUCE

1 tablespoon vegetable oil
½ cup chopped green pepper
2 tablespoons chopped onion
1 can (8¼ ounces) pineapple slices in syrup
Syrup reserved from crushed pineapple
4 teaspoons cornstarch
¾ cup water
1 chicken bouillon cube
1 tablespoon brown sugar
¼ teaspoon dried leaf tarragon
2 tablespoons vinegar
1 tablespoon soy sauce
2 tablespoons diced pimiento

1. Heat vegetable oil in saucepan. Add green pepper and onion; cook 2 minutes.

2. Drain syrup from pineapple slices and add to saucepan with syrup reserved from the crushed pineapple in stuffing.

3. Blend cornstarch with water; add to saucepan.

4. Add bouillon cube, brown sugar, tarragon, vine-

gar and soy sauce. Cook, stirring constantly, until mixture thickens and comes to a boil.

5. Cut pineapple slices in half; add to sauce with pimiento. Heat and serve over chicken breasts.

# ITALIAN CHICKEN BAKE

*Perfect for a large buffet dinner you want to enjoy.*

Bake at 350° for 30 minutes.
Makes 16 servings.

3 broiler-fryers (about 3 pounds each), cut up
1 medium-size onion, peeled and sliced
2½ teaspoons salt
½ teaspoon peppercorns
1 pound mushrooms, trimmed and sliced
1 cup (2 sticks) butter or margarine
1 cup fine soft bread crumbs
½ cup regular flour
¼ teaspoon pepper
¼ teaspoon ground nutmeg
2 cups light cream or table cream
½ cup dry sherry
1 package (1 pound) thin spaghetti, broken in 2-inch lengths
1 cup grated Parmesan cheese

1. Combine chicken, onion, 1 teaspoon of the salt, peppercorns and enough water to cover in a kettle. Heat to boiling; cover. Cook 40 minutes, or until chicken is tender. Remove from broth and cool until easy to handle. Strain broth into a 4-cup measure and set aside for making sauce.

2. Pull skin from chicken and take meat from bones; cube meat; place in a large bowl.

3. Sauté mushrooms in ¼ cup of the buttter or margarine until soft in a large frying pan; combine with chicken.

4. Melt remaining butter or margarine in a saucepan. Measure out ¼ cup and toss with bread crumbs in a bowl; set aside.

5. Stir flour, the remaining 1½ teaspoons salt, pepper and nutmeg into remaining butter or margarine in saucepan; cook, stirring constantly, until bubbly. Stir in 3½ cups of the chicken broth and cream. Continue cooking and stirring until sauce thickens and boils 1 minute; remove from heat. Stir in sherry.

6. While sauce cooks, cook spaghetti, following label directions; drain well. Spoon into two baking dishes, 13x9x2. Spoon chicken mixture over spaghetti; spoon sauce over all.

7. Add Parmesan cheese to bread-crumb mixture and toss lightly to mix. Sprinkle over mixture in baking dishes.

8. Bake in moderate oven (350°) 30 minutes, or until bubbly and crumb topping is toasted. Garnish with bouquets of watercress, sliced mushrooms and pimiento strips, if you wish.

DAY-BEFORE NOTE: Fix the 2 casseroles through Step 7; cover and chill. About an hour before serving, remove from refrigerator and uncover. Bake in moderate oven (350°) 40 minutes, or until bubbly. If casseroles must stand a bit before serving, leave in oven with heat turned off.

## BISCUIT-CHICKEN ROLLS

*Cheese, chicken and biscuits combined for an old-fashioned kind of treat.*

*Bake chicken at 450° for 15 minutes; then bake biscuit and chicken at 450° for 10 minutes.*

*Makes 10 snack servings, or 5 meal servings.*

5 **chicken thighs,**
   **boned**
½ **teaspoon salt**
¼ **teaspoon pepper**
1 **teaspoon instant**
   **minced onion**

¼ **teaspoon each,**
   **dried leaf basil and**
   **oregano**
1 **can (8 ounces) re-**
   **frigerated country-**
   **style or buttermilk**
   **biscuits**
**Swiss cheese slices**

1. To bone chicken thighs, cut along thinner side of thigh to the bone, slashing thigh the length of the bone. Holding one end of the bone, scrape the meat away until bone is free. Cut off rounded piece of cartilage. Remove skin and cut each boned thigh in half lengthwise.

2. Sprinkle on both sides with salt, pepper, instant minced onion, basil and oregano. Place in shallow baking pan and bake in hot oven (450°) 15 minutes.

3. Stretch each biscuit into oval. Cut strips of cheese slightly smaller than biscuit ovals; place on biscuits. Place pieces of cooked chicken across each biscuit. Fold cheese and biscuit over chicken and place, seam side down, on foil-lined baking sheet. Bake in hot oven (450°) 10 minutes, or until biscuit is browned.

## Broiled Chicken

### KEY LIME CHICKEN BROIL

*A zesty splash of lime and tarragon seasons tender broiled chicken.*

*Makes 6 servings.*

| | |
|---|---|
| 3 broiler-fryers (about 2 pounds each), split | 2 teaspoons tarragon, crushed |
| ½ cup lime juice | 1 teaspoon seasoned salt |
| ½ cup vegetable oil | ¼ teaspoon seasoned pepper |
| 1 tablespoon grated onion | |

1. Wash chickens; pat dry. Place, skin side down, on rack in broiler pan.

2. Mix lime juice, vegetable oil, onion, tarragon, and seasoned salt and pepper in a small bowl. Brush generously over chickens.

3. Broil, turning every 10 minutes and brushing with more lime mixture, 40 minutes, or until the chickens are tender and richly browned. Remove to a heated large serving platter.

# BROILED CHICKEN BING

*Elegant sweet-sour cherry sauce dresses up crisply broiled chicken.*

*Makes 6 servings.*

| | |
|---|---|
| **3 broiler-fryers (about 2 pounds each), split** | **2 cups Dark Cherry Sauce** |

1. Wash chickens; pat dry. Place, skin side down, on rack in broiler pan.
2. Broil, turning every 10 minutes, until the chickens are tender and brown—about 40 minutes. Remove to heated serving platter.
3. Spoon hot Dark Cherry Sauce over all and serve immediately.

# DARK CHERRY SAUCE

*Makes about 2 cups.*

| | |
|---|---|
| **1 can (1 pound) pitted dark sweet cherries** | **1 tablespoon molasses** |
| | **Few drops red-pepper seasoning** |
| **2 tablespoons cornstarch** | **Dash of salt** |
| **1 tablespoon prepared mustard** | **3 tablespoons lemon juice** |

1. Drain syrup from cherries into a 2-cup measure; add water to make 1½ cups. (Save cherries for Step 3.)
2. Blend a few tablespoons syrup into cornstarch until smooth in a small saucepan; stir in remaining syrup, mustard, molasses, red-pepper seasoning and salt. Cook over low heat, stirring constantly, until mixture thickens and boils 3 minutes.
3. Stir in cherries and lemon juice; heat slowly just until bubbly. Serve hot.

## Calorie- and Fat-Saver

Because of the fat in chicken skin, broiler-fryers can be broiled without additional fat. Simply sprinkle with salt, pepper, monosodium glutamate, lemon juice and an herb such as tarragon, thyme or basil. Broiled chicken may also be basted with a barbecue sauce near the end of cooking time.

# Roasted Chicken

## LITTLE CHICKEN ROASTS

*When you plan to make this delicious recipe, remember that everyone rates a half chicken and a portion of stuffing.*

*Roast at 400° for 1½ hours.*
*Makes 6 servings.*

3 whole broiler-fryers (1½ pounds each)
Salt
½ cup (1 stick) butter or margarine
1 can (about 9 ounces) crushed pineapple
3 cups soft bread crumbs (6 slices)
½ cup flaked coconut
½ cup chopped celery
½ teaspoon salt
¼ teaspoon poultry seasoning
2 tablespoons bottled steak sauce
Sweet-and-Sour Sauce

1. Rinse chickens inside and out with cold water; drain, then pat dry. Sprinkle inside with salt.
2. Melt butter or margarine in a small saucepan. Drain syrup from pineapple into a cup and set aside for Step 6.
3. Combine pineapple with bread crumbs, coconut and celery in a medium-size bowl; drizzle 4 tablespoons of the melted butter or margarine over; toss with a fork until crumbs are lightly coated. (Save remaining butter or margarine for Step 5.)

4. Stuff neck and body cavities of chickens lightly with the pineapple-bread mixture. Smooth neck skin over stuffing and skewer to back; close body cavity and tie legs to tail. Place chickens in a roasting pan.

5. Stir salt and poultry seasoning into saved 4 tablespoons butter or margarine in saucepan; brush part over chickens.

6. Roast for 1 hour in a hot oven (400°), basting several times with butter mixture. Stir saved pineapple syrup and steak sauce into any remaining butter in saucepan; brush generously over chickens.

7. Continue roasting, basting once or twice more, 30 minutes longer, or until drumsticks move easily and meaty part of thigh feels soft.

8. Remove chickens to heated serving platter; keep warm while making sauce.

9. When ready to serve, cut away strings from chickens. Garnish platter with watercress and preserved mixed fruits, if you wish. Pass sauce in a separate bowl.

## SWEET-AND-SOUR SAUCE

Blend 2 tablespoons cornstarch into drippings in roasting pan; stir in 1 cup water. Cook, stirring all the time, just until mixture thickens and boils 3 minutes. Stir in 2 tablespoons brown sugar and 1 tablespoon of lemon juice. Strain into heated serving bowl. Makes about 1¼ cups.

## ROAST CAPON

*This elegant fowl should be simply prepared so as not to detract from its own fine flavor.*

*Roast at 325° about 2½ hours.*
*Makes 6 servings.*

| | |
|---|---|
| 1 ready-to-cook capon (about 7 pounds) | 6 cups stuffing |
| Salt | Melted butter or margarine |
| Pepper | |

1. Sprinkle the chicken inside with salt and pepper.
2. Pack stuffing lightly into neck cavity. (Bread-and-Butter Stuffing is good with capon; for recipe, see section on STUFFINGS.) Smooth neck skin over stuffing and fasten with wooden picks or skewers to back of bird; twist wing tips until they rest flat against fastened neck skin.
3. Stuff body cavity lightly; fasten opening, and tie legs together and fasten to tailpiece.
4. Place capon, breast side up, on rack in a large open roasting pan; brush well with melted butter or margarine; cover breast with double-thick cheesecloth moistened with additional fat.
5. Roast in slow oven (325°) 2½ hours, or until meaty part of drumstick is tender when pierced with a 2-tine fork; baste frequently during roasting.
6. Place capon on heated serving platter and serve while hot.

# COUNTRY ROAST CHICKEN

*Corn bread stuffing makes this an extra special roast.*

*Bake at 375° for 1½ hours.*
*Makes 8 servings.*

2 broiler-fryers (about 3 pounds each)
1 cup water
½ teaspoon salt
1 package (8 ounces) corn bread-stuffing mix
1 medium-size onion, chopped (½ cup)
½ cup sliced celery
½ cup (1 stick) butter or margarine
¼ cup bacon drippings OR ¼ cup (½ stick) butter or margarine, melted

1. Remove giblets and necks from chicken packages and place (except livers) with water and salt in a small saucepan; cover. Simmer 45 minutes. Add livers; cover; simmer 15 minutes longer; cool.
2. Remove giblets and necks from broth; reserve

broth. Chop giblets and the meat from necks; place in a large bowl; stir in stuffing mix.

3. Simmer reserved broth until reduced to ½ cup; reserve.

4. Sauté onion and celery in the ½ cup butter or margarine for 5 minutes in a medium-size skillet. Add with reserved broth to stuffing mixture in bowl; toss until evenly moistened.

5. Stuff neck and body cavities lightly with stuffing. Skewer neck skin to back; close body cavity and tie legs to tail. Place chickens on rack in roasting pan. Brush with part of bacon drippings or butter or margarine.

6. Roast in moderate oven (375°) basting every 30 minutes with bacon drippings or butter or margarine, 1½ hours, or until tender.

7. To serve: Place on heated serving platter. Cut chickens into quarters with poultry shears.


## SAVORY ROAST CHICKEN

*Attention beginners: You almost can't muff this one. Look for the good-buy young roasters, heavy with meat on their frames.*

*Roast at 375° about 2 hours.*
*Makes 4 servings.*

| | |
|---|---|
| **1 roasting chicken** | **2 cups Savory Stuffing** |
|   **(about 4 pounds)** | **1 to 2 tablespoons** |
| **½ teaspoon salt** |   **butter or margarine** |

1. Wash chicken and pat dry. Sprinkle inside with salt.

2. Stuff neck and body cavities lightly with Savory Stuffing. Skewer neck skin to body, secure body closed, tie legs to tailpiece.

3. Place chicken on rack in shallow roasting pan; rub with butter or margarine. Roast at 375° about 2 hours (figure time at 30 minutes per pound), or until drumstick moves easily at joint.

# GLAZED CHICKEN WITH PEACHES

*A mouth-watering masterpiece of glossy little roasters on a bed of rice with golden peaches.*

*Roast at 375° for 1½ to 2 hours.*
*Makes 6 servings.*

2 roasting chickens
   (about 3½ pounds
   each)
1 teaspoon salt
2 cups stuffing

2 tablespoons melted
   butter or margarine
Golden Glaze and
   Golden Peaches

1. Wash and dry chickens; sprinkle the inside with salt; stuff neck and body cavities lightly with stuffing. (Savory Stuffing is good with this chicken.) Skewer neck skin to body, close body cavity and tie legs to tailpiece; place on rack in shallow roasting pan; brush with butter or margarine.

2. Roast in moderate oven (375°) 1½ to 2 hours (figure roasting time at 30 minutes per pound for one bird), or until drumstick moves easily at joint.

3. About 20 minutes before chickens are done, brush with Golden Glaze; continue roasting (brush once more after 10 minutes) until chickens are done.

4. Serve on a bed of rice on a heated platter, garnished with Golden Peaches.

# GOLDEN GLAZE AND GOLDEN PEACHES

*Bake at 375° for 20 minutes.*

1 can (about 1 pound)
   peach halves

2 tablespoons bottled
   meat sauce

1. Drain peach halves, saving syrup in small bowl; arrange peaches, cut side up, in shallow baking dish.

2. Blend meat sauce into syrup for Golden Glaze and brush over chickens; brush peach halves with rest of glaze for Golden Peaches; bake peaches in oven along with chicken during last 20 minutes of roasting time.

## Stuffings

### HAWAIIAN STUFFING

*Makes about 2½ cups.*

1½ cups soft bread
  crumbs
⅓ cup flaked coconut
¼ cup finely chopped
  celery

¼ cup drained,
  crushed pineapple
1 tablespoon grated
  orange peel
2 tablespoons melted
  butter or margarine

Combine all ingredients in a bowl and toss lightly to blend.

### FRUIT STUFFING

*Makes 7 cups.*

1 can (pound) sliced
  apples
Water
½ cup (1 stick) butter
  or margarine

1 package (2 cups)
  ready-mix bread
  stuffing
1 cup chopped peanuts
½ cup seedless raisins

1. Drain apples and add water to apple liquid to make 1 cup. Heat to boiling in large saucepan.
2. Stir in butter or margarine until melted.
3. Add ready-mix stuffing, apples, peanuts and raisins, tossing lightly to mix.

### SAVORY STUFFING

*Makes 2 cups.*

½ cup chopped celery
  leaves
2 tablespoons chopped
  onion
4 tablespoons (½
  stick) butter or
  margarine

½ cup water
2 cups ready-mix bread
  stuffing (½ of an
  8-ounce package)

1. Sauté celery leaves and onion in butter or margarine in medium-size saucepan. Add water; heat to boiling.

2. Stir in bread stuffing; toss with fork just until moistened.

## BREAD-AND-BUTTER STUFFING

*Makes about 3 cups.*

3 cups (about 6 slices) small dry bread cubes. To make dry bread cubes: Spread cubes out on baking sheet; bake in a very slow oven (300°) 15 minutes, or until cubes are dry but not brown
1 small onion, finely chopped (¼ cup)

2 tablespoons chopped parsley
1½ teaspoons crumbled basil
¼ teaspoon salt
⅛ teaspoon pepper
1 egg
¼ cup (½ stick) melted butter or margarine

1. Combine bread cubes, onion, parsley, basil, salt, pepper and egg in medium-size bowl.

2. Sprinkle melted butter or margarine over bread mixture; toss with fork until blended.

## GOURMET STUFFING

*Makes 2 cups.*

3 chicken livers
4 tablespoons (½ stick) butter or margarine
2 cups soft bread crumbs (4 slices)

2 tablespoons chopped onion
1 tablespoon water
1 teaspoon Worcestershire sauce
½ teaspoon salt

1. Sauté livers in butter or margarine, stirring often, in frying pan 5 minutes, or until livers lose their pink color.

2. Remove livers and chop, then add to bread crumbs in medium-sized bowl. Sauté onion just until soft in same frying pan.

3. Stir water, Worcestershire sauce and salt into onions in the frying pan; pour over crumb mixture. Toss lightly to mix well. (Mixture will be crumbly, not wet.)

## APRICOT-WALNUT STUFFING

*Makes 4 cups.*

1 medium-size onion, chopped (½ cup)
4 tablespoons (½ stick) butter or margarine
½ cup chopped dry apricots

1 envelope instant chicken broth OR
1 chicken bouillon cube
⅓ cup water
6 slices white bread, cubed (about 3 cups)
½ cup chopped walnuts

1. In a large frying pan, sauté onion in butter or margarine until soft; stir in apricots, chicken broth or bouillon cube and water. Heat to boiling, crushing bouillon cube if used; remove from heat.

2. Add cubed bread and walnuts; toss until evenly moist.

## HILO STUFFING

*Makes 4 cups.*

1 cup uncooked white rice
4 tablespoons (½ stick) butter or margarine
1 medium-size onion, chopped (½ cup)

2 envelopes instant chicken broth OR
2 chicken bouillon cubes
2½ cups water
½ cup chopped macadamia nuts (from a 6-ounce jar)
½ cup flaked coconut

1. In a large saucepan, sauté rice in butter or margarine, stirring often, just until golden.

2. Stir in onion, chicken broth or bouillon cubes and water; heat to boiling, crushing cubes, if using, with a spoon; cover. Simmer 20 minutes, or until rice is tender and liquid is absorbed.

3. Sprinkle with nuts and coconut; toss lightly to mix.

## Chapter 7

# Fried Favorites

Pasta is Italian, fish 'n chips are English and cheese soufflés are French. But there's no question about the fact that fried chicken is American. It's so integral a part of our heritage, it's difficult to imagine life without it. Every year, fried chicken is carried in picnic baskets to open fields and baseball games (another American tradition). It's brought to the backyard; sent to school in lunch pails, and served on Sunday tables all across the country.

To celebrate this tradition, we bring you a delightful recipe for basic fried chicken. However, in the true American style of adventure, we don't stop here. There are also recipes for fried chicken with gravy and ones that include special herbs for the crust.

Whichever you prefer, get out your frying pan or electric skillet—it's time to uphold an American custom!

## BASIC FRIED CHICKEN

*Essential to any good cook's repertoire, this chicken can't be hurried—but it is certainly worth waiting for.*

*Makes 4 servings.*

1 broiler-fryer (about 3 pounds)
½ cup flour
1 teaspoon salt
⅛ teaspoon pepper
1 cup bacon drippings or part drippings and shortening

1. Cut chicken into 8 serving-size pieces—2 breasts, 2 wings, 2 thighs, 2 drumsticks. (Simmer bony back pieces to make broth for gravy, if you wish.) Wash chicken, but do not dry. This is important so skin will take on a thick flour coating.

2. Mix flour, salt and pepper in a bag. Shake pieces, a few at a time, to coat evenly.

3. Heat bacon drippings ¼-inch deep in a large heavy frying pan on medium heat, or in an electric skillet to 360°. Arrange chicken in a single layer in hot fat.

4. Brown slowly for 15 minutes. When pink juices start to show on top, turn and brown the other side 15 minutes. Slow cooking, plus turning just once, gives the chicken its crisp coating.

5. When pieces are browned, pile all back into pan or skillet and cover. Lower range heat to simmer or reset control at 260°. Let chicken cook 20 minutes longer, or until it's richly golden and fork-tender.

## VARIATIONS

For added flavor, mix ½ teaspoon dried leaf thyme, tarragon, basil or poultry seasoning, or 1 teaspoon curry powder to the flour.

### Coatings that Stick

Chicken coated with seasoned flour before frying has a very thin crust. For a crisp, heavier crust, lightly dust chicken with flour and dip pieces in buttermilk or in a mixture of 1 egg beaten with ⅓ cup milk and 2 tablespoons lemon juice. Then roll in seasoned flour and place on wire racks. Let the chicken stand for 30 minutes for the coating to dry; roll in flour again if the coating is still moist. Proceed as usual for skillet-fried or oven-fried chicken.

# IOWA FRIED CHICKEN

*A convenient chicken that requires only 5 easy-to-get ingredients.*

*Makes 8 servings.*

1½ cups yellow corn-
   meal
1 envelope Italian
   salad dressing mix
½ cup cream for
   whipping

2 broiler-fryers (about
   2 pounds each), cut
   up
Vegetable oil

1. Combine cornmeal and salad dressing mix on a sheet of waxed paper; pour cream into a pie plate.
2. Dip chicken pieces into cream, then roll in cornmeal mixture to coat well; let stand on wire racks about 5 minutes.
3. Pour vegetable oil to a depth of 1 inch into each of 2 large frying pans; heat until a few drops of water sprinkled into oil sizzle. Add chicken and brown slowly, turning several times; cover. Cook 20 minutes longer, or until chicken is tender. Drain on paper toweling. Serve hot.

# GOLDEN-COATED FRIED CHICKEN

*Bread the chicken pieces and chill them, then fry very slowly—this gives the crusty golden coat.*

*Makes 6 servings.*

2 broiler-fryers (about
   2 pounds each), cut
   in serving-size pieces
1 cup (8-ounce
   carton) dairy sour
   cream
2 tablespoons lemon
   juice
1 teaspoon salt

1 teaspoon garlic salt
1 teaspoon Worcester-
   shire sauce
1¼ cups fine dry
   bread crumbs
Shortening or vegetable
   oil for frying
1 package chicken
   gravy mix

1. Wash chicken pieces; pat dry.

2. Mix sour cream, lemon juice, salt, garlic salt and Worcestershire sauce in a small bowl; place bread crumbs in a pie plate. Brush chicken pieces with sour cream mixture, then roll in crumbs to coat well.

3. Place in a single layer on a cooky sheet. Chill at least 1 hour. Chill remaining sour cream mixture for Step 6.

4. Melt enough shortening or pour in enough vegetable oil to make ½-inch depth in a large frying pan.

5. Brown chicken, a few pieces at a time, very slowly in hot fat; return all pieces to pan; cover. Cook over *very low* heat 30 minutes or until chicken is tender.

6. Prepare chicken gravy mix, following label directions. Stir ¼ cup of the hot gravy into remaining sour cream mixture; stir back into remaining gravy in pan; heat slowly just until hot. Serve separately to spoon over chicken.

## COUNTRY FRIED CHICKEN

*Chicken the way it was served down on the farm in Grandma's day (if you were lucky). It's crisp and flavory, with gravy.*

*Makes 6 to 8 servings.*

| | |
|---|---|
| 2 broiler-fryers (about 2 pounds each), cut into serving-size pieces | 1 teaspoon paprika |
| | ¼ teaspoon pepper |
| | 1 cup bacon drippings |
| | 2 cloves garlic |
| ⅔ cup flour | 1 bay leaf |
| 2 teaspoons salt | 2 cups Milk Gravy |

1. Wash and dry chicken pieces. Shake, a few at a time, in mixture of flour, salt, paprika and pepper in a paper bag to coat well.

2. Heat bacon drippings with whole cloves of garlic and bay leaf in large frying pan.

3. Place chicken in single layer in hot drippings. (Do not crowd as pieces should have enough room to

brown without touching each other.) Cook slowly, turning once or twice to brown both sides. (It will take about 30 minutes.)

4. Return all chicken to frying pan; cover; cook slowly 20 minutes, or until tender. Uncover; cook 5 minutes longer to crisp coating. Remove chicken to heated platter; keep hot in slow oven long enough to make Milk Gravy.

## MILK GRAVY

Tip pan and pour off all drippings into a cup, leaving crusty brown bits in pan. (Be sure to remove garlic cloves and bay leaf.) Return 3 tablespoons drippings to pan; blend in 3 tablespoons flour; cook, stirring all the time, just until mixture bubbles. Stir in 1 cup water and 1 cup milk slowly; continue cooking and stirring, scraping brown bits from bottom and sides of pan, until gravy thickens and boils 1 minute. Season to taste with salt. Makes about 2 cups.

## FRIED CHICKEN DIVINE

*The chicken strips are served with a milk gravy over rice.*

*Makes 8 servings.*

| | |
|---|---|
| 4 large breasts, boned | 1 cup buttermilk |
| 1 cup flour | Shortening or vegetable |
| 2 teaspoons salt | oil for frying |
| 2 teaspoons paprika | 5 cups hot cooked rice |
| ¼ teaspoon pepper | |

1. Cut chicken breasts into ½-inch strips. Combine flour, salt, paprika and pepper. Dip chicken strips into buttermilk, then roll in seasoned flour.

2. Heat oil ½-inch deep in skillet until drop of water added to fat sizzles.

3. Add chicken strips and fry until golden brown. To serve, mound rice on platter. Pour over Sauce Divine and top with fried chicken strips.

## SAUCE DIVINE

| | |
|---|---|
| 5 tablespoons butter or margarine | ¼ teaspoon cayenne |
| 5 tablespoons flour | 2 chicken bouillon cubes |
| 1 teaspoon salt | 3 cups milk |

Melt butter or margarine in saucepan. Blend in flour, salt, cayenne and bouillon cubes. Gradually add milk and cook, stirring constantly, until mixture thickens and comes to a boil.

## GINGER CRISP CHICKEN

*Secret of this favorite is double cooking: First baking, then frying. The ginger in the golden crust gives it a slightly spicy flavor.*

*Bake at 350° for 1 hour.*
*Makes 6 servings.*

| | |
|---|---|
| 2 broiler-fryers (about 2 pounds each), cut in serving-size pieces | ½ cup water |
| | 1½ cups Ginger Batter |
| 2 teaspoons salt | Shortening or salad oil for frying |
| 1 teaspoon rosemary | |

1. Wash chicken pieces; pat dry. Place in a single layer in a large shallow baking pan; sprinkle with the salt and rosemary; add water; cover.
2. Bake in moderate oven (350°) for 1 hour.
3. While chicken cooks, make Ginger Batter.
4. Remove chicken from pan; pull off skin and remove small rib bones, if you wish; drain chicken thoroughly on paper toweling.
5. Melt enough shortening or pour in enough salad oil to make a depth of 2 inches in a large frying pan or electric deep-fat fryer. Heat until hot (350° in electric fryer).
6. Dip chicken pieces, 2 or 3 at a time, into Ginger Batter; hold over bowl to let excess drip back.

7. Fry in hot shortening 3 minutes, or until golden-brown. Lift out with a slotted spoon; drain well. Keep warm on a hot platter, covered with foil, until all pieces are cooked.

## GINGER BATTER

*Makes about 1½ cups.*

| | |
|---|---|
| 1¼ cups sifted regular flour | ½ teaspoon ground ginger |
| 1 teaspoon baking powder | 1 egg |
| 1 teaspoon salt | 1 cup milk |
| | ¼ cup salad oil |

1. Sift flour, baking powder, salt and ginger into a medium-size bowl.
2. Add remaining ingredients all at once; beat with a rotary beater until smooth.

## BATTER-FRIED CHICKEN

*A Deep South style of fried chicken you'll want to try regardless where you live.*

*Bake at 375° for 45 minutes.*
*Makes 12 servings.*

| | |
|---|---|
| 3 broiler-fryers, cut in serving-size pieces | 2 teaspoons salt |
| ¼ cup water | 1 quart salad oil |
| | Batter |

1. Place chicken pieces in baking pan; add water and sprinkle with salt. Cover with foil; bake in moderate oven (375°) 45 minutes. Remove chicken pieces from liquid; dry well. If desired, remove skin.
2. Heat salad oil to 350° in a heavy 3-quart saucepan.
3. Dip chicken pieces in Batter; drain off excess. Fry, 2 to 3 pieces at a time, until golden brown, about 3 minutes. Drain on paper towels.

## BATTER

1¼ cups sifted all-
   purpose flour
1 teaspoon baking
   powder

½ teaspoon salt
1 egg
1 cup milk
¼ cup salad oil

Sift flour, baking powder and salt into mixing bowl. Add remaining ingredients; beat with rotary beater until smooth.

## SOUTHERN FRIED CHICKEN

*Time-honored, trusty, crusty chicken with cream gravy.*

*Makes 6 servings.*

2 broiler-fryers (about
   2 pounds each), cut
   up
3 cups light cream or
   table cream

2 cups plus 1 table-
   spoon sifted flour
2½ teaspoons salt
½ teaspoon pepper
Shortening or vegetable
   oil

1. Wash chicken pieces; pat dry. Place in a single layer in a large shallow dish; pour 1 cup of the cream over top; chill at least 20 minutes.
2. Shake chicken pieces, a few at a time, in a mixture of the 2 cups flour, 2 teaspoons salt and ¼ teaspoon pepper in a paper bag to coat well. Dip each again in remaining cream in dish; shake again in flour mixture.
3. Melt enough shortening or pour enough vegetable oil into each of two large heavy frying pans to make a depth of 1½ inches; heat. Add chicken pieces, skin side down. Brown slowly, turning once, then continue cooking 30 minutes, or until tender. Remove; keep warm while making gravy.
4. Pour all drippings from frying pans into a small bowl; measure 2 tablespoonfuls and return to one pan. Stir in 1 tablespoon of flour, remaining ½ teaspoon

salt and ¼ teaspoon pepper. Cook, stirring constantly, until bubbly. Stir in remaining 2 cups cream; continue cooking and stirring, until gravy thickens and boils 1 minute. Serve separately.

## TEMPURA FRIED CHICKEN

*This tender golden-brown chicken is covered with a crispy coat that will make your family shout "More!"*

Bake at 325° for 15 minutes.
Makes 8 servings.

| | |
|---|---|
| 2 broiler-fryers (about 2½ pounds each) | 1 teaspoon salt |
| Salt and pepper | ½ teaspoon ground ginger |
| 1 egg | ½ teaspoon ground cloves |
| 1 cup cold water | |
| 1¼ cups sifted all-purpose flour | Oil or shortening for frying |

1. Cut chickens into serving-size pieces. Sprinkle with salt and pepper. Refrigerate while preparing batter.

2. Beat egg until foamy in a medium-size bowl. Stir in cold water. Sift flour, salt, ginger and cloves into same bowl and beat until smooth. Chill at least 1 hour.

3. Add enough oil or shortening to a large heavy skillet to make a 2-inch depth when heated. Heat to 360° on a deep fat thermometer, or until a cube of bread turns golden in 15 seconds.

4. Dip chilled chicken pieces into batter with tongs. Hold over bowl several seconds to allow excess batter to run off.

5. Fry chicken, a few pieces at a time, turning often, until rich golden brown. Transfer browned chicken to a shallow baking pan. (Do not stack in pan, keep in one layer.)

6. Bake in slow oven (325°) 15 minutes, or until chicken is tender when pierced with a fork. Serve with duck sauce or spicy preserves, if you wish.

# BUTTERMILK FRIED CHICKEN

*A crunchy chicken topped with a creamy buttermilk gravy.*

*Makes 4 servings.*

1 broiler-fryer (about 2½ pounds)
2½ cups buttermilk
1 cup flour
1½ teaspoons salt
½ teaspoon leaf rosemary, crumbled
¼ teaspoon pepper
Shortening or vegetable oil

1. Cut chicken into serving-size pieces.
2. Pour ½ cup of the buttermilk into a shallow dish. Combine flour, salt, rosemary and pepper in a plastic bag.
3. Dip chicken pieces in buttermilk; shake in flour mixture to coat well. Dip again in buttermilk and flour mixture to build a thick coating. Place chicken pieces on wire rack for 15 minutes to allow coating to set. Reserve remaining flour mixture.
4. Melt enough shortening, or pour enough oil, into a large heavy skillet with a cover to ½-inch depth. Place over medium heat. When a few drops of water sizzle when flicked into the hot fat, add the chicken pieces skin-side down. Cook slowly, turning once, 20 minutes, or until chicken is golden.
5. Reduce heat; cover skillet. Cook 30 minutes longer, or until chicken is tender. Remove cover for last 5 minutes for a crunchy crust. Place chicken on platter; keep hot.
6. Pour off all fat into a cup. Return 2 tablespoons to skillet; blend in 3 tablespoons of the reserved flour mixture; cook, stirring constantly just until bubbly. Gradually add remaining 2 cups buttermilk; continue cooking and stirring, scraping to loosen brown bits in pan, until gravy is thickened and bubbles 1 minute. Taste; season with additional salt and pepper, if you wish. Spoon over chicken.

## Chapter 8

# Chicken in Parts

Someone once noted that it's the little things in life that mean a lot. Chicken is no exception. It doesn't take a whole bird to make dinner a success. Chicken parts, which include the breasts, thighs, drumsticks, wings and livers, can be used in a great number of imaginative ways.

For white meat fans, breasts offer the most meat for the money. The thighs, drumsticks and wings offer less meat but no less flavor.

And chicken livers are a delicately-flavored part that finds many uses on your menu.

Buying chicken in parts is an economy move, too, particularly for a small family, or for one whose preference is for only white or dark meat.

And for those who generally prepare a whole chicken, the parts are a nice change of pace.

These little things can mean a great big delicious meal.

# Breasts

## CHICKEN BREASTS MORNAY

*A nippy cheese sauce sparks bland and delicate white meat.*

*Bake at 350° for 55 to 60 minutes.*
*Makes 4 servings.*

4 chicken breasts
¼ cup flour seasoned
  with ½ teaspoon
  salt and dash of
  pepper

¼ cup (½ stick)
  melted butter or
  margarine
Mornay Sauce

1. Dust chicken breasts with seasoned flour.
2. Place in small, shallow baking dish, skin side down; pour melted butter or margarine over and around chicken.
3. Bake in moderate oven (350°) 30 minutes; turn chicken breasts; bake 25 to 30 minutes longer, basting 2 or 3 times during baking, until chicken is golden-brown and tender when pierced with a fork.
4. Place on heated serving platter; serve with Mornay Sauce.

## MORNAY SAUCE

*Makes about 1¼ cups.*

2 teaspoons butter or
  margarine
2 tablespoons flour
½ teaspoon salt
⅛ teaspoon pepper
½ cup milk
½ cup chicken stock

¾ cup grated sharp
  Cheddar cheese
½ teaspoon prepared
  mustard
½ teaspoon Worcester-
  shire sauce
1 tablespoon chopped
  parsley

1. Melt butter or margarine in small saucepan; remove from heat.

2. Blend in flour, salt and pepper; stir in milk and chicken stock.

3. Cook over low heat, stirring constantly, until sauce thickens and boils 1 minute.

4. Add cheese, mustard and Worcestershire sauce; continue cooking, stirring occasionally, until cheese melts; remove from heat.

5. Stir in parsley; serve hot.

## GOURMET CHICKEN BREASTS

*Rich creamed chicken breasts are sparked with water chestnuts and pimientos for a fancy touch.*

*Makes enough for 2 meals, 4 servings each.*

| | |
|---|---|
| 4 chicken breasts (about 12 ounces each) | ½ cup flour |
| | ¼ teaspoon nutmeg |
| | Dash of pepper |
| 1 small onion, quartered | 1 tablespoon lemon juice |
| Few celery tops | 2 pimientos, chopped |
| 2 teaspoons salt | 1 can (5 ounces) water chestnuts, drained and sliced |
| 6 peppercorns | |
| 1½ cups water | |
| ½ cup (1 stick) butter or margarine | 1 cup cream |

1. Simmer chicken with onion, celery tops, 1 teaspoon of the salt, peppercorns and water in a large saucepan 30 minutes, or until tender. Remove chicken from broth; cool until easy to handle. Strain broth into a 2-cup measure; add water, if needed, to make 2 cups; set aside for making the sauce in Step 3.

2. Remove skin from chickens, then pull chicken from bones; dice meat. (There should be about 4 cups.)

3. Melt butter or margarine in a large saucepan; blend in flour, remaining 1 teaspoon salt, nutmeg and pepper; cook, stirring constantly, just until bubbly. Stir in the 2 cups chicken broth; continue cooking and

stirring until sauce thickens and boils 1 minute. (It will be very thick.) Remove from heat.

4. Stir in lemon juice, diced chicken, pimientos and water chestnuts.

5. Spoon half of mixture into a 6-cup freezer container then cool, cover, label, date and freeze.

6. Stir cream very slowly into remaining mixture in saucepan. Heat, stirring often, just until hot. (If you prefer mixture thinner, stir in about ½ cup milk.) Spoon into patty shells, or over your choice of buttered toast, rice or mashed potato.

NOTE: To heat frozen chicken, set container in a pan of hot water, replacing water as it cools just until mixture is thawed enough to slide into top of a large double boiler. Add 2 tablespoons butter or margarine and 1 cup cream; heat, stirring several times, over simmering water, until hot. (Thin slightly with milk as above, if you wish.)

## CHICKEN BREASTS SUPREME

*An easygoing concoction of creamed white meat baked over rice with a crust of buttery crumbs topping it all.*

*Bake at 400° for 20 minutes.*
*Makes 6 servings.*

| | |
|---|---|
| 3 whole chicken breasts (about 2½ pounds) | 1 can (about 11 ounces) chicken gravy |
| 3 cups water | |
| 1 teaspoon salt | 1 tablespoon butter or margarine |
| 4 peppercorns | |
| Handful of celery tops | ½ cup ready-mix bread stuffing (from an 8-ounce package) |
| 2 cups precooked rice | |

1. Combine chicken breasts with water, salt, peppercorns and celery tops in a medium-size saucepan; cover. Cook 20 minutes, or until tender. Strain broth into a 4-cup measure; pour in water, if necessary, to make 2½ cups.

2. Let chicken stand until cool enough to handle, then remove skin and bones; cut meat into serving-size pieces.

3. Cook rice in 2 cups of the broth in same saucepan, following label directions. Stir remaining ½ cup broth into chicken gravy in small saucepan; heat slowly just until bubbly.

4. Spoon rice into 8-cup baking dish; top with chicken pieces; pour gravy over. Melt butter or margarine in small saucepan; stir in bread stuffing. Sprinkle on top.

5. Bake in a hot oven (400°) 20 minutes, or until bubbly-hot.

# MANDARIN CHICKEN BREASTS

*These chicken breasts are completely gourmet.*

*Makes 6 servings.*

6 chicken breasts
  (about 12 ounces
  each), boned
Salt
1½ cups hot cooked
  rice
3 tablespoons butter
  or margarine
1 tablespoon chopped
  parsley
¼ teaspoon leaf rose-
  mary, crumbled
¼ teaspoon leaf basil,
  crumbled
¼ cup flour
½ teaspoon paprika

2 envelopes instant
  chicken broth or
  2 teaspoons granu-
  lated chicken
  bouillon
1¾ cups water
1 tablespoon instant
  minced onion
2 tablespoons lemon
  juice
1 bay leaf
1 tablespoon corn-
  starch
1 can (about 11
  ounces) mandarin-
  orange segments,
  drained
1 cup seedless green
  grapes

1. Sprinkle insides of chicken breasts lightly with salt.

2. Combine rice, 1 tablespoon of the butter or margarine, ¼ teaspoon salt, parsley, rosemary and basil in a large bowl; toss lightly to mix; spoon into hollows in chicken breasts. Fold edges over stuffing to cover completely; fasten with wooden picks.

3. Mix flour, paprika and ½ teaspoon salt in a pie plate; dip chicken breasts into mixture to coat well. Brown slowly in remaining 2 tablespoons butter or margarine in a large frying pan.

4. Stir in chicken broth, water, onion, lemon juice and bay leaf; heat to boiling; cover.

5. Simmer 25 minutes, or until chicken is tender; remove bay leaf. Place chicken on a heated deep serving platter; keep warm. Reheat liquid to boiling.

6. Smooth cornstarch with a little water to a paste in a cup; stir into liquid in frying pan. Cook, stirring constantly, until sauce thickens and boils 3 minutes. Stir in mandarin-orange segments and grapes; heat until bubbly. Spoon over chicken. Garnish with additional grapes and mandarin-orange segments, if you wish.

## CURRIED CHICKEN AND VEGETABLES

*A different curry—tender, boneless chicken breasts in an aromatic curried vegetable sauce, served over steaming rice.*

*Makes 8 servings.*

4 whole chicken breasts, split (about 12 ounces each)

¼ cup flour (for chicken)

½ teaspoon salt (for chicken)

⅛ teaspoon pepper (for chicken)

¼ cup (½ stick) butter or margarine

1 large onion, chopped (1 cup)

1 green pepper, halved, seeded and diced

1 tablespoon flour (for sauce)

1 teaspoon salt (for sauce)

⅛ teaspoon pepper (for sauce)

2 tablespoons curry powder

1 can (8 ounces) tomatoes

2 envelopes or teaspoons instant chicken broth

2¼ cups water

6 cups hot cooked rice

1. Pull skin from split chicken breasts; bone. Flatten each half by placing between 2 pieces of wax paper and pounding with the back of a heavy knife or mallet. Cut each half into 2 pieces (fillets).

2. Combine ¼ cup flour, ½ teaspoon salt and ⅛ teaspoon pepper in a plastic bag. Add chicken fillets; shake well to coat.

3. Melt butter or margarine in a large skillet; sauté chicken fillets until brown on both sides. Remove from skillet.

4. Sauté onion and green pepper until almost tender in same skillet. Stir in the 1 tablespoon flour, 1 teaspoon salt, ⅛ teaspoon pepper and curry powder. Add tomatoes, instant chicken broth and water; bring to boiling.

5. Lower heat; simmer, covered, 20 minutes. Remove the cover and simmer 5 minutes longer, or until sauce thickens.

6. Return chicken fillets to sauce and cover. Simmer 15 minutes longer, or until chicken is tender.

7. Do-ahead note: Line a 10-cup shallow freezer-to-table baking dish with heavy foil. Arrange chicken in dish and spoon sauce over; wrap; label and freeze. When frozen, remove foil-wrapped food from dish; return to freezer.

8. Party day: Remove food from freezer and peel off foil. Place in same dish. Bake, covered, in moderate oven (350°) 1 hour, or until bubbly-hot. Serve with hot rice.

## BROILED CHICKEN WITH CREAM SAUCE

*Broiled chicken breasts are served on crisp bacon and blanketed with creamy sauce.*

*Makes 6 servings.*

3 large whole chicken breasts, split (about 2 pounds)

¼ cup (½ stick) butter or margarine, melted

1 can (about 11 ounces) chicken gravy

¼ cup light or table cream

1 teaspoon lemon juice

2 or 3 drops red-pepper seasoning

12 slices Canadian-style bacon (about ½ pound)

1. Remove skin from chicken and cut away meat from bones in one piece. (Use a sharp thin-bladed knife, cutting close to bones, and meat will pull away easily; simmer bones in water for a broth for another day, if you wish.)

2. Place chicken, rounded side down, on greased broiler rack; brush with half the melted butter or margarine; broil about 10 minutes; turn; brush again with

remaining butter or margarine; broil 10 to 12 minutes longer, or until golden-brown and tender when pierced with a fork.

3. While chicken cooks, combine chicken gravy, cream, lemon juice and red-pepper seasoning in small saucepan; heat, stirring often, just to boiling.

4. Arrange bacon slices in single layer in shallow pan; 2 to 3 minutes before chicken is done, slide pan into hot oven (from broiling chicken) to cook bacon and crisp any fat edges.

5. Put 2 slices bacon on each dinner plate; top with half a chicken breast; spoon about ¼ cup heated sauce over.

## SOUTH PACIFIC CHICKEN BREASTS

*Fruity, spicy—a glorious example of Island cuisine.*

*Makes 6 servings.*

| | |
|---|---|
| 6 whole chicken breasts (about 12 ounces each) | ½ cup honey |
| | ¾ cup grapefruit juice |
| 1 tablespoon cinnamon | 1 can (about 8 ounces) crushed pineapple |
| 1½ teaspoons curry powder | |
| 1½ teaspoons garlic salt | |

1. Place chicken breasts in a large frying pan or kettle. Blend cinnamon, curry powder, garlic salt and honey in a 2-cup measure; stir in grapefruit juice; pour over chicken; cover.

2. Simmer, stirring liquid in bottom of pan often so honey won't scorch, 20 minutes, or until chicken is tender.

3. Remove from liquid, letting any excess drip back into pan; slip off skin, if you wish. Place chicken on broiler rack.

4. Stir pineapple and syrup into liquid in pan; brush over chicken.

5. Broil, 4 to 5 inches from heat, 5 minutes, or until lightly glazed.

# CHICKEN AND MUSHROOM DUET

*Tender chicken breasts with mushrooms and noodles in a creamy gravy.*

*Makes 6 servings.*

3 whole chicken breasts (2½ to 3 pounds), split
2 cups water
1 slice onion
Handful of celery tops
1 teaspoon salt
4 peppercorns

1 package (8 ounces) noodles
½ pound fresh mushrooms, sliced
2 tablespoons butter or margarine
1 can (about 11 ounces) chicken gravy

1. Combine chicken breasts, water, onion, celery tops, salt and peppercorns in large saucepan. Simmer, covered, 20 minutes, or until chicken is tender.

2. While chicken simmers, cook noodles in large amount boiling salted water, following label directions; drain; place in greased shallow 8-cup casserole.

3. Sauté mushrooms in butter or margarine in large frying pan; arrange in clusters on top of noodles. (Keep casserole warm in heated oven while browning the chicken and heating the gravy.)

4. Drain chicken breasts (strain broth and save for soup). Brown chicken quickly in same frying pan, adding more butter or margarine, if needed; place on noodles.

5. Stir chicken gravy into frying pan; heat to boiling; pour over and around chicken.

## CHICKEN BREASTS MANDALAY

*This delectable chicken has a light curry-and-fruit-flavored sauce.*

*Bake at 350° for 2 hours.*
*Makes 8 servings.*

4 chicken breasts
(about 12 ounces
each)
3 tablespoons flour
1 tablespoon curry
powder
2 teaspoons salt
4 tablespoons vege-
table oil
1 tablespoon sugar

2 envelopes instant
beef broth or 2 beef
bouillon cubes
1 large onion, chopped
(1 cup)
1 cup water
1 jar (about 5 ounces)
baby-pack apricots
2 tablespoons lemon
juice
2 teaspoons soy sauce

1. Pull skin from chicken breasts; halve each.
2. Shake with mixture of flour, curry powder and salt in a paper bag to coat lightly and evenly.
3. Brown pieces in vegetable oil in a large frying pan; place in a 10-cup baking dish.
4. Stir sugar, beef broth or bouillon cubes, onion, water, apricots, lemon juice and soy sauce into drippings in frying pan; heat to boiling, crushing bouillon cubes, if used, with a spoon. Pour over chicken.
5. Bake, covered, in moderate oven (350°) 1 hour, or until chicken is tender and sauce is bubbly hot. Serve over hot fluffy rice or noodles, if you wish.

# Drumsticks

## DRUMSTICK FRICASSEE

*Meaty chicken legs, sweet potato and peas in rich gravy are topped with lemon-flecked dumplings.*

*Makes 2 servings.*

| | |
|---|---|
| **4 drumsticks (about 1 pound)** | **2 teaspoons flour** |
| **½ small onion, sliced** | **1 large sweet potato, pared and sliced ½ inch thick** |
| **¼ cup chopped celery tops** | |
| **1 teaspoon salt** | **1 cup frozen peas (from a 1½-pound bag)** |
| **⅛ teaspoon pepper** | |
| **1½ cups water** | **Lemon Dumplings** |

1. Cook chicken with onions, celery tops, salt and pepper in 1 cup water 30 minutes, or until tender.
2. Blend flour into ½ cup water; stir into broth; cook, stirring constantly, until gravy thickens and boils 1 minute.
3. Add potato and peas; heat to boiling, then simmer 10 minutes while making Lemon Dumplings.
4. Drop batter in 4 mounds on top of hot chicken and vegetables; cover tightly. Cook 20 minutes, or until dumplings are fluffy-light.
5. Lift off dumplings; spoon chicken, vegetables and gravy into serving dishes; top with dumplings. Garnish with grated lemon rind, if you wish.

## LEMON DUMPLINGS

Combine ⅔ cup sifted flour, 1 teaspoon baking powder, ½ teaspoon grated lemon rind and ¼ teaspoon salt. Stir 1 teaspoon lemon juice into ⅓ cup milk. (No need to fuss if mixture curdles.) Add all at once to dry ingredients; stir just until flour mixture is moistened completely.

# STUFFED DRUMSTICKS NAPOLI

*Each golden leg contains a zippy salami stuffing.*

*Makes 8 servings.*

| | |
|---|---|
| **8 chicken drumsticks with thighs (about 5 pounds)** | **2 teaspoons salt** |
| | **1 teaspoon paprika** |
| **1 piece (4 ounces) salami** | **1 teaspoon leaf oregano, crumbled** |
| **½ cup flour** | **⅛ teaspoon pepper** |
| | **½ cup vegetable oil** |

1. Cut through chicken legs at joints to separate drumsticks and thighs, then cut an opening along bone of each drumstick and in meaty part of each thigh to make a pocket for a salami slice.

2. Cut salami into 16 strips; stuff 1 strip into each piece of chicken.

3. Shake pieces, a few at a time, in a mixture of flour, salt, paprika, oregano and pepper in a paper bag to coat evenly.

4. Cook pieces slowly in vegetable oil in a large frying pan 20 minutes; turn; cover loosely. Cook 20 minutes longer, or until tender and crisply golden. Serve warm or cold.

# DRUMSTICK BAKE

*Convenience foods serve as a base for this oven treat.*

Bake at 425° for 50 minutes.
Makes 6 servings.

½ cup (1 stick) butter or margarine
1 package (5 ounces) barbecue-flavor potato chips
⅓ cup undiluted evaporated milk
12 chicken drumsticks

2 cans (15 ounces each) macaroni with cheese sauce
1 can (about 15 ounces) spaghetti with tomato sauce
1 tablespoon instant minced onion
1 large tomato, cut in 6 wedges

1. Melt butter or margarine in a jelly-roll pan.
2. Crush potato chips coarsely. (Tip: Leave chips in bag and simply squeeze it with your hands.) Slit bag; spread open.
3. Pour milk into a shallow dish. Dip drumsticks, 1 at a time, into milk, then roll in potato chips to coat well all over; place in a single layer in butter in pan.
4. Bake in hot oven (425°) 25 minutes; spoon drippings in pan over chicken. Bake 25 minutes longer, or until tender.
5. While chicken bakes, mix macaroni, spaghetti and onion in a 12-cup baking dish; cover. Heat in oven with chicken 20 minutes, or until bubbly.
6. To serve, arrange drumsticks, spoke fashion, over macaroni mixture in dish; place tomato wedges in a circle in center. Garnish with parsley, if you wish.

## DRUMSTICKS PIERRE

*Not for timid palates, this highly seasoned dish.*

*Makes 4 servings.*

| | |
|---|---|
| 8 drumsticks (about 2 pounds) | 2 tablespoons vinegar |
| ¼ cup flour seasoned with ½ teaspoon salt and a dash of pepper | 2 tablespoons Worcestershire sauce |
| | 1 teaspoon salt |
| 3 tablespoons butter or margarine | 1 teaspoon chili powder |
| 1 can (about 1 pound) tomatoes | 1 teaspoon dry mustard |
| ½ cup water | ½ teaspoon celery seeds |
| 2 tablespoons brown sugar | 1 clove garlic, minced |
| | Few drops hot-pepper sauce |

1. Dust drumsticks with the seasoned flour.
2. Melt butter or margarine in large heavy frying pan with tight-fitting cover; brown chicken over medium heat on all sides; drain on absorbent paper.
3. Combine all remaining ingredients in same pan.
4. Bring to boil; reduce heat; return chicken to pan; cover.
5. Simmer chicken 40 to 45 minutes, or until tender.
6. Serve with pan sauce.

# SKILLET CHICKEN AND VEGETABLES

*You can start this meal-in-one well beforehand and refrigerate it, then finish cooking it just before dinner-time.*

*Makes 6 servings.*

| | |
|---|---|
| 6 **drumsticks with thighs (about 3 pounds)** | 2 **cans (12 ounces each) Mexican-style corn** |
| 6 **slices bacon, halved** | ¾ **cup milk** |
| ⅓ **cup flour** | 2 **packages (10 ounces each) frozen Fordhook lima beans** |
| 1 **teaspoon salt** | |
| ¼ **teaspoon pepper** | 1 **cup thinly sliced celery** |

1. Cut through chicken legs at joints to separate drumsticks and thighs; wash pieces and dry.

2. Sauté bacon until crisp in a large heavy frying pan; remove and drain on paper toweling. Wrap and chill until just before serving time.

3. Brown chicken pieces in bacon drippings in same pan; remove and set aside.

4. Stir flour, salt and pepper into drippings; cook, stirring constantly, until bubbly. Drain liquid from corn into a small bowl; stir milk into corn liquid, then stir into flour mixture in frying pan. Continue cooking and stirring until gravy thickens and boils 1 minute. Return chicken, arranging pieces in a single layer; cover. Chill, along with corn.

5. An hour before serving, heat chicken and gravy very slowly to boiling; simmer 45 minutes; pile chicken in center of pan.

6. Pour boiling water to cover over limas and celery in a medium-size bowl; let stand 3 minutes, breaking up limas as they thaw; drain. Place at one side of chicken in pan; place corn at other side; cover. Simmer 10 minutes. Arrange bacon over chicken; continue

cooking 5 minutes, or until beans are tender and bacon is heated through. Just before serving, garnish with parsley, if you wish.

# Thighs

## CHICKEN SCALLOPINE

*Garnish with lemon and serve on toast points.*

*Makes 4 servings.*

8 **chicken thighs, boned**
1 **teaspoon salt**
2 **tablespoons butter or margarine**
1 **tablespoon lemon juice**

2 **tablespoons chopped parsley**
1 **tablespoon chopped chives**
¼ **teaspoon dried leaf marjoram**

1. Place boned thighs between 2 pieces of foil; pound with side of cleaver or rolling pin to flatten. Sprinkle with salt.

2. Melt butter over medium heat in a large skillet. Add chicken, skin side down. Cook about 10 minutes, until lightly browned. Turn; sprinkle with lemon juice and herbs. Cook about 10 minutes, until tender.

3. Serve on buttered toast points; garnish with thin lemon slice.

## PIZZA CHICKS

*Use 12 small skewers or stuffing pins to secure these delicious chicken-cheese rolls.*

*Bake at 400° for 40 minutes.*
*Makes 4 servings.*

8 chicken thighs, boned
½ teaspoon salt
1 teaspoon instant minced onion
1 teaspoon parsley flakes
4 ounces Mozzarella cheese

8 ounces spaghetti or linguini
2 cans (8 ounces each) tomato sauce
½ teaspoon dried leaf basil
½ teaspoon dried leaf oregano
Grated Parmesan cheese

1. Place boned thighs skin side down on cutting board. Sprinkle with the salt, instant minced onion and parsley flakes.
2. Cut Mozzarella cheese into 8 pieces, about 2½"x½"x¾". Place a piece of cheese on each boned thigh; fold sides over cheese and fasten with skewer.
3. Place skewered side down in foil-lined pan. Bake in hot oven (400°) 40 minutes.
4. While mini-rolls are baking, cook spaghetti according to package directions. Combine tomato sauce with basil and oregano in a small saucepan; heat.
5. Place mini-rolls on cooked spaghetti on serving platter. Pour tomato sauce over all. Serve sprinkled with the grated Parmesan cheese.

## Wings

### KENTUCKY BURGOO

*A delicious soup-stew for cold days.*

*Makes 6 servings.*

1½ pounds chicken
   wings (about 12)
1 medium-size onion,
   chopped (½ cup)
5 cups water
1 can (1 pound)
   stewed tomatoes
2 tablespoons bottled
   steak sauce
⅛ teaspoon cayenne
3½ teaspoons salt

½ pound ground beef
2 cans (1 pound each)
   mixed vegetables
1 small head cabbage
   (about 1 pound),
   shredded
2 cups instant mashed
   potato flakes
¼ cup chopped
   parsley

1. Cut apart chicken wings at joints with a sharp knife. Combine with onion, water, tomatoes, steak sauce, cayenne and 3 teaspoons of the salt in a large heavy kettle or Dutch oven. Heat to boiling; reduce heat; cover. Simmer 30 minutes.

2. Mix ground beef lightly with remaining ½ teaspoon salt; shape into 18 little meatballs.

3. Add mixed vegetables and cabbage to chicken mixture; bring to a boil; add meatballs; reduce heat; cover. Simmer 10 minutes. Stir in potato flakes. Remove from heat.

4. Sprinkle with parsley. Spoon into soup bowls. Serve with hot corn bread, if you wish.

# BREADED CHICKEN WINGS

*A batch of tasty tidbits for nibblers.*

*Bake at 350° for 1 hour.*
*Makes 50 pieces.*

3 pounds chicken
   wings (about 25)
½ cup vegetable oil
1 teaspoon seasoned
   salt

1½ cups corn-flake
   crumbs or bread
   crumbs

1. Trim tips from chicken wings. (Save for soup kettle.) Divide wings in half by cutting through remaining joints with a knife.
2. Mix vegetable oil and seasoned salt in a pie plate; place corn-flake or bread crumbs in a second pie plate. Roll chicken pieces in oil mixture, then in crumbs to coat evenly. Place, not touching, in a large shallow pan.
3. Bake in moderate oven (350°) 1 hour, or until golden. Serve hot.

# CRUSTY CHICKEN WINGS

*Crusty wing drumsticks, hot and savory from the oven, great with frosty drinks.*

*Bake at 375° for 40 minutes.*
*Makes 30 pieces.*

3 pounds chicken
   wings (about 15)
1 small can evaporated
   milk (⅔ cup)
1 tablespoon prepared
   mustard
1 clove of garlic,
   minced
1 cup fine dry bread
   crumbs

1 teaspoon instant
   minced onion
1 teaspoon seasoned
   salt
¼ teaspoon seasoned
   pepper
1 envelope or teaspoon
   instant chicken broth

1. Trim tips from chicken wings. (Save for soup kettle.) Divide each wing in half by cutting through joint.

2. Blend milk, mustard and garlic in a shallow dish. Combine bread crumbs, onion, salt, pepper and broth in another dish.

3. Dip chicken pieces into milk mixture, then into crumbs to coat well.

4. To freeze: Place chicken wings in a single layer in buttered foil pans. Cover with foil or transparent wrap; freeze.

5. Bake in moderate oven (375°) 40 minutes, turning once, until chicken is tender.

## PICKUP CHICKEN STICKS

*Luscious finger-food to serve at an open house, buffet lunch or cocktail party.*

*Bake at 350° for 1 hour.*
*Makes 50 pieces.*

| | |
|---|---|
| 3 pounds chicken wings (about 25) | ⅓ cup finely crushed toasted almonds |
| 1 cup (2 sticks) butter or margarine | 1 tablespoon salt |
| 1½ cups sifted flour | ½ teaspoon ground ginger |

1. Singe chicken wings, if necessary; cut off tips. (Save for soup kettle.) Divide each wing in half by cutting through joint. Wash and drain on paper toweling.

2. Melt butter or margarine in large shallow baking pan. Mix flour, crushed almonds, salt and ginger in pie plate.

3. Roll chicken pieces, one at a time, in butter or margarine in pan, letting any excess drip back. Roll in flour to coat. Arrange, not touching, in single layer in same pan.

4. Bake in moderate oven (350°) 1 hour, or until tender and richly golden on bottom. Brown in broiler for 3 to 5 minutes.

## Livers

### HERBED CHICKEN LIVERS

*Sautéed with a delightful blend of herbs, these livers will take only minutes to prepare.*

*Makes 4 servings.*

1 pound chicken livers, cut in half
¾ teaspoon salt
⅛ teaspoon pepper
1 tablespoon minced onion

1 tablespoon minced parsley
½ teaspoon dried leaf tarragon
Flour
2 tablespoons butter or margarine

1. Sprinkle livers with salt, pepper, onion, parsley, tarragon. Dust lightly with flour.
2. Melt butter or margarine in skillet over medium heat; add livers and cook about 5 minutes, turning occasionally.

### CHICKEN LIVERS AND EGGS

*A perfect dish to whip up for brunch, light supper or midnight snack.*

*Makes 4 servings.*

6 eggs
6 tablespoons milk
¾ teaspoon salt
Dash of pepper

½ pound chicken livers OR 1 package (8 ounces) frozen chicken livers, thawed
Salt and pepper
2 teaspoons butter or margarine

1. Combine eggs, milk, salt and pepper in medium-size bowl; beat until foamy; save.

2. Cut chicken livers into small pieces; sprinkle with salt and pepper.

3. Melt butter or margarine in medium-size frying pan; fry livers over medium heat, stirring several times, 3 to 4 minutes, or until lightly browned.

4. Add milk-egg mixture; cook over low heat, stirring several times, 3 to 4 minutes, or until eggs are set.

# CHICKEN-LIVER-MUSHROOM KEBABS

*An interesting variation on the popular kebab theme.*

*Makes 4 servings.*

| | |
|---|---|
| 4 bacon strips, cut in quarters | 12 chicken livers (about 1 pound) |
| 12 small mushroom caps | 2 tablespoons melted butter or margarine |
| | Salt and pepper |

1. On a 7-inch skewer, string a folded-over piece of bacon, a mushroom cap and a chicken liver; repeat 2 more times, ending with bacon; repeat to fill 4 skewers.

2. Place in shallow baking pan; brush with melted butter or margarine.

3. Place in broiler with top of food 4 inches from unit or tip of flame, and broil 10 minutes, or until livers are cooked through and bacon is crisp, turning once and basting once or twice with drippings. Sprinkle with salt and pepper to taste.

4. Remove food from each skewer onto a hot plate and serve.

# CHICKEN LIVERS WITH BACON CRISPS

*Harmonious morsels, oven baked and served on toast.*

*Bake at 400° for 30 minutes.*
*Makes 6 servings.*

| | |
|---|---|
| 12 slices (about ½ pound) bacon | 1 teaspoon salt |
| 1 pound chicken livers | ½ teaspoon paprika |
| 4 tablespoons flour | 6 slices hot toast |
| | Pepper |

1. Lay bacon slices in single layer on rack of broiler pan. (If slices don't separate easily, heat in oven for a few minutes.) Bake in hot oven (400°) 10 minutes, or until crisp. (No need to turn.) Remove rack with bacon on it; keep warm. (Leave oven heat on.)

2. Shake chicken livers in mixture of flour, salt and paprika in paper bag to coat well; lay in hot drippings in broiler pan.

3. Bake in hot oven (400°) 10 minutes, or until browned on underside; turn; bake 10 minutes longer, or until browned on other side. Drain on paper toweling.

4. Arrange toast slices in single layer on heated large serving platter; brush very lightly with bacon drippings from broiler pan. Arrange livers on top; sprinkle with pepper; top with criss-crossed bacon slices.

## CHICKEN LIVERS STROGANOFF

*Sour cream sauce turns these delicacies into a Continental dish.*

*Makes 6 servings.*

| | |
|---|---|
| 1 pound chicken livers | 2 tablespoons flour |
| 2 tablespoons butter or margarine | ½ teaspoon salt |
| | Dash of pepper |
| ½ teaspoon oregano | 1 can (6 ounces) |
| ½ teaspoon Worcestershire sauce | sliced mushrooms |
| | ¼ cup dairy sour |
| 1 medium-size onion, chopped (½ cup) | cream |

1. Halve chicken livers; snip out any veiny parts or skin with scissors.

2. Brown livers slowly in butter or margarine seasoned with oregano and Worcestershire sauce; remove from pan. Add onion to pan; sauté until soft.

3. Blend in flour, salt and pepper; stir in mushrooms and liquid. Heat, stirring constantly, to boiling; return livers; cover. Simmer 3 minutes, or just until livers lose their pink color.

4. Stir about ¼ cup liver mixture into sour cream, then stir back into remaining in pan. Heat very slowly just until hot. Serve over fluffy rice and garnish with crisp bacon slices, if you wish.

# CHICKEN LIVERS GREEK STYLE

*Specially flavored chicken livers combine with tender eggplant for a different dinner idea.*

*Makes 6 servings.*

1 eggplant (about 1 pound), sliced ½ inch thick
5 tablespoons flour
1 teaspoon salt
2 tablespoons vegetable oil
4 tablespoons (½ stick) butter or margarine
1½ pounds chicken livers, washed and cut in half

1 medium-size onion, sliced
½ teaspoon leaf basil, crumbled
1 can condensed chicken broth
2 tomatoes, peeled and cut in eighths
2 tablespoons chopped parsley

1. Dip eggplant slices in mixture of 3 tablespoons of the flour and salt. Sauté in oil and 2 tablespoons of butter or margarine about 3 minutes on each side, or until soft in a large skillet. Arrange, overlapping, around edge of serving dish. Keep warm.

2. Sauté chicken livers and onion in remaining butter or margarine in same skillet 6 minutes, or until browned. Stir in remaining 2 tablespoons flour and basil. Gradually stir in broth.

3. Heat, stirring constantly, until mixture thickens and bubbles 1 minute. Add tomatoes; cover; reduce heat; simmer 5 minutes. Spoon into center of serving dish with eggplant border. Sprinkle with parsley and serve with hot cooked rice, if you wish.

# CHICKEN-LIVER-TOMATO KEBABS

*A light and pretty dish bound to boost a hostess' reputation.*

*Makes 4 servings.*

| | |
|---|---|
| 12 chicken livers (about 1 pound) | 16 cherry tomatoes |
| 4 slices bacon, halved | 2 tablespoons Worcestershire sauce |

1. Halve chicken livers; snip out any veiny parts or skin with scissors.
2. Sauté bacon slices until partly cooked in a medium-size frying pan; remove and drain well on paper toweling. Wrap slices around 8 of the liver halves; hold in place with wooden picks, if needed.
3. Thread each of 8 long thin skewers this way: Cherry tomato, plain chicken liver half, bacon-wrapped liver, plain liver half and cherry tomato, allowing about ¼ inch between each. Place on rack in broiler pan; brush with part of the Worcestershire sauce.
4. Broil, 6 inches from heat, 7 minutes; turn. Brush with remaining Worcestershire sauce, then continue broiling 7 minutes, or until bacon is crisp. Remove wooden picks before serving.

# LITTLE LIVERS SPECIALTY

*Don't overcook these delicious tidbits.*

*Makes 4 servings.*

| | |
|---|---|
| 1 pound chicken livers | 1 can (3 or 4 ounces) sliced mushrooms |
| ¼ cup sifted flour | 1½ teaspoons Worcestershire sauce |
| ½ teaspoon salt | |
| ⅛ teaspoon pepper | |
| 2 tablespoons butter or margarine | |

1. Shake chicken livers, a few at a time, in mixture of flour, salt and pepper in paper bag to coat evenly.

2. Brown in butter or margarine in large frying pan over low heat. Stir in mushrooms and liquid and Worcestershire sauce.

3. Cover loosely; cook slowly 10 minutes, or just until liquid is absorbed.

*Chapter 9*

# Meal-in-One Chicken

A chicken in every pot? Hardly. The theme of this chapter is a chicken in one pot—an idea that makes dinner child's play for even the busiest cook.

Casseroles, one of the housewife's dreams come true, are joined here by chicken pies and stews. All are cooked in one pot, be it a Dutch oven, large kettle or oven-proof dish. And all provide a complete meal-in-one dinner (add salad and rolls if the spirit moves you).

The casseroles and pies can be made with leftover chicken, or from scratch; the stews provide the basis for leftovers. They'll keep after the first serving, to be frozen or refrigerated, and then reheated on another night. As you can see, this is not only one-pot, meal-in-one cooking—it's more than anyone could ask for.

## Casseroles

## MOCK COQ AU VIN

*Long slow cooking gives this aristocrat a mellow flavor. Its seasoning secrets: Apple cider, mixed vegetable juices.*

*Bake at 350° for 2 hours and 15 minutes.*
*Makes 4 servings.*

1 stewing chicken (about 4 pounds), cut in serving-size pieces
⅓ cup flour
1½ teaspoons salt
3 tablespoons butter or margarine
½ cup diced cooked ham
12 small white onions, peeled
1 can (12 ounces) mixed vegetable juices (1½ cups)
1½ cups apple cider
1 can (3 or 4 ounces) mushroom caps
1 clove garlic, minced
6 peppercorns
6 whole cloves
1 bay leaf

1. Wash chicken pieces; pat dry. Shake with the flour and salt in a paper bag to coat thoroughly.

2. Brown pieces, a few at a time, in butter or margarine in a large frying pan; place in a 12-cup baking dish; sprinkle with ham and top with onions.

3. Stir the vegetable juices, cider, mushrooms and their liquid and garlic into drippings in pan; heat to boiling, scraping brown bits from bottom of pan. Pour over chicken.

4. Tie seasonings in a tiny cheesecloth bag; add to casserole; cover.

5. Bake in moderate oven (350°) 2 hours and 15 minutes, or until chicken is very tender.

6. Uncover; remove spice bag and let chicken stand for 5 to 10 minutes, or until fat rises to top, then skim off. Garnish chicken with parsley, if you wish.

## DIXIE CHICKEN DINNER

*A lively dish with layers of chicken, beans, olives and tomatoes.*

*Bake at 350° for 1 hour.*
*Makes 8 servings.*

2 broiler-fryers (about 2 pounds each)
¾ cup flour
2 teaspoons salt
1 teaspoon leaf basil, crumbled
4 tablespoons vegetable oil
2 cans (1 pound each) cooked dried lima beans

1 can (1 pound) cut green beans, drained
½ cup sliced stuffed green olives
½ cup sliced pitted ripe olives
4 medium-size firm ripe tomatoes, sliced ½-inch thick
1 clove garlic, minced
½ cup apple juice or water

1. Cut chicken into serving-size pieces. Shake pieces with a mixture of ½ cup flour, salt and basil in a paper bag to coat evenly.

2. Brown slowly in vegetable oil in a large frying pan 10 minutes on each side; remove and set aside.

3. While chicken browns, drain liquid from lima beans into a 2-cup measure; combine limas with green beans, and green and ripe olives in a greased 12-cup shallow baking dish. Place tomato slices in a single layer over vegetables.

4. Pour all drippings from frying pan, then measure 4 tablespoonfuls and return to pan; stir in remaining ¼ cup flour and garlic; cook, stirring constantly, just until bubbly.

5. Combine apple juice with saved bean liquid and additional water to make 2 cups; stir into flour mixture in frying pan. Continue cooking and stirring until sauce thickens and boils 1 minute; pour over vegetables in baking dish. Arrange browned chicken in a single layer on top, then press pieces down into vegetables slightly.

6. Bake in moderate oven (350°) 1 hour, or until chicken is tender and sauce bubbles up. Sprinkle with chopped parsley, if you wish.

## CHICKEN MARENGO

*This dish originated in the Italian town of Marengo; they say it was invented to serve to Napoleon.*

*Bake at 350° for 1½ hours.*
*Makes 8 servings.*

6 slices bacon, cut in
  1-inch pieces
2 broiler-fryers (about
  2 pounds each),
  cut up
½ cup flour
2 teaspoons salt
¼ teaspoon pepper
2 medium-size onions,
  chopped (1 cup)

1 clove garlic, minced
1 can (3 or 4 ounces)
  whole mushrooms
2 cans (1 pound each)
  tomatoes
¼ cup chopped
  parsley
Few drops bottled red-
  pepper seasoning
1 cup Golden Croutons

1. Fry bacon until almost crisp in large frying pan. Lift out with slotted spoon; drain on paper toweling and set aside for Step 6. Leave drippings in pan.

2. Wash and dry chicken pieces well. Snip off small rib bones with kitchen scissors, if you wish. Shake chicken in mixture of flour, salt and pepper in paper bag to coat well. (Save any leftover flour mixture for Step 4.)

3. Brown chicken, a few pieces at a time, in bacon drippings; place in a 12-cup shallow baking dish.

4. Sauté onion and garlic until soft in same frying pan; stir in saved flour mixture. Drain liquid from mushrooms. (Save mushrooms for Step 6.) Stir liquid, tomatoes, parsley and the red-pepper seasoning into frying pan; heat to boiling, stirring constantly.

5. Spoon over chicken in baking dish; cover. (Casserole can be put together up to this point, then chilled. Remove from refrigerator and let stand at room temperature 30 minutes before baking.)

6. Bake in moderate oven (350°) 1 hour and 20 minutes, or until chicken is tender. Uncover; sprinkle with saved bacon pieces and mushrooms. Bake 10 minutes longer, or until bacon is crisp.

7. Just before serving, sprinkle Golden Croutons over top; garnish with more chopped parsley, if you wish.

## GOLDEN CROUTONS

Trim crusts from 2 slices of white bread; cut into 1½-inch cubes. Spread in single layer in shallow baking pan. Toast in moderate oven (350°) 10 minutes, or until golden. Makes 1 cup.

## NEOPOLITAN CHICKEN

*Families that love spaghetti will welcome this chicken-and-potatoes with spaghetti-sauce flavor.*

*Bake at 350° for 1½ hours.*
*Makes 6 servings.*

| | |
|---|---|
| 2 broiler-fryers (about 2 pounds each), cut up | 1 envelope spaghetti-sauce mix |
| ¼ cup flour | 3 medium-size tomatoes, chopped |
| 1 teaspoon salt | |
| ⅛ teaspoon pepper | ¼ cup chopped parsley |
| 2 tablespoons olive or salad oil | 6 medium-size potatoes, pared and cut in 1-inch cubes |
| 1 medium-size onion, chopped (½ cup) | |
| 1 clove garlic, minced | 1 large green pepper, seeded and cut into wide strips |
| 1 cup water | |

1. Shake chicken with flour, salt and pepper in a paper bag to coat well. Brown, a few pieces at a time, in olive oil or salad oil in frying pan; place in an 8-cup baking dish.

2. Sauté onion and garlic until softened in same

frying pan; stir in water, then spaghetti-sauce mix; heat to boiling. Stir in tomatoes and parsley. Simmer, uncovered, 15 minutes.

3. Pour over chicken in baking dish; top with potato cubes and pepper strips; cover.

4. Bake in moderate oven (350°) 1½ hours, or until chicken is tender.

## The Disappearing Casserole Trick

**Line a freezer-to-oven baking dish with foil, add the ingredients and freeze. When frozen, remove the food wrapped in the foil, relieving the dish for duty. To serve, remove food from foil, return to the same baking dish and bake.**

## CHICKEN TIJUANA

*A casserole with a saucy seasoning of olives, green pepper, tomatoes and herbs.*

*Bake at 350° for 50 minutes.*
*Makes 4 servings.*

| | |
|---|---|
| 1 broiler-fryer (about 2½ pounds) | 1 large onion, chopped (1 cup) |
| 2 cups water | 1 large green pepper, halved, seeded and chopped |
| ¼ teaspoon salt | |
| ½ cup flour | |
| 2 tablespoons butter or margarine | 1 teaspoon leaf basil, crumbled |
| 3 tablespoons vegetable oil | 1 teaspoon seasoned salt |
| 3 medium-size tomatoes, peeled and quartered | 1 teaspoon paprika |
| | ⅓ cup grated Parmesan cheese |
| ¼ cup pimiento-stuffed olives, sliced | |

1. Cut wings from chicken. Remove giblets and neck from chicken package and place (except liver) with wings, water, and the ¼ teaspoon salt in a small sauce-

pan; cover. Simmer 45 minutes. Add liver; cover; cook 15 minutes longer. Strain broth into a small bowl; reserve for Step 4. Chop giblets and the meat from wings and neck; reserve.

2. Cut chicken into serving-size pieces. Shake chicken, a few pieces at a time, in a plastic bag with flour to coat; tap off excess. Reserve 1 tablespoon of the flour for Step 4.

3. Sauté chicken in butter or margarine and oil, turning once, about 15 minutes, or until golden brown, in a large skillet. Place chicken in a 10-cup baking dish. Add tomatoes and olives.

4. Add onion and green pepper to drippings in skillet; sauté until tender. Stir in basil, the 1 tablespoon reserved flour, seasoned salt and paprika. Cook 1 minute, stirring constantly. Stir in 1 cup of the reserved broth; cook and stir until sauce thickens and bubbles 1 minute. Stir in chopped chicken and giblets, and cheese. Pour over chicken and vegetables; cover.

5. Bake in moderate oven (350°) 50 minutes, or until chicken is tender.

# CHICKEN AND ONIONS AU CASSEROLE

*White meat and onions in a creamy sauce, with green peas mixed in like little gems.*

*Bake at 350° for 1½ hours.*
*Makes 8 servings.*

| | |
|---|---|
| 1 package (8 ounces) medium noodles | 1 package (10 ounces) frozen green peas |
| 1 package (9 ounces) frozen onions in cream sauce | 4 chicken breasts (about 12 ounces each) |
| 2 cans condensed golden mushroom soup | Chopped pistachio nuts (optional) |

1. Cook noodles, following the label directions; drain. Combine with onions and 1 can of the mush-

room soup in a greased shallow 12-cup baking dish; sprinkle with peas.

2. While noodles cook, pull skin from chicken breasts; cut each in half. Arrange in a single layer over peas; spread with remaining can of soup; cover.

3. Bake in moderate oven (350°) 1½ hours, or until chicken is tender and sauce is bubbly. Garnish with chopped pistachio nuts, if you wish.

## BRUNSWICK CHICKEN

*This chicken dish includes corn, lima beans, a peppy tomato sauce.*

*Bake at 350° for 1½ hours.*
*Makes 8 servings.*

2 broiler-fryers (about 2 pounds each), cut up
½ cup flour
1 envelope herb-salad-dressing mix
¼ cup shortening
1 large onion, chopped (1 cup)
1 tablespoon sugar

2 cans (about 1 pound each) tomatoes
1 package (10 ounces) frozen whole-kernel corn, cooked and drained
1 package (10 ounces) frozen Fordhook lima beans, cooked and drained

1. Shake chicken in mixture of flour and salad-dressing mix in paper bag to coat well. Brown, a few pieces at a time, in shortening in large frying pan; arrange in a 12-cup baking dish.

2. Sauté onion in same frying pan; blend in any remaining seasoned flour, and sugar; stir in tomatoes. Heat to boiling, stirring constantly.

3. Spoon corn and lima beans around chicken in baking dish; pour tomato sauce over; cover with lid or foil; chill. Remove from refrigerator and let stand at room temperature 30 minutes before baking.

4. Bake in moderate oven (350°) 1½ hours, or until chicken is tender.

# CASEROLE-ROASTED CHICKEN

*Here's one potato lovers will really enjoy.*

*Bake at 325° for 1¼ hours.*
*Makes 4 servings.*

1 broiler-fryer (about
   3 pounds)
1½ teaspoons salt
¼ teaspoon pepper
16 small white onions,
   peeled
12 small red, new
   potatoes
3 tablespoons butter
   or margarine
3 tablespoons vege-
   table oil

½ cup boiling water
1 envelope instant
   chicken broth OR
1 teaspoon granu-
   lated chicken
   bouillon
1 teaspoon leaf basil,
   crumbled
1 tablespoon chopped
   parsley

1. Sprinkle chicken cavities with ½ teaspoon of the salt and pepper. Peel onions. Scrub potatoes; pare a band around the center of each.

2. Melt butter or margarine with the vegetable oil in a large heavy flameproof casserole or Dutch oven. Add chicken; brown on all sides.

3. Combine boiling water and chicken broth in a 1-cup measure, stirring until dissolved; add to casserole with chicken.

4. Place onions and potatoes around chicken; sprinkle with basil and remaining 1 teaspoon salt; cover.

5. Bake in slow oven (325°), basting once or twice with juices, 1¼ hours, or until chicken and vegetables are tender. Sprinkle with parsley.

# SENEGALESE CHICKEN CASSEROLE

*Mildly spiced with curry, chicken and noodles baked in a custard-type sauce.*

*Bake at 325° for 1¼ hours.*
*Makes 8 servings.*

| | |
|---|---|
| 1 broiler-fryer (about 3 pounds) | 1 package (8 ounces) fine noodles |
| 1 small onion, sliced | 1 package (10 ounces) frozen peas |
| Few celery tops | |
| 1½ teaspoons curry powder | 1 can (5 ounces) toasted slivered almonds |
| 2 teaspoons salt | |
| ⅛ teaspoon pepper | 4 eggs |
| 1½ cups water | 1 cup cream for whipping |
| Milk | |

1. Combine chicken with onion, celery tops, curry powder, salt, pepper and water in a large saucepan; cover. Simmer 45 minutes, or until tender.

2. Remove chicken from broth; cool until easy to handle. Strain broth into a 2-cup measure; skim any excess fat, then add milk, if needed, to make 2 cups; set aside for Step 5.

3. Pull skin from chicken and take meat from bones. Cut meat into bite-size pieces.

4. While fixing chicken, cook noodles and peas in separate saucepans, following label directions; drain. Combine with chicken and almonds in a buttered 10-cup baking dish.

5. Beat eggs slightly in a medium-size bowl; stir in the 2 cups chicken broth from Step 2 and cream. (This much can be done ahead.)

6. Pour custard mixture over chicken mixture, then stir lightly so liquid seeps to bottom. Bake in slow oven (325°) 1 hour and 15 minutes, or until custard sets. (Cover lightly with foil during last 15 minutes to keep top moist.) Garnish with diced red apple and coconut, if you wish.

MAKE-AHEAD NOTE: Cover chicken-noodle mixture in baking dish and custard mixture in bowl and chill. About 1¼ hours before serving combine both, following Step 6; place in a cold oven; set heat control at slow (325°). Bake 1 hour and 15 minutes.

# CHICKEN AND NOODLE CASSEROLE

*Comforting, old family friend—always good and dependable.*

*Bake at 350° for 2 hours.*
*Makes 4 to 6 servings.*

1 **stewing chicken (4 to 5 pounds), cut into serving-size pieces**

2 **medium-size onions, chopped (1 cup)**

1 **tablespoon Worcestershire sauce**

1 **can condensed cream of mushroom soup**

**Hot noodles**

1. Trim any excess fat from chicken pieces; remove skin from legs and breast.

2. Spread onion in bottom of a 12-cup baking dish; arrange chicken in 2 layers on top.

3. Stir Worcestershire sauce into soup in can; spoon over chicken; cover.

4. Bake in moderate oven (350°) 1 hour; uncover and stir to mix soup and chicken juices; cover again.

5. Bake 1 hour longer, or until chicken is very tender. Let casserole stand about 1 minute, or until fat rises to the top; skim. Serve chicken with hot noodles, gravy.

# CHICKEN IN THE GARDEN

*Fresh asparagus, new potatoes and celery combine with chicken quarters in this meal-in-one dish.*

*Bake at 375° for 1 hour.*
*Makes 4 servings.*

1 broiler-fryer,
  quartered
1½ teaspoons salt,
  divided
1 teaspoon dried leaf
  tarragon, divided
2 tablespoons butter
  or margarine
1 pound small new
  potatoes, pared
2 tablespoons snipped
  fresh chives

2 tablespoons chopped
  fresh parsley
2 cups diagonally cut
  celery pieces
1 pound asparagus
  (break off ends of
  stems where they
  snap easily)
1 tablespoon fresh
  lemon juice

1. Sprinkle chicken on both sides with ½ teaspoon salt and ½ teaspoon tarragon. Heat butter or margarine in large skillet; add chicken, skin side down, and brown slowly; turn, and brown other side. Transfer the chicken to a shallow 3- or 4-quart casserole.

2. Add potatoes to the butter in skillet; cook slowly over low heat for about 5 minutes and add to casserole. Sprinkle chicken and potatoes with chives, parsley and drippings from skillet. Cover tightly with casserole lid or aluminum foil.

3. Bake in 375° oven 30 minutes. Remove from oven and remove cover.

4. Add celery pieces and asparagus. Sprinkle vegetables with remaining 1 teaspoon salt and ½ teaspoon tarragon; spoon juices in casserole over asparagus and celery. Drizzle with lemon juice.

5. Cover tightly and bake 30 minutes longer, or until chicken and vegetables are tender; baste occasionally with the juices in the casserole.

## Stews

## POT-ROASTED CHICKEN WITH CREAM GRAVY

*A French way of simmering a large chicken to savory tenderness.*

*Makes 4 to 6 servings.*

4 tablespoons (½ stick) butter or margarine
1 stewing chicken (4 to 5 pounds)
2 teaspoons leaf thyme
1 can condensed beef broth
3 tablespoons flour
1 small can evaporated milk (⅔ cup)

1. Melt butter or margarine in heavy kettle or Dutch oven; brush part on inside of chicken, then sprinkle chicken with 1 teaspoon thyme. Brown chicken lightly on all sides in remaining butter or margarine.

2. Turn chicken, breast side up; pour beef broth over; sprinkle with remaining 1 teaspoon thyme; cover tightly.

3. Simmer, basting a few times with pan juices, 1½ hours, or until tender. Remove to heated serving platter; keep hot while making gravy.

4. Pour broth from kettle into 4-cup measure. Let fat rise to top, then skim off. Add water to broth, if needed, to make 2½ cups.

5. Return 2 tablespoons fat to kettle; blend in flour; stir in broth. Cook, stirring constantly, until gravy thickens and boils 1 minute. Blend in evaporated milk; heat just to boiling.

6. Serve chicken with buttered noodles and spoon gravy over all.

# BROWN CHICKEN FRICASSEE

*Chicken browned with onions and topped off with cornmeal dumplings should please all grown men and little boys.*

*Makes 6 servings.*

| | |
|---|---|
| 1 **stewing chicken** (about 5 pounds), cut up | 3 **tablespoons salad oil** |
| ¼ **cup flour** | 2 **medium-size onions,** sliced and separated into rings |
| 2 **teaspoons salt** | 1 **bay leaf** |
| 1 **teaspoon poultry** seasoning | 4 **cups water** |
| ¼ **teaspoon pepper** | **Cornmeal Dumplings** |

1. Wash chicken; drain. Shake pieces, a few at a time, in mixture of flour, salt, poultry seasoning and pepper in a paper bag to coat well.

2. Brown slowly in salad oil in a large heavy frying pan; remove. Add onion rings, sauté until they are soft.

3. Return chicken to pan; add bay leaf and water; cover. Simmer 1½ hours or until chicken is tender.

4. Prepare Cornmeal Dumplings. Heat chicken until boiling rapidly; drop dough into 12 small mounds on top; cover.

5. Cook, covered, 20 minutes. (No peeking, or the dumplings won't puff properly.)

6. Remove chicken and dumplings to a heated serving platter; remove bay leaf; serve gravy in a separate bowl.

## CORNMEAL DUMPLINGS

Sift 1½ cups sifted flour, ¼ cup yellow cornmeal, 3 teaspoons baking powder and 1 teaspoon salt into a medium-size bowl. Cut in 2 tablespoons shortening with a pastry blender until mixture is crumbly. Stir in 1 cup milk just until flour mixture is moistened. (Dough will be soft.)

# DAPPLED DUMPLING FRICASSEE

*Kettle chicken cooked tender, served with gravy and topped with parsley-sprigged dumplings.*

*Makes 6 servings.*

| | |
|---|---|
| 1 **stewing chicken** (about 5 pounds), cut up | 1 **medium-size carrot,** scraped and sliced |
| 4 **cups plus ½ cup** cold water | 2 **teaspoons salt** |
| 1 **large onion, sliced** | ¼ **teaspoon pepper** |
| 1 **cup chopped celery** and leaves | 6 **tablespoons flour** |
| | **Dappled Dumplings** |

1. Combine chicken, 4 cups water, onion, celery and leaves, carrot, salt and pepper in large kettle or Dutch oven with tight-fitting cover. Cover; heat to boiling, then simmer 1½ to 2 hours, or until chicken is tender.

2. Remove from broth; cool slightly; slip off skin, if you wish. Strain and measure broth; add water, if needed, to make 5 cups. Press vegetables through strainer into broth in kettle; heat to boiling.

3. Stir ½ cup cold water into flour in cup to make a smooth paste; stir into hot broth. Cook, stirring constantly, until gravy thickens and boils 1 minute. Season with salt and pepper to taste, if needed.

4. Return chicken to gravy in kettle; heat slowly to boiling while stirring up Dappled Dumplings.

5. Drop dough in 12 mounds on top of steaming chicken. Cook, covered, 20 minutes. (No peeking, or the dumplings won't puff properly.)

6. Arrange chicken and dumplings on a heated serving platter; pass gravy in separate bowl.

# DAPPLED DUMPLINGS

Sift 2 cups sifted flour, 3 teaspoons baking powder and 1 teaspoon salt into medium-size bowl. Cut in 2 tablespoons shortening with pastry blender until mixture is crumbly. Stir in ¼ cup chopped parsley and 1 cup milk just until flour is moistened. (Dough will be soft.)

## Herb Idea

Add a touch of rosemary to broth when cooking chicken stew. Just be sure to strain the broth for gravy.

## CHICKEN, HUNTER'S STYLE

*This is an easy-to-prepare blend of chicken and vegetables.*

*Makes 4 servings.*

1 broiler-fryer (about 3 pounds)
1 tablespoon vegetable oil
1 tablespoon butter or margarine
¼ pound mushrooms, trimmed and sliced
2 large tomatoes, peeled, seeded and chopped (2 cups)
¼ cup sliced green onions
1 small clove of garlic, crushed
¾ cup water
2 tablespoons lemon juice
1 teaspoon leaf chervil or thyme, crumbled
1 teaspoon salt
⅛ teaspoon pepper
1 tablespoon cornstarch

1. Cut chicken into serving-size pieces. Brown in oil and butter or margarine in a large skillet with a cover.

2. Add mushrooms, tomatoes, green onions, garlic, ½ cup of the water, lemon juice, chervil, salt and pepper; cover. Simmer 45 minutes, or until chicken is tender. Remove chicken to a heated serving platter; keep hot while making gravy.

3. Blend cornstarch with remaining water in a cup; stir into liquid in skillet. Cook, stirring constantly, until mixture thickens and bubbles 3 minutes. Pour over chicken.

## COUNTRY CAPTAIN

*A classic Southern dish with a touch of the Orient.*

*Makes 8 servings.*

| | |
|---|---|
| 2 broiler-fryers (about 2½ pounds each) | 1 large clove of garlic, crushed |
| ¼ cup flour | 3 teaspoons curry powder |
| 2 teaspoons salt | |
| ½ teaspoon pepper | 1 can (1 pound) tomatoes |
| 3 tablespoons vegetable oil | ½ cup raisins or currants |
| 1 large onion, chopped (1 cup) | Hot cooked rice |
| 1 large green pepper, halved, seeded, and chopped | |

1. Cut chicken into serving-size pieces.
2. Combine flour with 1 teaspoon of the salt and ¼ teaspoon of the pepper in a plastic bag. Shake chicken, a few pieces at a time, in flour mixture to coat; tap off excess.
3. Brown chicken, part at a time, in oil in a kettle. Remove chicken; keep warm.
4. Add onion, green pepper, garlic and curry powder to drippings remaining in kettle; sauté until soft. Add tomatoes (breaking with spoon), raisins and reserved chicken; cover. Simmer 1 hour, or until chicken is tender. Arrange chicken on a bed of rice. Spoon sauce over top.

# PIMIENTO CHICKEN STEW

*A hearty meal topped with peppy pimiento biscuits.*

*Makes 8 servings.*

1 stewing chicken (4 to 5 pounds), cut in serving-size pieces
½ cup flour
1 envelope herb salad-dressing mix
1 large onion, chopped (1 cup)
2 cans (about 1 pound each) tomatoes
2 cups water
1 teaspoon sugar
2 cups diced celery
2 cups fresh lima beans OR 1 can (about 1 pound) lima beans and liquid (cut water to 1½ cups)
1½ cups fresh corn kernels or 1 can (12 or 16 ounces) whole-kernel corn
1 can (4 ounces) pimientos
¼ cup chopped parsley
Pimiento Biscuits

1. Remove all fat from chicken, and skin from breasts, thighs and drumsticks; melt fat in large heavy kettle or Dutch oven.
2. Shake chicken with flour and herb salad-dressing mix in paper bag to coat evenly; brown, a few pieces at a time, in fat in kettle. Remove chicken and set aside.
3. Sauté onion until soft in same kettle; stir in tomatoes, water and sugar; add celery, lima beans, corn and chicken; cover.
4. Simmer 1 hour, or until chicken is tender; let stand 5 to 10 minutes; skim excess fat.
5. Save 1 pimiento for Pimiento Biscuits; dice remaining; stir into stew with parsley; serve with Pimiento Biscuits.

## PIMIENTO BISCUITS

*Bake at 400° for 10 minutes.*
*Makes 12 biscuits.*

1¾ cups biscuit mix
½ cup yellow cornmeal
2 tablespoons melted
 butter or margarine
1 pimiento, chopped
⅔ cup milk

1. Mix biscuit mix, cornmeal, melted butter or margarine and pimiento with a fork in a medium-size bowl; stir in milk just until no dry mix appears; spoon in 12 mounds onto ungreased cooky sheet.
2. Bake in hot oven (400°) 10 minutes, or until golden.

## CHICKEN 'N MUSHROOMS

*Serve this fricassee with homemade gravy over hot biscuits.*

*Makes 6 servings.*

1 stewing chicken
 (about 5 pounds),
 cut up
½ cup sliced celery
1 large onion, sliced
2 medium-size carrots,
 pared and sliced
 (1 cup)
1 bay leaf
½ teaspoon pepper-
 corns
3 teaspoons salt
Water
2 tablespoons butter or
 margarine
1 can (3 or 4 ounces)
 sliced mushrooms,
 drained
½ cup flour

1. Place chicken in a kettle or Dutch oven; add celery, onion, carrots, bay leaf, peppercorns, salt and water to cover. Heat to boiling; reduce heat; cover. Simmer 2½ hours, or until chicken is tender.
2. Remove chicken to heated deep serving dish; keep hot while making gravy.

3. Strain broth into a large bowl; let stand until fat rises to top. Skim off fat, then measure 3 tablespoonfuls back into kettle; reserve broth.

4. Heat the butter or margarine with the chicken fat until melted. Blend flour into fat; cook, stirring constantly, just until bubbly. Stir in 4 cups of the broth and mushrooms.

5. Cook, stirring constantly, until gravy thickens and bubbles 1 minute. Pour over the chicken. Serve over hot biscuits.

NOTE: Any leftover broth may be used for chicken soup for the next day.

## KETTLE CHICKEN

*A hearty meal-in-one that's great for cold winter nights.*

*Makes 8 servings.*

| | |
|---|---|
| 2 **broiler-fryers (about 2½ pounds each), cut up** | 1 **stalk celery, chopped (½ cup)** |
| 2 **tablespoons butter or margarine** | 2 **teaspoons salt** |
| 2 **tablespoons vegetable oil** | 1 **teaspoon leaf basil, crumbled** |
| 4 **cups water** | 6 **peppercorns** |
| 1 **medium-size onion, chopped (½ cup)** | 4 **whole cloves** |
| 1 **medium-size carrot, pared and sliced thin (½ cup)** | 1 **bay leaf** |
| | 6 **tablespoons flour** |
| | 1 **package (10 ounces) frozen peas** |
| | **Mashed potatoes** |

1. Brown chicken parts, part at a time, in butter or margarine and oil in a kettle or Dutch oven. Remove chicken pieces as they brown, then return all to kettle. Add water, onion, carrot, celery, salt, basil, peppercorns, cloves and bay leaf.

2. Heat to boiling; reduce heat; cover. Simmer 45 minutes, or until chicken is tender. Remove chicken and reserve.

3. Strain broth into a 4-cup measure; add water, if needed, to make 4 cups. Press vegetables through a sieve into broth.

4. Skim fat from broth, returning 6 tablespoons to kettle; stir in flour; heat, stirring constantly, just until bubbly. Stir in the 4 cups of broth; continue cooking and stirring until gravy thickens and bubbles 1 minute. Season to taste with salt and pepper, if needed. Add peas and chicken; reheat to boiling. Lower heat; simmer 10 minutes. Serve with mashed potatoes.

## Pies

# CRISSCROSS CHICKEN PIE

*This would be grandmother's idea of a stick-to-the-ribs dinner.*

*Bake at 400° for 20 minutes, then at 350° for 25 minutes.*
*Makes 6 servings.*

| | |
|---|---|
| 1 broiler-fryer (3 pounds), cut up | 1 package (10 ounces) frozen peas, cooked and drained |
| 3 cups water | |
| Handful of celery tops | 1 pimiento, chopped |
| 2 teaspoons salt | 2 cups sifted flour |
| 6 peppercorns | ⅓ cup shortening |
| Curry Cream Sauce | ⅔ cup milk |

1. Simmer chicken with water, celery tops, 1 teaspoon salt and peppercorns in kettle 1 hour, or until tender. Remove from broth and let cool until easy to handle.

2. Strain broth into a 4-cup measure; add water, if needed, to make 3 cups. Make Curry Cream Sauce.

3. Slip skin from chicken, then remove meat from bones. (It comes off easily while still warm.) Cut into

bite-size pieces; toss with peas, pimiento and 2 cups of Curry Cream Sauce in medium-size bowl. Set aside for Step 5. (Save remaining sauce to reheat and serve over pie.)

4. Sift flour and 1 teaspoon salt into medium-size bowl; cut in shortening with pastry blender until mixture is crumbly; stir in milk with a fork just until dough holds together.

5. Turn out onto lightly floured pastry cloth or board; knead lightly 5 to 6 times. Roll out ⅔ of dough to a rectangle, 16x12; fit into a baking dish, 10x6x2. Spoon filling into shell.

6. Roll out remaining pastry to a rectangle about 14x7; cut into 9 long strips, each about ¾ inch wide, with knife or pastry wheel. Lay 5 strips lengthwise over filling. Halve remaining 4 strips; weave across long strips to make a crisscross top. Trim overhang to 1 inch; fold under; flute.

7. Bake in hot oven (400°) 20 minutes; reduce heat to moderate (350°). Bake 25 minutes longer, or until golden. Cut into 6 servings. Serve with remaining hot Curry Cream Sauce.

## CURRY CREAM SAUCE

Melt 6 tablespoons (¾ stick) butter or margarine over low heat in medium-size saucepan. Stir in 6 tablespoons flour, 1 teaspoon salt, 1 teaspoon curry powder and ⅛ teaspoon pepper. Cook, stirring all the time, just until mixture bubbles. Stir in 3 cups chicken broth slowly; continue cooking and stirring until sauce thickens and boils 1 minute. Stir in 1 tall can evaporated milk. Makes about 4½ cups.

## OLD-FASHIONED CHICKEN PIE

*It's so good it's no wonder this dish has been around for ages.*

*Bake at 400° for 30 minutes.*
*Makes 8 servings.*

2 broiler-fryers (about 2½ pounds each)
Water
2 teaspoons salt
¼ teaspoon pepper
2 cups sliced carrots
1 package (10 ounces) frozen peas

¼ cup (½ stick) butter or margarine
6 tablespoons flour
1½ cups biscuit mix
½ cup dairy sour cream
1 egg
2 teaspoons sesame seeds

1. Place chickens in a large heavy kettle or Dutch oven; add 2 cups water, salt, pepper and carrots. Heat to boiling; reduce heat; cover; simmer 45 minutes. Add peas; simmer 15 minutes longer, or until chicken is tender. Remove chicken to a bowl to cool.

2. Skim fat from chicken broth-vegetable mixture; reserve 2 tablespoons fat. Melt butter or margarine with reserved chicken fat in a medium-size saucepan; stir in flour; cook, stirring constantly, just until bubbly. Stir in chicken broth-vegetable mixture; continue cooking and stirring until gravy thickens and bubbles 1 minute.

3. When chickens are cool enough to handle, pull off skin and slip meat from bones; cut meat into bite-size pieces; stir into gravy; pour into an 8-cup baking dish, 8x8x2.

4. Combine biscuit mix and sour cream in a small bowl; stir to form a stiff dough; turn out onto a lightly floured board; knead a few times; roll out dough to ¼-inch thickness; trim to make an 8½-inch square; cut into 8 strips, each about one inch wide.

5. Using 4 of the strips, make a lattice design on top of the chicken mixture, spacing evenly and attach-

ing ends firmly to edges of the dish. Place remaining strips, one at a time, on edges of dish, pinching dough to make a stand-up rim; flute rim. (Or, roll out dough to a 9-inch square and place over chicken mixture; turn edges under, flush with rim; flute to make a stand-up rim. Cut slits near center to let steam escape.)

6. Combine egg with 1 tablespoon water in a cup; mix with a fork until well blended; brush mixture over strips and rim; sprinkle with sesame seeds.

7. Bake in hot oven (400°) 30 minutes, or until chicken mixture is bubbly-hot, and crust is golden. Serve immediately.

## DEEP-DISH CHICKEN PIE

*Not for dieters but guaranteed to fill up a famished family.*

*Bake at 425° for 30 minutes.*
*Makes 6 servings.*

| | |
|---|---|
| 6 medium-size potatoes, pared, quartered | 2 tablespoons butter or margarine |
| 6 medium-size carrots, scraped and quartered | 1 can condensed cream of chicken soup |
| 1 small onion, chopped (¼ cup) | 3 cups chunks of cooked chicken (boiled, roasted or broiled) |
| ¼ cup chopped green pepper | Biscuit Wedge Topping |

1. Cook potatoes and carrots in boiling salted water in large saucepan 15 to 20 minutes, or until tender; drain, saving 1 cup of liquid for next step.

2. While vegetables cook, sauté onion and green pepper in butter or margarine until soft in saucepan; stir in chicken soup and 1 cup saved liquid.

3. Spoon vegetables and chicken into 8-cup casserole; pour sauce over.

4. Bake in hot oven (425°) 15 minutes while making Biscuit Wedge Topping; arrange biscuits on top of hot mixture; bake 15 minutes longer, or until biscuits are golden.

## BISCUIT WEDGE TOPPING

Sift 1½ cups sifted flour, 2 teaspoons baking powder and ½ teaspoon salt into medium-size bowl; cut in ¼ cup (½ stick) butter or margarine; add ½ cup milk all at once; stir just until blended. Turn dough out onto lightly floured pastry cloth or board; knead lightly ½ minute; roll out to a 7-inch round; cut into 6 wedges; brush tops lightly with milk; sprinkle with ¼ teaspoon poppy seeds.

## JUMBO CHICKEN POPOVER

*This turns out to be an oversize puffy popover containing browned chicken parts.*

*Bake at 350° for 1 hour.*
*Makes 4 servings.*

1 broiler-fryer (about 3 pounds)
4 tablespoons plus 1½ cups flour
2 teaspoons salt
1 teaspoon paprika
¼ teaspoon pepper
Fat for frying
1½ teaspoons baking powder
4 eggs
1½ cups milk
3 tablespoons melted butter or margarine
Cream Gravy

1. Cut chicken into 8 pieces—2 breasts, 2 wings, 2 thighs, 2 drumsticks. Cut away back and any small bones from breasts; simmer bones with neck and giblets in 1 cup water in small saucepan. Strain to make broth for Cream Gravy (for recipe, turn to chapter on GRAVIES).

2. Shake chicken pieces with 4 tablespoons flour, 1 teaspoon salt, paprika and pepper in paper bag to coat lightly.

3. Brown, a few at a time, in hot fat in heavy frying pan; drain on paper towel.

4. Sift 1½ cups flour, baking powder and 1 teaspoon salt into medium-size bowl.

5. Beat eggs slightly in second medium-size bowl; blend in milk and melted butter or margarine. Stir into dry ingredients; beat with rotary beater until smooth.

6. Pour batter into buttered shallow 8-cup baking dish; arrange chicken in batter.

7. Bake in moderate oven (350°) 1 hour, or until golden. (Keep oven door closed for full hour.) Serve with Cream Gravy.

## Chapter 10

# Company's Coming

Unexpected or invited, it's always nice to be prepared
for company—and that includes having dinner under
control. When the occasion is an elegant dinner party,
you'll want to put your best entertaining foot forward.
The recipes here are for just such moments.

Incidentally, a whole roast chicken is a particularly
good choice for company. It looks wonderful and can
be stretched easily to feed an extra last-minute guest.
(See Chapter 6 for roast chicken recipes in addition
to the ones in this chapter.)

Some of the recipes are also geared to be made
ahead of time—with only details left for the end.

Also, while dinner normally means from 4 to 8
people, there are times when it's necessary to put an
extra leaf in the dining room table. For help with
dinner for more than 8 people, see the section in this
chapter entitled "Dinners for a Large Crowd."

# Dinner for a Small Crowd

## CHICKEN IMPERIAL

*A bit of a production to make, but a splendid dish to serve. And if guests are late, this dinner will wait.*

*Bake at 350° for 1 hour and 15 minutes.*
*Makes 8 servings.*

2 cups soft bread crumbs (4 slices)
¾ cup finely diced cooked ham
½ cup chopped parsley
8 tablespoons (1 stick) hard butter or margarine, sliced thin
4 chicken breasts (about 12 ounces each)

4 chicken drumsticks with thighs
1 cup milk
1 cup fine dry bread crumbs
1 can or 1 envelope (2 to a package) cream of mushroom soup mix
2 cups cold water
¼ cup chili sauce

1. Mix soft bread crumbs, ham and parsley in a large bowl; cut in butter or margarine quickly with a pastry blender; chill while fixing chicken so butter doesn't melt.

2. Pull skin from chicken pieces; halve breasts, then cut out rib bones with scissors. Separate thighs and drumsticks at joints with a sharp knife. To make pockets for stuffing, pull each breast piece open on its thick side, and cut an opening along bone in each leg and thigh.

3. Stuff about ¼ cup chilled stuffing into each half breast and 2 tablespoonfuls into each leg and thigh.

4. Place ½ cup of the milk in a pie plate and dry bread crumbs on a sheet of waxed paper. (Set remaining ½ cup milk aside for making sauce.) Roll stuffed chicken pieces in milk, then in bread crumbs to coat; chill while making sauce.

5. Combine mushroom soup mix and water in a

small saucepan; cook, following label directions. Stir in remaining ½ cup milk and chili sauce; pour 1 cup into shallow 12-cup baking dish.

6. Place chicken pieces, standing on edge if needed to fit, in sauce in dish; drizzle remaining sauce between pieces.

7. Bake in moderate oven (350°) 1 hour and 15 minutes, or until tender and richly golden. Garnish with parsley, if you wish.

HOSTESS NOTE: If dinner is delayed, simply lower oven heat to very slow (250°) and fit a sheet of foil, tent fashion, over casserole. It will hold about an hour.

## EAST-WEST BROILED CORNISH HENS

*The flavor trick is, when broiling these little birds, to baste frequently with the marinade which keeps them especially moist.*

*Makes 6 servings.*

3 frozen Rock Cornish game hens (about 1 pound each), thawed
½ cup soy sauce
1½ cups water
2 green onions, trimmed and chopped

¼ teaspoon crushed red pepper
1 small head romaine, shredded (about 4 cups)
2 tablespoons dry sherry
Chinese noodles

1. Cut hens in half with poultry shears or kitchen scissors. Place in a large shallow broiling pan, without rack.

2. Combine soy sauce, ½ cup of the water, green onions and red pepper; pour over hens. Marinate 1 hour.

3. Broil hens, 4 inches from heat, turning often and basting with marinade, 40 minutes, or until hens are a rich brown.

4. Line a heated serving platter with shredded romaine. Arrange hens on romaine; keep warm.

5. Stir remaining 1 cup water and sherry into broiling pan.

6. Cook, stirring and scraping cooked-on bits from sides of pan, until liquid comes to boiling. Spoon over hens. Serve with Chinese noodles.

# CHAFING-DISH CHICKEN ROYALE

*Perfect for a company buffet. Shrimps and tiny meat balls add the royal touches.*

*Makes 6 servings.*

3 chicken breasts (about 12 ounces each), halved
4 cups water
Few celery tops
2½ teaspoons salt
½ pound meat-loaf mixture (ground beef and pork)
6 tablespoons flour
Dash of pepper
1 egg
2 teaspoons grated onion
¼ cup milk
3 medium-size carrots, pared and sliced

1 cup frozen peas (from a 1¼ pound bag)
4 tablespoons (½ stick) butter or margarine
1 tablespoon lemon juice
Few drops red-pepper seasoning
1 can (about 5 ounces) deveined shrimp, drained and rinsed
2 tablespoons chopped parsley

1. Combine chicken breasts, water, celery tops and 2 teaspoons of the salt in a large saucepan; cover. Simmer 30 minutes, or until chicken is tender.

2. Remove from broth and cool until easy to handle. Pull off skin and take meat from bones in one piece; set aside for Step 7. Set broth aside for Step 4.

3. Combine meat-loaf mixture, 2 tablespoons of the

flour, remaining ½ teaspoon salt, pepper, egg, onion and milk in a medium-size bowl; mix with a fork until well-blended. Shape into 18 small balls. (Set remaining flour aside for making sauce.)

4. Reheat chicken broth to boiling; add meat balls; cover. Poach 10 minutes or until cooked through; lift out with a slotted spoon and place in a bowl.

5. Cook carrots, covered, in part of the same chicken broth 20 minutes, or until tender; cook peas in remaining broth, following label directions. Drain liquid from each and strain into a 4-cup measure; add more water if needed, to make 4 cups. Keep carrots and peas hot for Step 7.

6. Melt butter or margarine in a large saucepan; blend in remaining 4 tablespoons flour; cook, stirring constantly, just until bubbly. Stir in the 4 cups chicken broth; continue cooking and stirring until sauce thickens and boils 1 minute. Stir in lemon juice and red-pepper seasoning.

7. Cut each half chicken breast into three pieces; add to sauce with meat balls, carrots and peas. Heat slowly just to boiling; spoon into a chafing dish or heated serving dish. Arrange shrimps on top; sprinkle with parsley.

# APPLE CIDER CHICKEN

*This chicken-in-sauce makes a fine company dinner served over hot buttered noodles.*

*Makes 4 servings.*

| | |
|---|---|
| 1 broiler-fryer (about 3 pounds, cut in serving-size pieces | 1 envelope instant chicken broth |
| 6 tablespoons flour | ½ teaspoon salt |
| ¼ cup salad oil | ⅛ teaspoon pepper |
| 1 small onion, sliced and separated into rings | ½ cup apple cider |
| | ½ cup water |
| | 2 tablespoons catsup |
| ½ clove garlic, minced | 1 teaspoon grated lemon rind |

1. Wash chicken pieces; pat dry. Shake, a few at a time, in 4 tablespoons of the flour in a paper bag to coat well. (Save remaining flour for sauce in Step 3.)

2. Brown chicken slowly in salad oil in a large frying pan; remove from pan and set aside for Step 4.

3. Stir onion and garlic into drippings in pan; sauté just until soft. Blend in saved 2 tablespoons flour, chicken broth, salt and pepper; cook, stirring all the time, just until mixture bubbles. Stir in cider, water, catsup and lemon rind; continue cooking and stirring until sauce thickens and boils 1 minute.

4. Return chicken to pan; cover. Simmer 45 minutes or until tender.

## DOUBLE-TREAT ROAST CHICKEN

*Let your guests choose their favorite dressing and share the delicious gravy.*

*Roast at 375° for 1¼ hours.*
*Makes 8 servings.*

| | |
|---|---|
| 2 broiler-fryers (about 2½ pounds each) | 4 tablespoons (½ stick) butter or margarine, melted |
| 3 cups water | Fruited Giblet Dressing |
| Handful of celery leaves | Jardiniere Dressing |
| 2 onion slices | 2 teaspoons aromatic bitters |
| ½ teaspoon salt | Chicken Gravy |
| Dash of pepper | |

1. Remove chicken giblets from chickens and return chicken and livers to refrigerator. Combine giblets, water, celery leaves, onion slices, salt and pepper in medium-size saucepan. Heat to boiling; reduce heat and simmer 50 minutes. Add chicken livers and cook 10 minutes longer, or until giblets are tender. Trim and finely chop giblets. Strain and reserve broth.

2. Stuff one chicken with Fruited Giblet Dressing and one chicken with Jardiniere Dressing. Place in shallow roasting pan. Brush with part of butter or margarine.

3. Roast in moderate oven (375°), basting several times with pan drippings, 1 hour. Stir bitters into remaining melted butter. Brush over chickens. Roast 15 minutes longer, or until chickens are golden. Place on heated serving platter and keep warm while making Chicken Gravy. Garnish platter with bundles of cooked carrots and green beans and parsley, if you wish.

## FRUITED GIBLET DRESSING

*Makes 1½ cups or enough to stuff one 2½-pound chicken.*

| | |
|---|---|
| 1 large apple, pared, cored and chopped | 3 tablespoons giblet broth |
| 2 tablespoons butter or margarine | ½ teaspoon salt |
| Chopped giblets | ¼ teaspoon ground allspice |
| 1½ cups soft bread crumbs (3 slices) | Dash of pepper |

Sauté apple until soft in butter or margarine in skillet. Stir in chopped giblets and cook 2 minutes. Stir in bread crumbs, broth, salt, allspice and pepper until well-blended.

## JARDINIERE DRESSING

*Makes 1½ cups or enough to stuff one 2½-pound chicken.*

| | |
|---|---|
| 1 medium-size onion, chopped (½ cup) | 1 cup soft bread crumbs (2 slices) |
| ½ cup finely chopped celery | ½ teaspoon leaf savory, crumbled |
| ½ cup finely chopped carrots | ½ teaspoon salt |
| 2 tablespoons butter or margarine | Dash of pepper |

Sauté onion, celery and carrots until soft in butter or margarine in skillet. Stir in bread crumbs, savory, salt and pepper until well-blended.

## CHICKEN GRAVY

*Makes about 2½ cups.*

Stir 4 tablespoons flour into pan drippings. Cook, stirring constantly, 3 minutes. Blend in remaining giblet broth. (You should have 2½ cups.) Cook, stirring constantly, until mixture thickens and bubbles 3 minutes.

## CRISP CORNISH HENS

*Midget chickens in coats of seasoned crumbs bake themselves to a golden turn.*

*Bake at 350° for 1¼ hours.*
*Makes 6 servings.*

6 frozen Rock Cornish hens (about 1 pound each), thawed
Salt
½ cup buttermilk
2 packages seasoned coating mix for chicken

1 package (1 pound) spinach noodles
½ teaspoon onion salt
2 tablespoons butter or margarine

1. Remove giblets from Cornish hens and chill or freeze to simmer for gravy another day. Rinse hens inside and out; pat dry. Sprinkle cavities lightly with salt.
2. Brush hens, one at a time, with buttermilk, then shake in coating mix. Place, breast side up and not touching, in a jelly-roll pan.
3. Bake in moderate oven (350°) for 1¼ hours, or until tender and golden.
4. While hens bake, cook noodles in a kettle, following label directions; drain; return to kettle. Add onion salt and butter or margarine; toss lightly to mix.
5. Spoon noodles onto a large deep serving platter; arrange Cornish hens on top.

# HERBED CHICKEN ROLLS

*Chicken thighs wrapped around a cheese and herb butter are fried to a delicious finish.*

*Makes 6 servings.*

¾ cup shredded sharp
   Cheddar cheese
6 tablespoons (¾
   stick) butter or
   margarine
2 tablespoons freeze-
   dried chives
1 teaspoon garlic salt
½ teaspoon leaf rose-
   mary, crumbled
⅛ teaspoon liquid
   red-pepper seasoning

12 chicken thighs,
   skinned and boned
¾ teaspoon salt
¾ teaspoon mono-
   sodium glutamate
¼ cup flour
2 eggs, beaten
1 cup fine cheese-
   cracker crumbs
4 tablespoons vege-
   table oil
3 tablespoons water

1. Blend cheese with 4 tablespoons of the butter or margarine, chives, garlic salt, rosemary and red-pepper seasoning in a small bowl. Spread in a square, ½ inch thick, on waxed paper; chill until very firm.

2. Place each boned chicken thigh between sheets of waxed paper and pound with a mallet to flatten; sprinkle with salt and monosodium glutamate.

3. Cut chilled butter mixture into 12 squares; place one on each piece of chicken. Fold edges of meat over butter to cover completely; fasten with wooden picks.

4. Dip rolls in flour, then in beaten egg and cracker crumbs to coat well. Brown slowly in vegetable oil and remaining 2 tablespoons butter or margarine in a large frying pan 5 minutes. Add water to pan; cover. Cook 10 minutes; uncover. Cook 5 minutes longer, or until chicken is tender.

# MOLDED CHICKEN INDIENNE

*All white meat blends with curry and chutney for this inviting company-supper mold.*

*Makes 6 servings.*

| | |
|---|---|
| 2 whole chicken breasts (about 12 ounces each) | 2 envelopes unflavored gelatin |
| 3½ cups water | 1 tablespoon sugar |
| 2 teaspoons salt | 2 tablespoons lemon juice |
| 1 teaspoon curry powder | ⅓ cup chutney (from a 6-ounce bottle), finely chopped |
| Few celery tops | 1 cup chopped celery |

1. Combine chicken breasts with water, salt, curry powder and celery tops in a large saucepan; cover; simmer 30 minutes, or until tender.

2. Remove chicken from broth; cool until easy to handle. Strain broth into a 4-cup measure; add water, if needed, to make 3½ cups. Pull skin from chicken and take meat from bones; chill meat; dice.

3. Soften gelatin with sugar in 1 cup of the broth in a medium-size saucepan; heat, stirring constantly, just until gelatin dissolves; remove from heat. Stir in remaining 2½ cups broth.

4. Measure ½ cup of the gelatin mixture into a small bowl; set aside for next step. Stir lemon juice into remaining gelatin in saucepan. Chill about 50 minutes, or until as thick as unbeaten egg white.

5. Stir chutney into gelatin in small bowl; pour into a 6-cup mold; chill about 30 minutes, or just until sticky-firm.

6. Fold chicken and celery into thickened gelatin in saucepan; spoon over sticky-firm chutney layer in mold. Chill overnight, or several hours until firm.

7. To unmold, run a sharp-tip thin-blade knife around top of mold, then dip very quickly in and out of a pan of hot water. Cover mold with serving plate; turn upside down; gently lift off mold. Garnish with

leaves of Belgian endive, halved seedless grapes and flaked coconut.

## CHICKEN PERFECTION

*Chicken baked with this spicy sweet-sour glaze can best be described as gorgeous.*

*Bake at 400° about 1 hour.*
*Makes 8 servings.*

Curry Glaze
2 broiler-fryers (about
   3 pounds each),
   quartered
6 tablespoons flour
1½ teaspoons salt

1 teaspoon ground
   ginger
6 tablespoons (¾
   stick) butter or
   margarine
Buttered hot rice

1. Make Curry Glaze.
2. Cut away backbones and any small rib bones from chickens. (Kitchen scissors do a fast neat job.) Pull off skin, if desired. Shake chicken pieces in mixture of flour, salt and ginger in paper bag to coat well.
3. Melt butter or margarine in large shallow baking or roasting pan. Roll chicken in melted butter to coat well, then arrange, skin side up, in single layer in pan.
4. Bake, uncovered, in hot oven (400°) 20 minutes, or until beginning to turn golden. Spoon about half of Curry Glaze on top of chicken to make a thick coating; bake 20 minutes. Spoon on remaining glaze; bake 20 minutes longer, or until chicken is tender.
5. Arrange chicken around a mound of buttered hot rice on serving platter. Garnish with lemon cups filled with your own or store-bought pepper relish, if you wish.

## CURRY GLAZE

*Makes about 2 cups.*

1 medium-size onion,
chopped (½ cup)
6 slices bacon, finely
diced
2 tablespoons flour
1 tablespoon curry
powder
1 tablespoon sugar

1 can condensed beef
broth
2 tablespoons flaked
coconut
2 tablespoons apple-
sauce
2 tablespoons catsup
2 tablespoons lemon
juice

Combine all ingredients in medium-size saucepan. Heat
to boiling, stirring constantly, then simmer uncovered,
stirring often, 15 minutes.

## GOURMET STUFFED CHICKEN

*White meat with a chicken liver stuffing, topped with
crumbs and a dollop of gravy—serve this one to visit-
ing celebrities, or maybe your in-laws.*

*Bake at 350° for 1 hour.*
*Makes 6 servings.*

3 whole chicken
breasts (about 2½
pounds)
2 cups Gourmet
Stuffing
4 tablespoons (½
stick) butter or
margarine

½ cup packaged corn
flake crumbs
1 can or 1 envelope
(2 to a package)
mushroom soup mix

1. Halve breasts this way: Pull off skin, then cut
along breastbone on either side, loosening meat as you
go along, until each side can be pulled away in one
piece. Snip out small bones. Pull each half breast open

in the middle to form a pocket for stuffing. (Meat will come apart easily between its two large muscles.)

2. Make Gourmet Stuffing. Spoon into breast pockets to fill; press edges together and fasten with wooden picks.

3. Melt butter or margarine in large shallow baking pan; roll chicken in butter to coat well; arrange in single layer in same pan. Sprinkle crumbs over top.

4. Bake in moderate oven (350°) 1 hour, or until chicken is tender and golden.

5. Prepare mushroom soup mix, following label directions for gravy or sauce.

6. Place chicken on heated serving platter; remove wooden picks. Pass gravy in separate bowl to spoon over chicken.

## GOURMET STUFFING

*Makes 2 cups.*

3 chicken livers
4 tablespoons (½ stick) butter or margarine
2 cups soft bread crumbs (4 slices)

2 tablespoons chopped onion
1 tablespoon water
1 teaspoon Worcestershire sauce
½ teaspoon salt

1. Sauté chicken livers in butter or margarine, stirring often, in small frying pan 5 minutes, or until livers lose their pink color.

2. Remove livers and chop, then add to bread crumbs in medium-size bowl. Sauté onion just until soft in same frying pan.

3. Stir water, Worcestershire sauce and salt into onions in frying pan; pour over crumb mixture. Toss lightly to mix well. (Mixture will be crumbly, not wet.)

# ORANGE GLAZED CHICKENS

*This one is a showpiece: Two glistening roasters, plumped with apricot stuffing.*

*Roast at 350° for 2 hours.*
*Makes 8 servings.*

**2 roasting chickens**
  **(about 4 pounds**
  **each)**
**Apricot-Walnut Stuffing**

**3 tablespoons butter or**
  **margarine, melted**
**Double Orange Glaze**

1. Rinse chickens inside and out with cold water, drain, then pat dry.
2. Make Apricot Stuffing; pack lightly into neck and body cavities. Smooth neck skin over stuffing and skewer to back; twist wing tips flat against skewered neck skin; tie legs to tails with string. Place chickens on a rack in a roasting pan; brush with melted butter or margarine.
3. Roast in moderate oven (350°), basting several times with drippings in pan, 1¾ hours, or until chickens are almost tender.
4. While chickens cook, make Double Orange Glaze; brush part over each to coat generously.
5. Continue roasting, brushing twice with remaining glaze 15 minutes, or until drumsticks move easily and chickens are richly glazed.
6. Remove to a heated large serving platter; take out skewers and cut away strings. Garnish platter with dried apricot halves topped with canned mandarin-orange segments, if you wish. Carve chickens into serving-size pieces.

## DOUBLE ORANGE GLAZE

Combine ½ cup thawed frozen concentrated orange juice (from a 6-ounce can), ¼ cup of orange marmalade and 2 tablespoons bottled meat sauce in a small saucepan. Heat slowly, stirring constantly, until marmalade melts and mixture is blended; remove from heat. Makes enough to glaze two 4-pound chickens.

## APRICOT-WALNUT STUFFING

*Makes 4 cups, or enough to stuff two 4-pound chickens.*

1 **medium-size onion, chopped (½ cup)**

4 **tablespoons (½ stick) butter or margarine**

½ **cup chopped apricots**

1 **envelope instant chicken broth OR**

1 **chicken bouillon cube**

⅓ **cup water**

6 **slices white bread, cubed (about 3 cups)**

½ **cup chopped walnuts**

1. In a large frying pan, sauté onion in butter or margarine until soft; stir in apricots, chicken broth or bouillon cubes and water. Heat to boiling; remove from heat.

2. Add bread and walnuts; toss until moist.

# Dinner for a Large Crowd

## OUTDOOR CHICKEN PARTY TIME

*Allow plenty of grilling time so that the meat will almost fall off the bones.*

*Makes 12 servings.*

6 **broiler-fryers, split (1½ to 2 pounds each)**

2 **cups salad oil**

½ **cup lime or lemon juice**

2 **teaspoons salt**

¼ **cup honey**

1. Wash chicken halves, then dry. Mix salad oil, lime or lemon juice and salt in a small saucepan; brush part over chickens. Place, skin side up, on grill about 6 inches above hot coals.

2. Grill, turning and brushing often with more sauce, 1 hour.

3. Stir honey into remaining sauce; brush over chickens. Continue grilling, turning often and brushing with remaining sauce, 15 minutes, or until golden-brown and joints move easily.

# PAELLA

*From sunny Valencia comes this famous Spanish dish (pronounced pah-ay-ya). Made with chicken, shellfish, spicy sausages and rice, it arrives at the table right in its pan, steaming hot.*

Bake at 375° about 1 hour.
Makes 8 to 10 servings.

1 broiler-fryer, cut up
1 clove garlic, minced
¼ cup olive oil or salad oil
6 strands saffron
1½ cups raw long-grain rice
1 pound sweet Italian sausages, sliced 1-inch thick
1 large onion, chopped (1 cup)
1 green pepper, chopped
1 can (about 14 ounces) chicken broth
2 cans (about 7 ounces each) minced clams
1 teaspoon salt
1 teaspoon paprika
1 pound raw shrimps, shelled and deveined
4 tomatoes, sliced
1 pound fresh peas, shelled
1 can (4 ounces) pimientos, diced

1. Brown chicken with garlic in olive oil or salad oil in large frying pan; remove; stir in saffron and rice; sauté until rice is golden; add sausages, onion and green pepper; sauté 7 to 10 minutes longer; stir in chicken broth, minced clams and their liquid, salt and paprika; cover, and cook 10 minutes.

2. Layer the chicken, rice mixture, shrimps, tomatoes, peas and pimientos in a 12-cup baking dish; cover tightly. (Or use a metal paella pan.)

3. Bake in moderate oven (375°) 1 hour, or until rice is tender and liquid is absorbed.

4. Remove cover; garnish paella with more diced pimientos and a few freshly steamed clams in their shell, if you wish.

5. Serve from its baking dish at the table with thick slices of crusty bread and a big green salad; add fresh fruit and coffee for dessert, or in true Spanish style serve a chilled creamy baked caramel custard.

## CHICKEN AND FRUIT HARMONY

*For a summer party: An elegant melange of tender chicken and fruits tossed with a creamy curry dressing.*

*Makes 12 servings.*

2 broiler-fryers (2½ to 3 pounds each)
4 cups water
2 teaspoons salt
12 peppercorns
Handful of celery tops
2 carrots, scraped and sliced
Creamy Boiled Dressing
3 cups cantaloupe cubes
2 cups halved green grapes (about 1 pound)
2 cups thinly sliced celery
1 cup slivered almonds, toasted
2 heads of Boston or leaf lettuce
Paprika

1. Simmer broiler-fryers in water with salt, peppercorns, celery tops and carrots in large saucepan, covered, 45 minutes, or until tender.

2. Remove from broth and let cool just until easy to handle. (Save broth for soup for another meal.) Slip skin from chickens; remove meat from bones in large chunks and cut into cubes. (You should have about 6 cups.)

3. Place chicken in large bowl; toss with just enough Creamy Boiled Dressing to coat well; cover; chill.

4. When ready to serve, stir the cantaloupe, grapes, celery and almonds into chicken mixture; toss with enough of remaining dressing to coat well.

5. Line a salad bowl with lettuce; spoon salad in center; garnish with paprika.

# CREAMY BOILED DRESSING

*Makes 1½ cups.*

| | |
|---|---|
| 4 tablespoons sugar | 2 eggs, beaten |
| 2 tablespoons flour | 1 cup water |
| 1 teaspoon salt | ½ cup cider vinegar |
| ½ teaspoon curry powder | 2 tablespoons butter or margarine |

1. Combine sugar, flour, salt and curry powder in pan; stir in egg, water and vinegar.

2. Cook slowly, stirring constantly, 5 minutes, or until thickened. Remove from heat; stir in butter or margarine until melted. This dressing will keep well in a tightly covered jar in the refrigerator.

# CLUB NIGHT CASSEROLE

*This agreeable casserole will please all comers. It's best started the day before.*

Bake at 350° for 50 to 60 minutes.
Makes 8 to 12 servings.

| | |
|---|---|
| 1 stewing chicken (about 5 pounds), not cut up | 6 tablespoons flour |
| | 1 cup light or table cream |
| 3½ cups water | 2 cans (3 or 4 ounces each) sliced mushrooms |
| 1 medium-size onion, sliced | |
| 1 carrot, scraped and halved | 1 can (about 4 ounces) pimientos, diced |
| Handful of celery tops | |
| 2 teaspoons salt | 1 cup (about a 5-ounce can) toasted slivered almonds |
| 1 bay leaf | |
| 6 cups cooked rice (1½ cups raw) | |
| 6 tablespoons chicken fat | 1 cup buttered soft bread crumbs (2 slices) |

1. Combine chicken, water, onion, carrot, celery tops, salt and bay leaf in large kettle; cover; simmer 1 to 1½ hours, or until tender.

2. Cool chicken in stock; remove, and skin. Take meat from bones; cut meat into bite-size pieces; place in medium-size bowl. Pour ½ cup stock over to keep chicken moist; cover and chill.

3. Strain remaining stock into a medium-size bowl; chill; skim off fat and save for Step 5. (This much can be done the day before.)

4. When ready to complete dish, heat 1 cup stock and pour over cooked rice in large bowl; let stand while making sauce.

5. Melt chicken fat from Step 3 in medium-size saucepan, adding butter or margarine, if needed, to make 6 tablespoons. Remove from heat; blend in flour; stir in 2 cups stock.

6. Cook over low heat, stirring constantly, until sauce thickens and boils 1 minute. Remove from heat; gradually stir in cream, mushrooms and their liquid, pimientos, almonds and chicken; season to taste with salt and pepper.

7. Make alternate layers of chicken and rice mixtures in buttered 12-cup casserole; sprinkle buttered bread crumbs around edge.

8. Bake in moderate oven (350°) 50 to 60 minutes, or until sauce bubbles around edges and crumbs are golden-brown.

# JAMBALAYA

*A kettle of contrasts from Creole country: Chicken, ham, vegetables, rice.*

*Makes 12 servings.*

2 broiler-fryers (about 2 pounds each), cut up
3 cups diced cooked ham (1 pound)
4 tablespoons (½ stick) butter or margarine
2 cloves garlic, sliced
3 large onions, chopped (3 cups)
1 package (1 pound) frozen deveined shelled raw shrimps

3 cans (about 1 pound each) stewed tomatoes
2 teaspoons salt
¼ teaspoon liquid red-pepper seasoning
1 large bay leaf
3 cups thinly sliced celery
2 cups uncooked rice
¼ cup chopped parsley

1. Wash chicken pieces; pat dry.
2. Brown ham lightly in butter or margarine in a heavy roasting pan. Stir in garlic and onions; sauté 5 minutes, or until soft. Add chicken and shrimps.
3. Combine the tomatoes, salt, red-pepper seasoning and bay leaf in a large bowl; pour over ham and chicken.
4. Heat to boiling; cover. Simmer 30 minutes. Stir in celery and rice, making sure all rice is covered with liquid.
5. Simmer 30 minutes longer, or until chicken and rice are tender; remove bay leaf. Stir in parsley.

## Chapter 11

# Special Imports

They come from Europe, South America, Asia and Africa, yet they're completely at home here. They're chicken recipes that blend cooking secrets from many old worlds with ingredients found in your local supermarket. And while the names may sound foreign, the preparation is no more difficult than for other, more familiar American recipes. Some, in fact, have become as much a part of our cuisine as fried chicken and chicken pot-pie. So the next time you feel like getting away from it all, serve one of these dishes. They're your passport to international flavor—and there's no packing or unpacking involved.

## TAGINE

*In Morocco, ginger, paprika and olives are favorite seasoners for the ever-popular chicken.*

*Makes 6 servings.*

2 broiler-fryers (about 2 pounds each), cut up
4 tablespoons (½ stick) butter or margarine
4 medium-size onions, chopped (2 cups)
3 teaspoons salt
1½ teaspoons ground ginger
1 teaspoon paprika
¼ teaspoon pepper
Water
1 jar (7 ounces) stuffed green olives, drained and sliced
2 tablespoons flour
Bulgar
¼ cup chopped parsley
6 thin lemon wedges

174

1. Wash the chicken pieces; pat dry. Brown, a few pieces at a time, in butter or margarine in a heavy kettle or Dutch oven; remove all from kettle.

2. Stir onions into drippings in kettle; sauté until soft. Stir in salt, ginger, paprika, pepper and 1 cup water. Return chicken; cover.

3. Simmer, basting several times with liquid in kettle, 45 minutes, or until chicken is tender.

4. While chicken simmers, combine sliced olives with water to cover in a small saucepan; heat to boiling; drain. Keep hot for Step 7.

5. Remove chicken from the kettle; keep hot. Pour liquid into a 2-cup measure; let stand about 1 minute, or until fat rises to top, then skim off. Add water to liquid, if needed, to make 1½ cups, return to kettle; heat to boiling.

6. Blend flour and ¼ cup water until smooth in a cup; stir into boiling liquid. Cook, stirring constantly, until gravy thickens and boils 1 minute.

7. When ready to serve, combine olives with Bulgar; spoon onto a heated serving platter; arrange chicken on top; sprinkle with chopped parsley. Arrange lemon wedges, petal fashion, in center. Pass gravy separately.

## BULGAR (Cracked Wheat)

*Makes 6 servings.*

| | |
|---|---|
| 3½ cups water | 2 medium-size |
| ½ cup (1 stick) butter | eggplants |
| or margarine | 1 large onion, chopped |
| 3 teaspoons salt | (1 cup) |
| 1 package (1 pound) | ¼ cup vegetable oil |
| bulgar wheat | |

1. Heat water with butter or margarine and 2 teaspoons of the salt to boiling in a large heavy saucepan; slowly stir in wheat. Cook, stirring several times, 5 minutes, or until liquid is almost absorbed; cover.

2. Continue cooking very slowly, stirring several times with a fork, 45 minutes, or until wheat is very light and fluffy.

3. While wheat cooks, slice eggplants 1 inch thick; pare and cut into 1-inch cubes.

4. In a large frying pan sauté onion in vegetable oil until soft; stir in eggplant and remaining 1 teaspoon salt; cover. Cook slowly, stirring often, 30 minutes.

5. Add cooked wheat; toss lightly with two forks to mix well and to fluff up the wheat.

# GLAZED BUTTERFLY CHICKEN

*Breasts, fragrant with a fruit-curry glaze.*

Bake at 350° for 1½ hours.
Makes 8 servings.

Curry-Fruit Glaze
  (from page 180)
8 whole chicken
  breasts (12 ounces
  each)

6 tablespoons (¾
  stick) butter or
  margarine
1 teaspoon ground
  ginger
½ cup flaked coconut

1. Make Curry-Fruit Glaze and set aside.

2. Cut away rib bones from chicken breasts, leaving the V-shape bone at neck.

3. Melt butter or margarine in a large shallow baking pan; stir in ginger. Roll chicken in mixture to coat well, then arrange, skin side up, in a single layer in pan. Tuck edges of each breast under to give a rounded shape. Spoon glaze over.

4. Bake, uncovered, in moderate oven (350°), basting often with glaze mixture in pan, 1 hour and 20 minutes, or until richly glazed.

5. Top with coconut; bake 10 minutes more.

# CHICKEN PAPRIKA WITH PARSLEY DUMPLINGS

*Sour cream gravy and dumplings make chicken extra special and extra hearty.*

*Makes 8 servings.*

2 broiler-fryers (about 2½ pounds each), cut up
⅓ cup flour
2 teaspoons salt
¼ teaspoon pepper
2 tablespoons butter or margarine
1 tablespoon vegetable oil
1 large onion, chopped (1 cup)

2 envelopes instant chicken broth OR 2 teaspoons granulated chicken bouillon
1 tablespoon paprika
2 cups water
1 cup (8-ounce carton) dairy sour cream
¼ cup cream for whipping
Parsley Dumplings

1. Shake chicken in a mixture of flour, salt and pepper in a plastic bag to coat well. (Save any remaining seasoned flour mixture for gravy.)

2. Brown chicken, part at a time, in butter or margarine and vegetable oil in a kettle or Dutch oven; remove all from kettle. Pour off drippings, then measure 1 tablespoonful and return to kettle.

3. Stir in onion; sauté until soft. Stir in chicken broth or bouillon, paprika and water. Heat, scraping brown bits from bottom, to boiling; return chicken; cover. Simmer 30 minutes, or until chicken is tender. Remove from broth to a shallow pan; reheat broth to boiling.

4. Measure saved seasoned flour, adding more flour, if needed, to make 2 tablespoons. Blend with a small amount of water to a paste in a cup; stir into broth. Cook, stirring constantly, until gravy thickens and boils 1 minute.

5. Blend sour cream and cream in a small bowl; stir

into kettle; return chicken. Reheat slowly to boiling while mixing Parsley Dumplings.

6. Drop dough in 8 mounds on top of chicken; cover tightly. Cook 20 minutes. (Do not lift lid of kettle while the dumplings cook.) Serve from kettle.

## PARSLEY DUMPLINGS

Sift 1½ cups sifted regular flour, 2 teaspoons baking powder and ¾ teaspoon salt into a medium-size bowl; stir in 3 tablespoons chopped parsley. Combine ¾ cup milk and 2 tablespoons melted butter or margarine in a cup; stir into flour mixture just until moist. (Dough will be soft.)

## CHICKEN PAPRIKASH

*The esteemed concoction of paprika-flavored chicken in sour cream with noodles is one of Hungary's great contributions to the world of food.*

*Makes 8 servings.*

| | |
|---|---|
| 2 broiler-fryers (about 3 pounds each) | ¼ teaspoon pepper |
| 1 large onion, chopped (1 cup) | 1 can (8 ounces) tomatoes |
| 2 tablespoons butter or margarine | 1 package (1 pound) noodles |
| 2 tablespoons paprika | 1 cup (8-ounce carton) dairy sour cream |
| 1 tablespoon flour | 1 tablespoon chopped parsley |
| 3 teaspoons salt | |

1. Cut the chickens into serving-size pieces.

2. Sauté onion in butter or margarine until soft in a large skillet with a cover. Stir in paprika and flour; cook, stirring constantly, 1 minute. Stir in salt, pepper and tomatoes (breaking with spoon).

3. Add chicken and giblets (except livers), turning to coat pieces well; cover. Simmer 30 minutes. Turn chicken pieces; add livers; simmer 15 minutes longer, or until chicken is tender.

4. Meanwhile, cook noodles, following label directions; drain; spoon onto hot serving platter. Remove chicken from skillet with a slotted spoon. Arrange on platter with noodles; keep warm.

5. Spoon sour cream into a medium-size bowl. Heat sauce in skillet to boiling; stir slowly into sour cream, blending well. Spoon over chicken. Garnish with chopped parsley.

## POLYNESIAN HILO PLATTER

*Many flavors join harmoniously in the stuffing and glaze of this exotic roast chicken.*

*Bake at 350° for 2 hours.*
*Makes 6 to 8 servings.*

| | |
|---|---|
| **2 roasting chickens** (about 4 pounds each) | **3 tablespoons butter or margarine, melted** |
| **4 cups Hilo Stuffing** | **1½ cups Curry-Fruit Glaze** |

1. Rinse chickens inside and out with cold water; drain, then pat dry. Stuff neck and body cavities lightly with Hilo Stuffing. Smooth neck skin over stuffing and skewer to back; tie legs to tail with strings.

2. Place chickens on a rack in roasting pan; brush with melted butter or margarine.

3. Roast in moderate oven (350°) for 1 hour.

4. Spoon part of the Curry-Fruit Glaze over each chicken to make a thick coating. Continue roasting, basting 2 or 3 times with remaining glaze, 1 hour, or until drumsticks move easily and chickens are glazed.

5. Remove to a heated serving platter; cut away strings and remove skewers.

## HILO STUFFING

*Makes 4 cups, or enough to stuff two 4-pound chickens.*

1 cup uncooked white
rice
4 tablespoons (½
stick) butter or
margarine
1 medium-size onion,
chopped (½ cup)

2 envelopes instant
chicken broth OR
2 chicken bouillon
cubes
2½ cups water
½ cup chopped maca-
damia nuts (from a
6-ounce jar)
½ cup flaked coconut

1. In a large saucepan, sauté rice in butter or margarine, stirring often, just until it is golden.
2. Stir in onion, chicken broth or bouillon cubes
and water; heat to boiling, crushing cubes, if using,
with a spoon; cover. Simmer 20 minutes, or until rice
is tender and liquid is absorbed.
3. Sprinkle with nuts and coconut; toss lightly to
mix.

## CURRY-FRUIT GLAZE

*Makes 1½ cups, or enough to glaze two 4-pound
chickens.*

4 slices bacon, diced
1 medium-size onion,
chopped (½ cup)
2 tablespoons flour
1 tablespoon sugar
2 teaspoons curry
powder
½ teaspoon salt

1 tablespoon bottled
steak sauce
1 cup water
2 tablespoons lemon
juice
1 jar (4 ounces)
baby-pack strained
apples-and-apricots

1. Sauté bacon until almost crisp in a medium-size
saucepan; remove and drain on paper toweling.
2. Stir onions into drippings in saucepan; sauté until
just soft. Stir in flour, sugar, curry powder and salt;
heat until bubbly.

3. Stir in remaining ingredients and bacon. Simmer, stirring several times, 15 minutes, or until thick.

# CHICKEN CACCIATORE

*Men especially like this zesty Italian dish. It's also a good choice for guests, because it waits well.*

*Makes 8 servings.*

2 broiler-fryers (about 3 pounds each), quartered
¾ cup flour
3 teaspoons salt
¼ teaspoon pepper
6 tablespoons olive oil or salad oil
2 medium-size onions, chopped (1 cup)

1 clove garlic, minced
1 can (about 2 pounds) Italian tomatoes
1 tablespoon sugar
1 teaspoon basil
½ teaspoon thyme
2 medium-size green peppers, halved, seeded and sliced

1. Wash the chicken quarters; pat dry. Shake with flour, salt and pepper in a paper bag to coat well.
2. Brown pieces, a few at a time, in olive oil or salad oil in a large frying pan; remove all from pan.
3. Stir onion and garlic into drippings in pan and sauté until soft; stir in tomatoes, sugar, basil and thyme; heat to boiling.
4. Return chicken to pan; spoon some of the tomato sauce over; lay sliced green peppers on top; cover.
5. Simmer, basting several times with sauce in pan, 1½ hours, or until chicken is tender.

# RISOTTO ALLA MILANESE

*This is a continental specialty that can be ready for the table in less than 1 hour.*

*Makes 6 servings.*

4 slices bacon, diced
1 pound chicken livers, halved
¼ cup all-purpose flour
1 teaspoon salt
¼ teaspoon pepper
1 large onion, chopped (1 cup)

1 cup uncooked regular rice
2 envelopes or teaspoons instant chicken broth
1 teaspoon leaf basil, crumbled
1 bay leaf
2½ cups water
Chopped parsley

1. Cook bacon until crisp in a large skillet. Remove bacon with a slotted spoon and reserve.

2. Shake chicken livers in a plastic bag with flour, salt and pepper.

3. Brown chicken livers in bacon drippings. Remove with slotted spoon and reserve.

4. Sauté onion in same skillet until soft. (If there is no fat remaining in the skillet, add 2 tablespoons vegetable oil.) Stir in rice, chicken broth, basil, bay leaf and water.

5. Heat to boiling. Lower heat; stir rice mixture well; cover.

6. Simmer 10 minutes. Spoon the browned chicken livers over rice. Return cover and simmer 20 minutes longer, or until liquid is absorbed and rice is tender; remove bay leaf. Sprinkle with reserved bacon and chopped parsley.

# TWIN CHICKENS PARISIENNE

*Stuffed with parsley, simmered in mushroom sauce, the birds are then bathed in gravy and presented on a bed of noodles.*

*Makes 6 to 8 servings.*

| | |
|---|---|
| 2 **whole broiler-fryers** (about 3 pounds each) | 2 **tablespoons butter or margarine** |
| 1 **teaspoon salt** | 1 **can (3 or 4 ounces) whole mushrooms** |
| ½ **teaspoon sugar** | ¼ **teaspoon pepper** |
| 2 **bunches parsley, washed and trimmed** | 2 **tablespoons flour** |
| | ¾ **cup cream** |
| | **Hot cooked noodles** |

1. Rinse chickens inside and out with cold water; drain, then pat dry. Sprinkle insides with ½ teaspoon of the salt and sugar; place parsley in body cavities, packing in lightly. Skewer neck skin to back; twist wing tips flat against skewered neck skin; tie the legs to tails with string.

2. Brown in butter or margarine in a heavy kettle or Dutch oven; turn breast side up.

3. Drain liquid from mushrooms into a 1-cup measure; add water to make ¾ cup; pour over chickens. Sprinkle with remaining ½ teaspoon salt and pepper; cover tightly. (Set mushrooms aside for Step 6.)

4. Simmer, basting several times with liquid in kettle, 1 hour and 15 minutes, or until tender. Remove from kettle and keep hot while making gravy.

5. Pour liquid from kettle into a 2-cup measure; let stand about a minute, or until fat rises to top, then skim off into a cup. Add water to liquid, if needed, to make 1 cup.

6. Measure 2 tablespoons of the fat and return to kettle; blend in flour; stir in the 1 cup liquid. Cook, stirring constantly, until gravy thickens and boils 1 minute. Stir in mushrooms and cream; heat slowly just to boiling. Darken with a few drops bottled gravy coloring, if you wish.

7. Spoon noodles into a heated large serving bowl. Take out skewers and cut string from chickens; arrange chickens on top of noodles; spoon gravy over all. Garnish with parsley, if you wish. Carve chickens into serving-size pieces.

## MEXICALI CHICKEN

*Chicken and peppers are steeped in a tangy tomato sauce—cook this in your gayest casserole.*

Bake at 350° for 1½ hours.
Makes 8 servings.

2 **broiler-fryers (about 3 pounds each), cut up**
2 **tablespoons butter or margarine**
2 **tablespoons olive oil or vegetable oil**
1 **large onion, chopped (1 cup)**
1 **large sweet green pepper, quartered, seeded and chopped**
1 **large sweet red pepper, quartered, seeded and chopped**
3 **teaspoons chili powder**
¼ **cup flour**
1 **can (about 2 pounds) Italian tomatoes**
3 **teaspoons salt**
1 **teaspoon sugar**
¼ **teaspoon pepper**

1. Wash chicken pieces and dry. Brown, part at a time, in butter or margarine and olive oil or vegetable oil in a large frying pan; remove all from pan and set aside while making the sauce.

2. Stir onion and green and red peppers into drippings in pan; sauté until soft. Stir in chili powder; cook 1 minute longer.

3. Sprinkle flour over top, then blend in; stir in tomatoes, salt, sugar and pepper. Cook, stirring constantly, until sauce thickens and boils 1 minute.

4. Layer browned chicken, topping each with part of the sauce, into a 12-cup baking dish; cover.

5. Bake in moderate oven (350°) 1 hour; uncover. Bake 30 minutes longer, or until chicken is tender and sauce is thickened slightly. Garnish with rings of red and green pepper, if you wish.

# ARROZ CON POLLO

*Chicken with rice, Spanish style, includes tomatoes, onion, mushrooms, pimientos—and a nip of garlic.*

*Bake at 350° for 1 hour and 10 minutes.*
*Makes 4 servings.*

| | |
|---|---|
| 1 broiler-fryer (about 3 pounds), cut up | 2 cans (about 1 pound each) tomatoes |
| ¼ cup salad or olive oil | 1 can (3 or 4 ounces) chopped mushrooms |
| 1 cup raw rice | 1 can (about 4 ounces) pimientos, diced |
| 1 large onion, chopped (1 cup) | 2 tablespoons chopped parsley |
| 2 cloves garlic, minced | |
| 1 strand saffron, crushed | 1½ teaspoons salt |
| | ⅛ teaspoon pepper |

1. Brown chicken on all sides in hot oil in large heavy frying pan; drain on absorbent paper; place in 3-quart baking dish; save for Step 4.
2. Sauté rice in same frying pan, stirring often, about 5 minutes, or until golden-brown; add onion and garlic; sauté over low heat 10 minutes, or just until tender.
3. Stir in saffron, tomatoes, mushrooms, diced pimientos, parsley, salt and pepper; heat to boiling, stirring often.
4. Pour hot tomato mixture over chicken in casserole; cover.
5. Bake in moderate oven (350°) 30 minutes; uncover; bake 40 minutes longer, or until chicken is tender and liquid is absorbed.

# CHICKEN SAUTÉ NORMANDY STYLE

*Chicken simmered in apple cider and served with a delicious cream and egg sauce.*

*Makes 6 servings.*

2 broiler-fryers (about 1½ pounds each)
1 tablespoon vegetable oil
2 tablespoons butter or margarine
2 tablespoons apple-jack
1 medium-size onion, finely chopped (½ cup)
½ cup sliced celery
2 tablespoons chopped parsley
1 teaspoon salt
¾ teaspoon leaf thyme, crumbled
⅛ teaspoon pepper
1 cup apple cider
2 egg yolks
1 cup light cream

1. Cut chickens into serving-size pieces. Brown well in oil and butter or margarine in a large kettle; remove from heat.

2. Warm the applejack in a small saucepan until small bubbles appear around edge. (Do not boil.) Carefully ignite with a wooden match held at arm's length. Quickly pour over chicken, shaking gently until flames die. Remove chicken to a heated platter; keep warm.

3. Sauté onion and celery until soft in same kettle. Stir in parsley, salt, thyme, pepper and cider; heat to boiling. Return chicken pieces; reduce heat; cover. Simmer 45 minutes, or until chicken is tender; remove from heat. Remove chicken pieces from cooking liquid to a heated serving platter; keep hot.

4. Beat egg yolks slightly in a small bowl; blend in light cream. Gradually add cooking liquid, beating vigorously; pour back into saucepan. Cook, over medium heat, stirring constantly, 1 minute, or until sauce thickens slightly. Pour a little of the sauce over chicken pieces. Pass remaining sauce separately.

# CHICKEN TEMPURA

*This delicately cooked Japanese-style chicken has a golden-rich batter coating.*

*Makes 8 servings.*

| | |
|---|---|
| 2 broiler-fryers (2 to 3 pounds each) | ¼ teaspoon pepper |
| 2 cups water | 2 eggs |
| 2 teaspoons salt | ½ cup milk |
| 1 teaspoon poultry seasoning | 1 cup sifted flour |
| | Fat for frying |

1. Cut each chicken into 8 pieces (2 breasts, 2 wings, 2 thighs, 2 drumsticks); cook 15 minutes in 2 cups water seasoned with 1 teaspoon salt, poultry seasoning and pepper. (Save broth to simmer backs, necks and giblets to make soup for another meal.)

2. Drain chicken on paper towels; remove all skin and cut any small rib bones; dry thoroughly.

3. Beat eggs slightly with milk in bowl; beat in flour and 1 teaspoon salt until smooth.

4. Melt enough fat (about 3 pounds) to make a 2-inch depth in large heavy saucepan; heat to 375°, or use an electric fryer, following manufacturer's directions.

5. Dip chicken, one piece at a time, into batter (tongs are a useful tool); let any excess batter drip back into bowl; fry 2 or 3 pieces at a time, turning once, about 4 minutes, or until golden; drain on paper towels; keep hot in warm oven while frying remaining chicken.

## CHICKEN KIEV

*These great Russian-style chicken breasts take fussing,
so fix them ahead for a special dinner.*

*Makes 6 servings.*

1½ sticks (6 ounces)
butter or margarine
6 whole chicken
breasts (about 12
ounces each)
4 tablespoons finely
chopped parsley
½ teaspoon sugar

2 eggs
1 cup fine dry bread
crumbs
1 teaspoon salt
⅛ teaspoon pepper
Shortening or salad oil
for frying

1. Cut the butter or margarine into 12 even-length
sticks; chill in freezer while fixing chicken, for butter
should be very cold.

2. Pull skin from the chicken breasts; halve breasts
and cut meat in one piece from bone. Place each half,
boned side up, between waxed paper and pound very
thin with a mallet or rolling pin to form a "cutlet."
(Do not pound holes in meat.)

3. Place 1 piece very cold butter or margarine, 1
teaspoon parsley and a dash of sugar on end of each
cutlet; fold sides over to seal in butter, then roll up.
Hold in place with wooden picks.

4. Beat eggs slightly in a pie plate; mix bread
crumbs, salt and pepper in a second pie plate. Dip
stuffed rolls in egg, then in crumb mixture to coat well.
Chill at least an hour. (This much can be done ahead.)

5. When ready to fry, melt enough shortening or
pour in enough salad oil to make a 2-inch depth in an
electric deep-fat fryer or large saucepan; heat to 350°.

6. Fry rolls, 3 or 4 at a time and turning often,
7 minutes, or until tender and crisply golden. Lift out
with a slotted spoon; drain well. Keep hot until all rolls
are cooked.

## CHINESE CHICKEN SALAD

*Chinese fried noodles and soy dressing give the touch of authenticity to this Oriental-style salad.*

*Makes 6 servings.*

| | |
|---|---|
| 1 whole broiler-fryer (about 3 pounds) | 6 cups broken salad greens |
| 2 cups water | 1 cup chopped celery |
| Handful of celery tops | 2 green onions, sliced |
| 1 teaspoon salt | 5 large radishes, sliced |
| 6 peppercorns | 1 can (3 ounces) |
| 1½ cups Soy Dressing | Chinese fried |
| 1 bunch fresh broccoli (about 2 pounds) | noodles |
| | 1 hard-cooked egg, shelled |

1. Simmer chicken with water, celery tops, salt and peppercorns in kettle 1 hour, or until tender. Take chicken from broth and let drain in shallow pan just until cool enough to handle. (Strain broth and save for soup.)

2. Remove skin from chicken, then pull meat from frame in large pieces. (It comes off easily while still warm.) Cut into bite-size pieces; place in shallow pan; pour ¼ cup Soy Dressing over. Cover; chill at least an hour to blend flavors.

3. Trim and discard outer leaves from broccoli. Cut off ends to make about 4-inch-long stalks; split large ones lengthwise. Cook, covered, in about 1-inch depth boiling salted water in large frying pan 15 minutes, or until crisply tender; drain well.

4. Place in shallow pan; pour ½ cup Soy Dressing over. Cover; chill at least an hour.

5. When ready to serve, pile salad greens, celery, green onions and radishes, saving about 8 slices for Step 7, into large shallow salad bowl. Pour remaining ¾ cup Soy Dressing over; toss lightly to mix.

6. Arrange marinated broccoli with stems toward center in a ring on top; fill ring with marinated chicken. Spoon noodles around broccoli.

7. Press white of egg, then yolk through a sieve onto separate sheets of waxed paper. Spoon white on top of chicken; top with saved radish slices, overlapping slightly; garnish with sieved egg yolk.

## SOY DRESSING

Combine ½ cup soy sauce, ½ cup salad oil or peanut oil and ½ cup wine vinegar or cider vinegar with 1 teaspoon salt and ½ teaspoon ground ginger in small jar with tight-fitting cover; shake to mix well. Makes 1½ cups.

## CLASSIC CHICKEN ALMOND

*An Oriental favorite of white meat, delicate vegetables and toasted nuts. You can start it the day before, finish it up quickly at suppertime.*

*Makes 6 servings.*

3 **whole chicken breasts (about 12 ounces each), halved**
1 **large onion, peeled and sliced**
1½ **teaspoons salt**
⅛ **teaspoon pepper**
**Water**
2 **tablespoons vegetable oil**
1½ **cups chopped celery**

1 **package (10 ounces) frozen peas**
1 **can (3 or 4 ounces) sliced mushrooms**
2 **tablespoons cornstarch**
½ **teaspoon ground ginger**
2 **tablespoons soy sauce**
**Toasted slivered almonds (from a 5-ounce can)**

1. Combine chicken breasts, 2 slices of the onion, salt, pepper and 1 cup water in a large saucepan; cover. Simmer 20 minutes, or until chicken is tender.

2. Remove from broth and cool until easy to handle; strain broth into a small bowl. Pull skin from chicken and take meat from bones in one piece; chill, then cut into thin strips. Chill broth separately, then skim fat, if needed.

3. When ready to finish cooking, sauté remaining onion in vegetable oil in a large frying pan 2 to 3 minutes; push to side. Stir in celery and sauté 2 to 3 minutes; push to side. Place peas, mushrooms and liquid and chicken strips in separate piles in pan; pour in broth; cover. Steam 10 minutes, or until peas are crisply tender.

4. Lift vegetables from pan with a slotted spoon; place in a serving bowl; lift out chicken strips and arrange on top of the vegetables.

5. Blend cornstarch and ginger with soy sauce in a cup; stir in 2 tablespoons water until smooth. Stir into liquid in pan; cook, stirring constantly, until sauce thickens and boils 3 minutes.

6. Spoon over chicken and vegetables; sprinkle with almonds. Garnish with thin strips of pimiento and drained canned mushroom caps and celery slices threaded onto kebab sticks, and serve with hot cooked rice or noodles, if you wish.

MAKE-AHEAD NOTE: Chicken may be cooked as much as a day ahead and chilled in its broth to keep moist. Chop celery ahead too, and place in a transparent bag in the refrigerator until ready to cook.

# MANDARIN SUPPER

*Cubed chicken, Chinese-style fried rice and soy-seasoned broccoli make this meal-in-a-skillet.*

*Makes 6 servings.*

2 chicken breasts
  (about 12 ounces
  each)
1 tablespoon packaged
  shrimp spice
1 tablespoon instant
  minced onion
1 teaspoon salt
2 cups water
1 cup uncooked rice
1 bunch fresh broccoli
  (about 1½ pounds)
2 large onions,
  chopped (2 cups)

6 tablespoons peanut
  oil or vegetable oil
4 tablespoons soy
  sauce
2 tablespoons wine
  vinegar or cider
  vinegar
¼ teaspoon ground
  ginger
¼ cup coarsely
  chopped salted
  peanuts

1. Combine chicken breasts, shrimp spice, instant onion, salt and water in a large saucepan; cover. Simmer 30 minutes, or until chicken is tender. Remove from broth and cool until easy to handle. Strain broth into a 4-cup measure; add water if needed to make 2¼ cups. Pull skin from chicken and take meat from bones; cut in cubes.

2. Combine the 2¼ cups chicken broth and rice in a medium-size saucepan. Cook 25 minutes, or until rice is tender and liquid is absorbed.

3. While rice cooks, trim broccoli; split any large stalks lengthwise, then cut into 2-inch lengths. Cook in boiling salted water in a saucepan 15 minutes; drain; keep warm.

4. Sauté chopped onions in 4 tablespoons of the peanut oil or vegetable oil until soft in a large frying pan; stir in cooked rice. Sauté, stirring constantly, 5 minutes; add chicken; toss lightly to mix. Arrange cooked broccoli around edge in pan.

5. Combine remaining 2 tablespoons peanut oil or vegetable oil, soy sauce, wine vinegar or cider vinegar and ginger in a cup; drizzle over broccoli. Sprinkle peanuts over rice. Serve warm right from the skillet it cooked in.

# HONG KONG CHICKEN ALMOND

*A simple version of the traditional Oriental dish.*

*Makes 4 servings.*

2 **whole chicken breasts (about 12 ounces each)**
3 **tablespoons salad oil**
1 **cup sliced celery**
½ **clove garlic, minced**
2 **envelopes instant chicken broth OR 2 chicken bouillon cubes**
1½ **cups water**
1 **tablespoon soy sauce**

1 **tablespoon chopped crystallized ginger**
1 **package (8 ounces) frozen Chinese pea pods**
2 **tablespoons cornstarch**
¼ **cup toasted slivered almonds (from a 5-ounce can)**
3 **cups hot cooked rice**

1. Pull skin from chicken breasts; halve the breasts and cut meat in one piece from bones, then slice meat into long thin strips.

2. Heat salad oil in a large frying pan; add chicken and sauté, stirring constantly, 5 minutes. Stir in celery and garlic; sauté 3 minutes more, or until meat is almost tender.

3. Stir in chicken broth or bouillon cubes, water, soy sauce and ginger; heat to boiling, crushing cubes, if using, with a spoon; add pea pods; cover. Simmer 5 minutes.

4. Smooth cornstarch with a little water to a paste in a cup; stir into chicken mixture. Cook, stirring constantly, until mixture thickens and boils 3 minutes.

5. Spoon into a serving dish; sprinkle with almonds. Serve with rice.

# Chapter 12

# Wine Cookery

Wine used to be considered the exception to cooking rather than the rule. Now, fortunately, the only thing that's exceptional about cooking with wine is the result—a dinner that's truly gourmet.

With most American wines and some European ones, wine doesn't have to be expensive either. In fact, it should be easy to make it part of your weekly menu (it doesn't take a large amount to make the difference in cooking). There's no secret to its use. You add it to chicken as you do any other ingredient . . . just follow the recipes in this chapter to get you started. Then, when you've got the knack, try substituting it for other liquids in recipes.

Serving wine with dinner is another way of saying you appreciate fine food. The guide in this chapter will give you a choice of wines to serve with every kind of chicken dish. Now, on to some exceptional dinners.

# CHICKEN MARENGO EN CASSEROLE

*This delightful casserole is easy to make and elegant to serve.*

*Bake at 350° for 45 minutes.*
*Makes 8 servings.*

4 slices bacon, diced
2 broiler-fryers, cut up
¼ cup flour
1 teaspoon salt
¼ teaspoon freshly ground pepper
1 large onion, chopped
1 clove of garlic, minced
2 large ripe tomatoes, pared, seeded and chopped

1 teaspoon leaf tarragon, crumbled
1 cup dry white wine
½ pound mushrooms
3 tablespoons butter or margarine
1 pound small white onions
1 envelope or teaspoon instant chicken broth
½ cup hot water

1. Brown bacon in a large skillet until very crisp; remove bacon with a slotted spoon; reserve.
2. Shake chicken parts in a plastic bag with flour, salt and pepper until all pieces are evenly coated.
3. Brown chicken, a few pieces at a time, in bacon drippings in skillet; remove to a 10-cup casserole with tongs.
4. Sauté onion and garlic in same skillet until soft; stir in chopped tomatoes and tarragon; cook 3 minutes; stir in white wine and bring to a boil. Spoon sauce over chicken in casserole and cover casserole.
5. Bake in moderate oven (350°) 45 minutes, or until chicken is tender.
6. While casserole bakes, reserving about 8 mushrooms for garnish, slice remaining mushrooms. Sauté whole and sliced mushrooms in butter or margarine in a large skillet; remove with spoon and reserve.
7. Peel white onions and cut a small cross in the bottom of each one to prevent onions from separating during cooking. Brown onions well in same skillet. Dissolve instant chicken broth in hot water and pour

over onions. Cover skillet and simmer onions until
onions are tender and liquid has almost evaporated;
remove skillet cover and cook onions slowly until they
are a rich golden brown.

8. When chicken is cooked, remove cover and add
reserved mushrooms and onions to casserole; sprinkle
crisp bacon over and garnish casserole with a tomato
peel rose and parsley, if you wish.

## CHICKEN IN WALNUT SAUCE

*All you do at the last minute is pop this delightful
casserole in the oven.*

Bake at 350° for 1¼ hours.
Makes 8 servings.

| | |
|---|---|
| 1 package (8 ounces) regular noodles | 1 medium-size onion, chopped (½ cup) |
| 2 broiler-fryers, weighing about 2 pounds each, cut in serving-size pieces | 4 tablespoons flour |
| | 1¾ cups milk |
| | ¼ cup dry white wine |
| 2 teaspoons salt | 1 can condensed cream of chicken soup |
| ½ teaspoon leaf rosemary, crumbled | 1 can (4 ounces) walnuts, chopped |
| ¼ teaspoon pepper | Paprika |
| 3 tablespoons butter or margarine | |

1. Cook noodles, following label directions; drain
well. Place in a refrigerator-to-oven baking dish,
13x9x2.

2. Season chicken with 1½ teaspoons of the salt,
rosemary, and pepper. Brown, part at a time, in butter
or margarine in a large frying pan; place in a single
layer over noodles.

3. Stir onion into drippings in pan; sauté until soft.
Blend in flour; cook, stirring constantly, until bubbly.
Stir in milk and wine; continue cooking and stirring
until sauce thickens and boils 1 minute. Stir in soup,

walnuts, and remaining ½ teaspoon salt. Pour over mixture in baking dish. Sprinkle with paprika. Cover; chill.

4. About 1 hour and 15 minutes before serving time, place baking dish, covered, in moderate oven (350°).

5. Bake 1 hour and 15 minutes, or until bubbly and chicken is tender.

# BLUE-RIBBON CHICKEN CASSEROLE

*A make-ahead casserole with a light touch of sherry.*

Bake at 350° for 25 to 30 minutes.
Makes 8 servings.

¼ cup butter or margarine
¼ cup flour
1 teaspoon salt
2 cups chicken broth
2 cups milk
1 can (6 or 8 ounces) sliced mushrooms
¼ cup sherry
½ teaspoon dried leaf marjoram

2 tablespoons snipped chives
1 package (8 ounces) medium noodles, cooked according to package directions
5 cups cut-up cooked chicken
¼ cup grated Parmesan cheese

1. Melt butter or margarine in saucepan. Blend in flour and salt. Gradually stir in chicken broth, milk and liquid from mushrooms. Cook, stirring constantly, until mixture thickens and comes to a boil. Add sherry, marjoram and chives.

2. Combine with cooked noodles, diced cooked chicken and mushrooms. Turn into 3-quart casserole. Sprinkle with grated cheese. Bake in moderate oven (350°) 25 to 30 minutes.

MAKE-AHEAD NOTE: If sauce, noodles and chicken are cool or chilled, bake casserole 50 to 60 minutes, until heated through.

# TENNESSEE CLUB CHICKEN

*Southern-fried chicken breasts and ham, in a milky sauce lightly touched with sherry.*

*Bake at 350° for 45 minutes.*
*Makes 8 servings.*

4 chicken breasts
(about 12 ounces
each)
8 small thin slices
cooked ham
½ cup flour
1½ teaspoons salt

¼ teaspoon pepper
4 tablespoons (½
stick) butter or
margarine
2½ cups milk
½ cup dry sherry

1. Halve chicken breasts; wash and pat dry. Cut a pocket, about 3x2, in thin side of each. Place breasts on waxed paper.

2. Sauté ham slices quickly in a large frying pan; cool slightly. Tuck one into pocket in each half chicken breast.

3. Mix ¼ cup of the flour, 1 teaspoon of the salt and pepper in a cup; sprinkle over chicken to coat evenly.

4. Melt butter or margarine in frying pan used for ham; add chicken breasts and brown slowly; place in a large shallow baking dish.

5. Blend remaining ¼ cup flour and ½ teaspoon salt into drippings in pan; cook, stirring constantly, just until bubbly. Stir in milk; continue cooking and stirring, scraping brown bits from bottom of pan, until sauce thickens and boils 1 minute; stir in sherry. Pour over chicken breasts; cover.

6. Bake in moderate oven (350°) 45 minutes, or until chicken is tender.

7. Arrange chicken on a heated deep serving platter; spoon sauce over top. Garnish with parsley, if you wish.

# APPLE-WINE BROILER CHICKEN

*True apple flavor comes through in this easy-going chicken.*

*Makes 8 servings.*

2 broiler-fryers (2½ to 3 pounds each), split
½ cup (8 tablespoons) melted butter or margarine

2 teaspoons salt
2 tablespoons apple jelly
¼ cup white wine

1. Brush chicken halves thoroughly with butter or margarine. Sprinkle with salt.
2. Mash apple jelly with a fork, then add wine gradually. Brush this mixture on both sides of chicken halves.
3. Place chicken, skin side down, in broiler pan (without rack). Broil 6 to 9 inches from the heat for 30 minutes. Then turn skin side up and continue broiling until chicken is evenly browned and cooked, about 20 minutes longer.
4. Cut each half into quarters for serving.

## SHREDDED CHICKEN AND VEGETABLES

*A little meat goes a long way in this vegetable-chicken combo.*

*Makes 4 servings.*

1 chicken breast (14 ounces), split, skinned and boned
2 tablespoons vegetable oil
1 clove of garlic, minced
3 carrots, thinly sliced
2 small zucchini, sliced
1 cup frozen sliced green beans
6 water chestnuts
2 teaspoons salt
⅛ teaspoon pepper
3 tablespoons soy sauce
1 cup water
1 tablespoon corn-starch
1 tablespoon dry sherry (optional)
2 cups hot cooked rice
2 tablespoons toasted sliced almonds (optional)

1. Cut chicken into thin shreds. Heat oil in a large skillet. Add chicken; quickly stir-fry until the color turns from pink to white, about 3 minutes.

2. Add garlic, carrots, zucchini, beans, water chestnuts, salt, pepper, soy sauce and ¾ cup of the water. Cover; reduce heat; simmer until vegetables are crisply tender, about 5 minutes (do not overcook).

3. Combine cornstarch, sherry and remaining ¼ cup of the water in a cup. Add to skillet; cook and stir gently just until sauce is thickened and bubbly. Spoon hot rice onto serving platter; spoon mixture over; sprinkle with almonds.

# HONG KONG CHICKEN

*This broiler-fryer is marinated in sherry-soy-honey, then basted while baked.*

Bake at 350° for 1½ hours.
Makes 4 servings.

| | |
|---|---|
| 1 broiler-fryer (about 3 pounds) | ¼ cup soy sauce |
| | ¼ cup honey |
| ¼ cup water | 2 teaspoons seasoned salt |
| ¼ cup dry sherry | |

1. Cut chicken into quarters; arrange in a single layer in a 13x9x2-inch baking dish.
2. Mix water, sherry, soy sauce, honey and seasoned salt in a small bowl; pour over chicken, turning to coat on all sides; cover. Marinate chicken in refrigerator about 4 hours, or overnight.
3. About 2 hours before serving time, remove chicken from refrigerator; let stand at room temperature 30 minutes, then drain; reserve marinade. Arrange chicken, skin side up, on rack in broiler pan, or in a shallow baking pan with a rack. Brush generously with part of the marinade.
4. Bake in moderate oven (350°), basting with remaining marinade every 20 minutes, 1½ hours, or until chicken is tender and deep golden brown. Place on heated serving platter; serve with cooked frozen Chinese pea pods and sliced water chestnuts, if you wish.

## Wines to Serve with Chicken

Red, white, rosé, sherry and champagne wines are all complementary to chicken . . . and these can be domestic or imported depending on your preference, pocketbook and the kind of chicken dish you're serving.

It's good to remember that full-flavored dishes (barbecued chicken; hearty stews, casseroles and baked dishes; and chicken with zesty sauces or spicy glazes) should be served with full-bodied rich wines. Dishes that are more delicate in flavor (fried or broiled chicken; simple roasts; lightly flavored stews and pies; salads and sandwiches) should be accompanied by light wines. The light wines are usually white, rosé or young red wines such as Beaujolais.

The following list is divided into full red and white wines and light red and white wines. It consists of both American and European wines.

The most important thing to remember about this list is to take a copy of it with you the next time you shop for chicken dinner.

# FULL RED WINES

*From California:*
    Zinfandel
    Pinot Noir
    Cabernet Sauvignon
*From France:*
    Bordeaux (such as St.-Émilion or Pomerol)
    Burgundy (such as Nuits-St.-Georges, Vosne-Ro-
        manée, Clos de Vougeot, Chambolle-Musigny,
        Morey-St.-Denis, Gevrey-Chambertin, Fixin)
    Rhône (such as Châteauneuf-du-Pape or Hermitage)
*From Italy:*
    Chianti
    Barolo

# FULL WHITE WINES

*From California:*
    Sauvignon Blanc
*From France:*
    Rhône (Hermitage Blanc)
*From Germany:*
    Traminer
    Gewürztraminer
    Sylvaner

## LIGHT RED WINES

*From California:*
  Mountain Red

*From France:*
  Rhône (such as Côtes du Rhône)
  Burgundy (such as Beaujolais, Côtes de Beaune-
      Villages, Chassagne-Montrachet, Volnay, Pom-
      mard, Santenay, Beaune, Monthélie)
  Bordeaux (such as Graves, Médoc, Haut-Médoc)

*From Italy:*
  Bardolino
  Valpolicella

## LIGHT WHITE WINES

*From California:*
  Mountain White
  Pinot Blanc
  Gray Riesling
  Pinot Chardonnay
  Johannisberger Riesling
  Sylvaner
  Traminer

*From France:*
  Loire (such as Pouilly-Fumé or Muscadet)
  Alsace (such as Pinot Gris or Riesling)
  Bordeaux (such as Graves)
  Burgundy (such as Pouilly-Fuissé or Meursault)
  Note: A white Burgundy such as Chablis, while too
      dry for most chicken, is excellent for pâtés,
      chicken liver dishes and dishes or stuffings that
      include shellfish.

*From Germany:*
  Liebfraumilch
  Steinwein
  Moselblümchen
  Mosel (one from Graach or Bernkastel)
  Rheinpfalz (one from Ruppertsberg or Forst)
  Rheinhessen (one from Oppenheim or Nierstein)
  Rheingau (one from Eltville or Erbach)

*From Italy:*
  Verdicchio
  Orvieto
  Soave

# ROSÉ WINES

Many people prefer pink, or rosé, wines to accompany Oriental or lightly-flavored chicken dishes. Good choices are the following:
  Grenache Rosé
  Cabernet Rosé
  Gamay Rosé
  Grignolino Rosé
  Zinfandel Rosé

## SHERRY

With chicken appetizers and soups, a dry chilled sherry is delicious, especially one called Fino or Manzanilla. Sherry is also the drink to serve when your chicken dish has sherry in the sauce.

## CHAMPAGNE

The all-purpose wine champagne can accompany any chicken dish. When served with food, a "sec" (dry) usually tastes better than one labeled "brut," which is very very dry.

## Chapter 13

# Indoor-Outdoor Chicken

Chicken is one of the most portable of foods. Hot or cold, it's the ideal choice for both indoor and outdoor eating. Previous chapters have offered chicken dishes that adapt well to being transported. The recipes in this chapter, however, are especially designed for carrying anywhere you choose.

We've divided the chapter into 3 sections that cover just about every outdoor occasion. The first, Patio Dinners, is a series of recipes you'll want to try on your barbecue or outdoor grill. (They can also be prepared indoors and then taken out.) This section is followed by Salads, and here there's no limit to the possibilities. Chicken salad is a welcome partner for bridge luncheons, warm summer night suppers or for winter dinners. Last, but not least, Chicken Sandwiches.

Need we say more?

## Patio Dinners

### CHICKEN ROMA

*Boned breast meat is filled with salami stuffing and grilled ever so slowly.*

*Makes 6 servings.*

6 chicken breasts,
  weighing about 12
  ounces each
2 tablespoons finely
  chopped green onion

½ cup (1 stick) butter
  or margarine
1½ cups fresh bread
  crumbs
¼ pound soft salami,
  finely chopped

1. Bone chicken breasts, leaving skin in place. Place flat, skin side down, on a cutting board.

2. Sauté onion in 3 tablespoons of the butter or margarine until soft in a small frying pan; stir in crumbs and salami until moist.

3. Divide stuffing into 6 parts; spoon along hollows in chicken breasts. Fold edges of chicken over stuffing to cover completely; fasten with wooden picks.

4. Melt remaining butter or margarine in a small saucepan on grill; brush part over chicken. Place breasts on grill, buttered side down, about 6 inches above hot coals. Grill 20 minutes. Brush again with melted butter or margarine; turn. Grill 20 minutes longer, or until chicken is tender and golden. Place on a large serving platter; remove picks. Garnish with carrot curls and sprigs of chicory, if you wish.

NOTE: If traveling a distance to your eating spot, make stuffing and chill well, then stuff into chicken breasts and keep chilled until cooking time.

## CHICKEN ON A SPIT

*Currant jelly glazes this chicken as it twirls on the rotisserie.*

*Makes 4 to 6 servings.*

| | |
|---|---|
| 2 cups ready-mix bread stuffing | 1 roasting chicken (about 4 pounds) |
| ½ cup (1 stick) butter or margarine, melted | ½ cup currant jelly, melted |
| ⅔ cup water | |

1. Prepare stuffing mix with ⅓ cup of the melted butter or margarine and water, following label directions on package.

2. Wash chicken, then dry. Stuff neck and body cavities lightly; skewer neck skin to body; secure body cavity closed and tie legs tightly to tail.

3. Place chicken on spit; brush with remaining butter or margarine. Set spit in position over hot coals; start spit turning.

4. Roast 1 hour; brush with melted jelly. Continue roasting, brushing often with more jelly, 15 minutes longer, or until chicken is tender and richly glazed.

## GRILLED CHICKEN BREASTS SUPREME

*This exotic chicken from the Far East is especially good with Tibetan rice and a tangy fruit sauce.*

*Makes 4 servings.*

| | |
|---|---|
| 4 whole chicken breasts | 4 green onions, chopped |
| ½ cup flour | 2 tablespoons chopped parsley |
| 1 teaspoon salt | |
| ⅛ teaspoon pepper | 4 tablespoons (½ stick) butter or margarine, melted |
| ⅛ teaspoon nutmeg | |
| 1 egg | |
| 1 tablespoon water | Tibetan Rice |
| 1 cup finely ground cashew nuts (½ pound) | 3 cups Piquant Fruit Sauce |

1. Wash and dry chicken; cut out any small rib bones and breastbones so breasts will lie flat, butterfly style. Shake in mixture of flour, salt, pepper and nutmeg in paper bag to coat well.

2. Beat egg with water in pie plate; place ground cashew nuts in second pie plate. Dip chicken in egg mixture, then in nuts.

3. Place each breast, skin side up, on a 12-inch square of heavy foil. Sprinkle with green onions and parsley; drizzle melted butter or margarine over.

4. Wrap foil around chicken and seal tightly with a drugstore fold; place on grill above hot coals. Grill, turning often, 1 hour, or until chicken is tender.

5. Split foil envelopes open; place each breast on a bed of Tibetan Rice; serve with Piquant Fruit Sauce.

## TIBETAN RICE

*Makes 4 servings.*

| | |
|---|---|
| ¾ cup raw rice | ¼ cup seedless raisins |
| 2 tablespoons salad oil | Water |
| ½ teaspoon turmeric | 1 can condensed chicken broth OR |
| ½ teaspoon curry powder | 2 chicken bouillon cubes |
| ½ teaspoon salt | |

1. Stir rice into salad oil in top of medium-size double boiler; heat over direct heat, stirring constantly, until rice is well coated with the oil.

2. Blend in turmeric, curry powder and salt; stir in raisins. Add enough water to the broth to make 1½ cups (or use bouillon cubes dissolved in 1½ cups boiling water); stir into rice mixture.

3. Cover; cook over simmering water 1 hour, or until rice is fluffed and tender and liquid is absorbed.

## PIQUANT FRUIT SAUCE

*Makes about 3 cups.*

| | |
|---|---|
| 2 tablespoons brown sugar | 1 tablespoon lemon juice |
| 1 teaspoon cornstarch | ¼ cup water |
| 1 teaspoon salt | 1 can (about 11 ounces) mandarin orange sections, drained |
| 1 can (1 pound, 4 ounces) pineapple chunks | |
| ½ cup orange juice | |

1. Blend brown sugar, cornstarch and salt in medium-size saucepan; stir in pineapple and syrup, orange and lemon juices, and water.

2. Cook, stirring constantly, until sauce thickens slightly and boils 3 minutes. Stir in mandarin orange sections; heat just to boiling.

# ROSEMARY CHICKEN

*Serve this flavory chicken on the patio for a summer supper.*

*Bake at 400° for 1 hour.*
*Makes 4 servings.*

2 broiler-fryers (2 pounds each), cut up
1 large onion, cut into thick slices
⅔ cup catsup
⅓ cup vinegar
4 tablespoons (½ stick) butter or margarine

1 clove garlic, minced
1 teaspoon rosemary, crushed
1 teaspoon salt
¼ teaspoon dry mustard

1. Place chicken, skin side down, in a single layer in a buttered shallow baking pan; top with onion slices.
2. Mix all remaining ingredients in a small saucepan; heat just to boiling; pour over chicken.
3. Bake in hot oven (400°) 30 minutes. Turn chicken, skin side up; baste with sauce in pan. Continue baking, basting once or twice, 30 minutes longer, or until tender and richly glazed.

# SIMPLE SIMON

*Chicken baked in a cheese-cracker coating—delicious hot or cold.*

*Bake at 375° for 1 hour.*
*Makes 6 servings.*

1 package (about 6 ounces) cheese crackers, crushed fine
2 teaspoons seasoned salt

½ cup salad oil
2 broiler-fryers (about 3 pounds each), cut in serving-size pieces

1. Place cracker crumbs in a pie plate; stir in seasoned salt. Pour salad oil into a second pie plate.

2. Dip chicken pieces into salad oil, then into crushed crumbs to coat well. Place in a single layer in an ungreased large shallow pan.

3. Bake in moderate oven (375°) 1 hour, or until tender and golden-brown. Serve warm or cold.

## STUFFED WHIRLYBIRD

*Rotisserie chicken with two stuffings.*

*Makes 4 servings.*

| | |
|---|---|
| 1 roasting chicken (about 4 pounds) | Butter or margarine (1 to 2 tablespoons) |
| Fruit Stuffing OR packaged Spanish Rice Stuffing | Salt<br>Pepper<br>Ginger-Honey Glaze |

1. Wash and dry chicken.

2. Stuff breast and body cavities with either Fruit Stuffing (recipe below) or Spanish Rich Stuffing (follow label directions).

3. Secure body and neck cavities tightly closed; tie legs and wings tightly to body. Rub bird with softened butter or margarine and sprinkle with salt and pepper.

4. Place on rotisserie spit and roast 1 hour, then begin basting with Ginger-Honey Glaze. Continue roasting, basting often, 30 to 45 minutes longer, or until chicken is richly browned and tender.

## GINGER-HONEY GLAZE

Combine ½ cup soy sauce, 6 tablespoons honey and 2 teaspoons ground ginger in a small saucepan. Heat, stirring constantly, just to boiling. Makes enough for two roasting chickens.

## FRUIT STUFFING

*Makes 7 cups.*

| | |
|---|---|
| 1 can (1 pound) sliced apples | 1 package (2 cups) ready-mix bread stuffing |
| Water | |
| ½ cup (1 stick) butter or margarine | 1 cup chopped peanuts |
| | ½ cup seedless raisins |

1. Drain sliced apples; add water to apple liquid to make 1 cup; heat to boiling in large saucepan.

2. Stir in butter or margarine until melted; add ready-mix bread stuffing, sliced apples, peanuts and raisins, tossing lightly to mix.

3. Stuff chicken. Wrap any remaining stuffing in foil; cook on grill about 1 hour, while chicken roasts.

## DUNKING CHICKEN

*Fine finger food—crackly crisp outside, juicy inside—for picnic or patio meals.*

*Makes 6 servings.*

| | |
|---|---|
| 2 broiler-fryers (about 2 pounds each), cut up | ½ teaspoon pepper |
| | Bacon drippings |
| 1 cup flour | Orange Curry Dunk |
| 2 teaspoons salt | Zippy Tomato Dunk |

1. Wash and dry chicken pieces well. Shake in mixture of flour, salt and pepper in paper bag to coat well.

2. Heat bacon drippings in large frying pan or electric skillet. It'll take about 1 cup, for fat should be about ½ inch deep. (If you like, use part shortening.)

3. Place chicken in a single layer in hot fat; cover lightly. Cook over *low heat* 20 minutes, or until golden; turn; cover again and cook 20 minutes to brown other side. (If using an electric skillet, follow manufacturer's directions.) Remove browned chicken and set aside

while cooking any remaining pieces, adding more drippings, if needed, to keep fat ½ inch deep.

4. Drain fat from frying pan, leaving just enough to keep chicken from sticking; return all chicken to pan. Cover; cook, turning once or twice, over very low heat 30 minutes longer, or until tender.

5. Serve hot or cold, with dunking sauces.

## ORANGE CURRY DUNK

*Makes 2 cups.*

1 cup orange marmalade

⅓ cup vinegar

¼ cup granulated sugar

2 tablespoons brown sugar

1 tablespoon curry powder

1 tablespoon Worcestershire sauce

1 teaspoon salt

½ teaspoon ground ginger

Combine all ingredients in small saucepan; heat to boiling, then simmer, stirring constantly, until marmalade is melted and sauce is blended. Serve warm or cold.

## ZIPPY TOMATO DUNK

*Makes 1½ cups.*

1 can (8 ounces) tomato sauce

½ cup finely chopped green pepper

½ cup finely chopped celery

2 tablespoons vinegar

2 tablespoons light molasses

1 tablespoon Worcestershire sauce

¼ teaspoon bottled red-pepper seasoning

Combine all ingredients in small saucepan; heat to boiling, then simmer, stirring constantly, 5 minutes, or until vegetables are softened and sauce is blended.

# HERB SPITTED CHICKEN

*Fresh herbs are a feature of this outdoor chicken.*

*Makes 4 servings.*

3 tablespoons minced
  fresh rosemary
3 tablespoons minced
  fresh tarragon OR
  2 tablespoons leaf
  rosemary, crumbled
2 tablespoons leaf
  tarragon, crumbled
Dry white wine or
  chicken broth

½ cup (1 stick) butter
  or margarine
1 teaspoon salt
¼ teaspoon freshly
  ground pepper
1 roasting chicken
  (about 3½ to 4
  pounds)

1. Combine fresh rosemary and tarragon in a small bowl. If you are using dried herbs, combine with ⅓ cup dry white wine or broth in a small bowl. Let stand 1 hour. Strain; reserve liquid. Add butter or margarine to the herbs; blend well.
2. Sprinkle the cavity of the chicken with part of the salt and pepper and put in about 1 tablespoon herb butter. Carefully loosen the skin over the breast with your fingers and press in about 1 to 2 tablespoons of the herb butter. Truss the bird, balance it on the spit and fasten it securely.
3. Melt the remaining herb butter and brush over bird. Sprinkle it with remaining salt and pepper. Combine the remaining herb butter with an equal quantity of wine or broth, or, if using dried herbs, with reserved wine or broth.
4. Roast the chicken for about 2½ hours, basting it frequently with the butter-wine mixture. Skim off the fat and pour a little juice over each piece of carved chicken.

## BONANZA-BOBS

*Thread the chunks on skewers with green pepper and onions and you're all set for the outdoor grill.*

*Makes 8 servings.*

4 **whole chicken breasts**
4 **green peppers, cut in pieces**
2 **cans (1 pound each) onions, well drained**
2 **teaspoons monosodium glutamate**
2 **teaspoons salt**
½ **cup butter or margarine, melted**
1 **tablespoon dried leaf tarragon**
1 **tablespoon lemon juice**

1. Bone chicken breasts; remove skin. Cut each breast half into 6 to 8 chunks, about 1½ inches square.
2. Alternate chunks on 8 skewers with green pepper and onions. Sprinkle with monosodium glutamate and salt.
3. Combine melted butter, tarragon and lemon juice. Brush over kabobs; grill 3 inches from heat for 5 minutes. Turn and grill 5 minutes longer, brushing occasionally with butter mixture.

## NAPOLI CHICKEN BROIL

*Grilled chicken breasts brushed with a butter mixture—great indoors or out.*

*Makes 8 servings.*

1 **cup (2 sticks) butter or margarine**
2 **envelopes Italian-flavor salad dressing mix**
¼ **cup lime juice**
8 **chicken breasts, weighing about 12 ounces each**

1. Melt butter or margarine in a small saucepan;

stir in salad dressing mix and lime juice. Brush part over both sides of chicken.

2. Place the chicken, skin side down, on grill about 10 inches above hot coals. Grill, turning and brushing pieces often with more butter mixture, 40 minutes, or until tender and richly glazed.

NOTE TO INDOOR COOKS: Place chicken pieces, skin side up, on rack in broiler pan; brush with butter mixture. Broil, 4 to 6 inches from heat, brushing several times with butter mixture, 15 minutes; turn. Brush again; broil 15 minutes longer.

## Salads

### CLASSIC CHICKEN SALAD

*Big, juicy chunks of chicken you can serve with either of two dressings.*

*Makes 8 servings.*

| | |
|---|---|
| 2 broiler-fryers, whole or cut in serving-size pieces | 2 bay leaves |
| | 2 teaspoons monosodium glutamate |
| 3 cups water | 2 teaspoons salt |
| 1 onion, sliced | 2 cups sliced or chopped celery |
| 4 celery tops | |

1. Put chickens in a large kettle or Dutch oven. Add water and all ingredients except the chopped celery; heat to boiling; cover tightly. Reduce heat and simmer 1 hour, or until tender.

2. Remove from heat; strain broth. Refrigerate chicken and broth at once. When chicken is cool, remove meat from bones; cut meat into large chunks.

3. Mix cut-up chicken with chopped celery; add either Creamy Mayonnaise Dressing or Old-Fashioned Cooked Dressing; mix well. Serve on salad greens and garnish with tomato wedges, carrot curls, olive or radish roses, if you wish.

## CREAMY MAYONNAISE DRESSING

Blend together ⅔ cup mayonnaise, ⅓ cup dairy sour cream, ½ teaspoon salt, ¼ teaspoon pepper and 1 teaspoon lemon juice. Makes 1 cup dressing.

## OLD-FASHIONED COOKED DRESSING

Mix together in top of double boiler 2 tablespoons flour, 1 teaspoon sugar, 1 teaspoon dry mustard, ½ teaspoon salt and ⅛ teaspoon pepper. Add 1 egg, 2 tablespoons butter or margarine, ¾ cup milk, 2 tablespoons vinegar and 1 tablespoon lemon juice; beat with rotary beater or wire whisk until well mixed. Cook, stirring constantly, over boiling water until slightly thickened, about 8 minutes. Refrigerate. Makes 1¼ cups dressing.

## CHICKEN-CORN SALAD

*Filling fare with all white meat chicken, hard-cooked eggs, corn nuggets and tender macaroni.*

*Makes 6 servings.*

| | |
|---|---|
| 2 chicken breasts (about 12 ounces each) | 1 can (12 or 16 ounces) whole-kernel corn, well drained |
| 2 cups water | 1 can thinly sliced celery |
| 1 slice onion | 1 large head Boston lettuce |
| Few celery tops | |
| 1¼ teaspoons salt | 3 hard-cooked eggs, shelled and coarsely chopped |
| 3 tablespoons cider vinegar | |
| 2 teaspoons sugar | ¼ cup mayonnaise or salad dressing |
| ¼ teaspoon pepper | |
| ½ cup vegetable oil | 3 tablespoons chopped parsley |
| 1 package (8 ounces) small macaroni shells | |

1. Combine chicken breasts with water, onion, celery tops and ¼ teaspoon of the salt in a medium-size sauce-

pan; cover. Simmer 30 minutes, or until chicken is tender. Remove from broth and cool until easy to handle. (Save broth to add to soup for another day.)

2. Pull skin from chicken and take meat from bones; cut meat into bite-size pieces.

3. Combine vinegar, sugar, remaining 1 teaspoon salt, pepper and vegetable oil in a jar with a tight fitting lid; shake well to mix. Drizzle 1 tablespoon over chicken; chill.

4. Cook macaroni in boiling salted water, following label directions; drain well. Combine with corn, celery and 1 tablespoon of the dressing in a large bowl; toss to mix well; chill. (Set remaining dressing aside for Step 7.)

5. When ready to serve, line 6 soup plates or shallow salad bowls with lettuce; shred remaining lettuce into pieces in centers. Spoon macaroni mixture on top.

6. Add chopped eggs to chicken mixture; toss lightly to mix; spoon over macaroni.

7. Beat remaining dressing into mayonnaise or salad dressing and parsley in a small bowl; pass separately.


## CURRIED CHICKEN CORONET

*A partylike rich chicken-salad mousse delicately spiced with curry.*

*Makes 8 servings.*

2 whole chicken
  breasts (about 2
  pounds)
2 cups water
1 medium-size onion,
  sliced
Handful of celery tops
1½ teaspoons salt
3 peppercorns
1 envelope unflavored
  gelatin
2 eggs, separated

½ cup chopped
  toasted almonds
1 teaspoon curry
  powder
¼ teaspoon pepper
1 cup mayonnaise
1 cup cream for
  whipping
1 can (about 13
  ounces) frozen
  pineapple chunks,
  thawed and drained
½ cup flaked coconut

1. Combine the chicken breasts, water, onion, celery tops, 1 teaspoon salt and peppercorns in large saucepan; simmer, covered, 45 minutes, or until chicken is tender. Let stand until cool enough to handle, then skin chicken and take meat from bones. Dice chicken fine (you should have about 2 cups diced chicken).

2. Strain stock into a bowl; measure out 1 cupful; pour into a medium-size saucepan and cool. (Save any remaining stock for soup for another day.)

3. Soften gelatin in cooled stock in saucepan; heat, stirring constantly, until dissolved.

4. Beat egg yolks slightly in small bowl; slowly stir in dissolved gelatin. Return mixture to saucepan and cook, stirring constantly, 1 minute or until slightly thickened; remove from heat.

5. Stir in diced chicken, almonds, curry powder, ½ teaspoon of salt and pepper, blending well. Chill 30 minutes, or until the mixture is syrupy-thick; blend in the mayonnaise.

6. Beat egg whites until stiff in large bowl; fold in chicken mixture until no streaks of white remain.

7. Beat cream until stiff in medium-size bowl; fold into chicken mixture.

8. Pour into a 6-cup ring mold; chill several hours, or until firm.

9. Unmold onto serving plate; fit a shallow bowl into center of mold; fill with pineapple chunks; sprinkle with coconut.

## CHICKEN-APPLE SALAD

*Mayonnaise and cream furnish the base for this Netherlands original.*

*Makes 4 servings.*

| | |
|---|---|
| 1 broiler-fryer (about 3 pounds), cut up | ½ cup mayonnaise or salad dressing |
| 2 cups water | 1 tablespoon lemon juice |
| 1½ teaspoons salt | Dash of pepper |
| 1 package (10 ounces) frozen broccoli spears | ½ cup cream for whipping |
| 1 tablespoon bottled French dressing | Iceberg lettuce |
| 2 medium-size apples | 2 tomatoes, cut in wedges |
| 1 cup chopped celery | 2 hard-cooked eggs, shelled and sliced |
| 1 small onion, chopped fine (¼ cup) | |

1. Place chicken in a large frying pan; add water and 1 teaspoon of the salt. Heat to boiling; cover. Simmer 50 minutes, or until chicken is tender. Remove from broth; cool until easy to handle, then skin chicken and take meat from bones; cut into bite-size pieces. Place in a large bowl; chill.

2. Cook broccoli spears, following label directions; drain. Place in a pie plate; drizzle with French dressing; let stand a half hour to season and blend flavors.

3. Pare apples; quarter, core and dice. Add to chicken with celery and onion.

4. Blend mayonnaise or salad dressing with lemon juice, remaining ½ teaspoon salt and pepper in a small bowl. Beat cream until stiff in a second small bowl. Beat cream until stiff in a second small bowl; fold into mayonnaise mixture; fold into the chicken mixture.

5. Line a large serving platter with lettuce. Spoon chicken mixture in a mound down center. Arrange broccoli spears on one side, tomato wedges on other side and egg slices at each end.

# PYRAMID PLATTER

*This main-course salad is a giant triple-decker built on chicken. To top it off, the work can all be done ahead of time.*

*Makes 4 servings.*

3 **chicken breasts (about 12 ounces each)**
2 **cups water**
¼ **cup chopped celery**
1 **small onion, chopped (¼ cup)**
2 **teaspoons salt**
¼ **teaspoon cayenne**
1 **pound sliced bacon**
**Romaine**
4 **large tomatoes, sliced thin**

2 **individual-portion wedges (about 1¼ ounces each) Roquefort cheese, crumbled**
2 **small ripe avocados**
**Lime juice**
½ **cup refrigerated Thousand Island dressing (from an 8-ounce jar)**
½ **cup dairy sour cream (from an 8-ounce carton)**
**Paprika**

1. Combine chicken breasts, water, celery, onion, salt and cayenne in a large frying pan; heat to boiling; cover. Simmer 30 minutes, or until chicken is tender. Remove from broth; cool. Chill about 45 minutes. Pull off skin and carefully remove meat from bones; cut meat into thin slices.

2. Sauté bacon until limp in a large frying pan. Pick up end of each bacon strip in tines of fork; wind around fork. Return bacon curls to frying pan to crisp and brown. Drain bacon on paper toweling.

3. Line a platter with part of the romaine leaves. Arrange layers of chicken slices in a neat circle over romaine; layer tomato slices in a smaller circle over chicken. Sprinkle cheese over tomatoes.

4. Halve and pit avocados; sprinkle with lime juice.

5. Mix Thousand Island dressing with sour cream in a small bowl; spoon into avocado halves; sprinkle with paprika. Place 2 avocado halves at each end of

platter. Arrange 3 of the bacon curls on top of cheese and remainder at sides of pyramid.

6. To serve, place one filled avocado half on each serving plate and surround with portions of the pyramid layers; garnish with bacon curls.

## CHICKEN VERONIQUE

*Fresh green grapes and apricots, plus a tangy cucumber dressing, add style to a favorite.*

*Makes 6 servings.*

| | |
|---|---|
| 4 chicken breasts (about 12 ounces each) | 1 cup water |
| | 1 cup chopped celery |
| Few celery tops | 1 cup seedless grapes, halved |
| 2 teaspoons salt | |
| 6 peppercorns | 2 cups Cucumber Dressing |
| 1 bay leaf | |
| 1 envelope instant chicken broth OR 1 chicken bouillon cube | Bibb lettuce |
| | 6 apricots, washed, halved and pitted |

1. Combine the chicken breasts, celery tops, salt, peppercorns, bay leaf, instant chicken broth or bouillon cube and water in a large frying pan; heat to boiling; cover. Simmer 30 minutes, until meat is tender.

2. Cool in broth until easy to handle, then remove and pull off skin; take meat from bones; cube. Place in a large bowl. (Strain broth and chill for making soup another day.)

3. Add celery and grapes to chicken; drizzle with about half of the Cucumber Dressing; toss lightly to mix. Chill at least an hour to season.

4. When ready to serve, line a large bowl with lettuce; pile chicken mixture in center; frame with apricot halves. Serve with remaining dressing.

## CUCUMBER DRESSING

Combine 6 tablespoons mayonnaise or salad dressing, 1½ teaspoons salt, 1 teaspoon chopped fresh dill, ¼ teaspoon pepper, 6 tablespoons lemon juice and 1 cup buttermilk in a small bowl; beat until well-blended. Stir in 1 small cucumber, pared, diced and drained well. Chill at least an hour to season. Makes about 2 cups.

## PARISIAN CHICKEN BOWL

*Halved chicken breasts are glazed, French style, and served cold with seasoned vegetables for this fancy bowl.*

*Makes 6 servings.*

3 whole chicken breasts (12 ounces each)
1 small onion, sliced
1 teaspoon salt
⅛ teaspoon pepper
1 bay leaf
2 cups water
1 envelope unflavored gelatin
½ cup mayonnaise or salad dressing
6 pitted ripe olives
1 package (10 ounces) frozen Fordhook lima beans
½ cup bottled Italian salad dressing
4 cups broken mixed salad greens
3 medium-size tomatoes, peeled and sliced
3 hard-cooked eggs, shelled and quartered

1. Combine chicken breasts with onion, salt, pepper, bay leaf and water in a large saucepan; cover. Simmer 30 minutes, or just until tender.

2. Remove from broth, cool until easy to handle, then pull off skin. Remove meat from each half of breast in one piece; place in one layer in a shallow dish. Chill.

3. Strain broth into a 2-cup measure; chill just until fat rises to top, then skim.

4. Soften gelatin in 1 cup of the broth in a small saucepan. (Save any remaining to add to soup.)

Heat gelatin mixture, stirring constantly, just until gelatin dissolves; pour into a small bowl. Blend in mayonnaise or salad dressing; chill, stirring several times, 20 minutes, or until as thick as unbeaten egg white.

5. Spoon part over chilled chicken breasts to make a thick layer, then repeat with remaining until chicken is evenly glazed. Cut each olive into 6 slivers, arrange, petal fashion, on top of each glazed chicken breast; chill until gelatin is firm.

6. Cook lima beans, following label directions; drain. Toss with ¼ cup of the Italian dressing in a small bowl; cover. (This much can be done early in the day, or even a day ahead.) If making ahead, store in the refrigerator until ready to use.

7. When ready to serve, place salad greens in a large shallow bowl; drizzle remaining ¼ cup Italian dressing over; toss lightly to mix. Top with tomato slices; mound lima beans in center, then arrange chicken breasts, spoke fashion, around beans; place quartered eggs around edge of bowl. Garnish with a cherry-tomato flower, if you wish. To make, cut a cherry tomato into eighths from tip almost to stem end; separate "petals" slightly; stuff with a ripe olive and top with a sprig of parsley.

## CHICKEN SALAD DELUXE

*Tender chicken is brightly flavored with a sour cream-mayonnaise combination.*

*Makes 4 servings.*

| | |
|---|---|
| 1 broiler-fryer (about 3 pounds) | 1 tablespoon lemon juice |
| 4 cups water | ¼ teaspoon pepper |
| 1 small onion, sliced | ¾ cup chopped celery |
| Few celery tops | 1 medium-size onion, chopped (½ cup) |
| ¼ teaspoon salt | ¼ cup chopped dill pickle |
| ⅓ cup mayonnaise or salad dressing | Lettuce |
| ⅓ cup dairy sour cream | Paprika |

1. Combine chicken with water, sliced onion, celery tops and salt in a kettle or Dutch oven. Heat to boiling; reduce heat; cover; simmer about 1 hour, or until chicken is tender. Remove from broth and cool until easy to handle. (Save broth to start a soup another day.)

2. Skin the chicken and take meat from bones. Cut meat into bite-size pieces; put in a medium-size bowl.

3. Blend mayonnaise or salad dressing, sour cream, lemon juice and pepper in a small bowl. Combine celery, onion and dill pickle with chicken; add the dressing; toss until evenly coated. Cover; chill at least an hour to season and blend flavors.

4. Line salad bowl with lettuce leaves. Spoon salad into bowl. Sprinkle with paprika.

# WINTER CHICKEN SALAD

*White meat, carrots and celery team up in a warm salad for cold weather.*

*Makes 6 servings.*

3 chicken breasts
(about 12 ounces
each)
1 pound carrots, pared
and sliced thin
2 cups sliced celery
1 small onion, chopped
(¼ cup)
¼ cup water

1 envelope instant
chicken broth OR
1 chicken bouillon
cube
2 teaspoons salt
½ cup mayonnaise or
salad dressing
Potato chips

1. Pull skin from chicken breasts, then cut meat from bones; dice meat.

2. Combine with carrots, celery, onion, water, chicken broth or bouillon cube and salt in a large frying pan; heat to boiling; cover.

3. Simmer 30 minutes, or until chicken is tender. Drain off any broth and save to add to soup or stew.

Fold mayonnaise or salad dressing into chicken mixture.

4. Spoon onto a large serving platter; frame with potato chips and garnish with parsley, if you wish.

## AVOCADO CHICKEN SALAD

*Chill, seasoned chicken and delicate avocado: A combination everybody loves.*

*Makes 6 servings.*

| | |
|---|---|
| 1 stewing chicken (about 4 pounds), cooked | ¼ teaspoon ground ginger |
| 4 tablespoons salad oil | 1 large head of iceberg lettuce, washed and dried |
| 2 tablespoons fresh lime juice | 1 cup sliced celery |
| | 1 large ripe avocado |

1. Cool chicken until easy to handle; remove skin and white and dark meat from frame in chunks as big as possible, then slice into thin bite-size pieces. (You should have about 4 cups.) Place in medium-size bowl. Save broth for making soup another day.

2. Combine salad oil, lime juice and ginger in a cup; sprinkle over chicken; toss to coat well; cover; chill.

3. At serving time, place a large lettuce leaf on each plate; shred remaining lettuce; toss with celery, and divide evenly onto lettuce leaves. Top with mounds of marinated chicken.

4. Peel avocado, remove seed and cut into thin lengthwise slices; arrange 3 on top of each mound of chicken to garnish.

# BARBECUED CHICKEN SUPPER SALAD

*You can use ready-cooked meat and salad from your supermarket for this hearty hot-weather meal.*

*Makes 4 servings.*

2 containers (1 pound each) prepared macaroni salad
1 package (4 ounces) shredded Cheddar cheese
1 can (8 ounces) lima beans, drained
½ cup chopped celery
½ teaspoon fines herbes

1 small head chicory, washed, drained
2 medium-size tomatoes, cut in wedges
2 ready-to-eat barbecued chickens, weighing about 2 pounds each
Sweet mixed pickles
Stuffed green olives

1. Combine macaroni salad, cheese, lima beans, celery and herbes in a large bowl; toss lightly to mix well. Chill about an hour to season.
2. Just before serving, line a large platter with chicory leaves; break remaining into bite-size pieces in center; spoon macaroni salad on top. Tuck tomato wedges around salad.
3. Cut chickens in half with kitchen scissors; place, skin side up, around edge of platter.
4. Thread pickles and olives, alternately, onto wooden picks; stick, kebab style, into macaroni salad. Serve with rye bread-and-butter sandwiches, if you wish.

# CHICKEN MOUSSE

*This refreshing gelatin salad is packed with fruits and vegetables to complement the chicken.*

*Makes 16 servings.*

2 large chicken breasts (about 1 pound each)
2 cups water
1 small onion, peeled and sliced
Few celery tops
1 teaspoon salt
1 bay leaf
4 peppercorns
1 can (about 9 ounces) pineapple tidbits

2 envelopes unflavored gelatin
1 cup mayonnaise or salad dressing
1 tablespoon lemon juice
1 teaspoon prepared mustard
½ pound cooked ham
1 can (5 ounces) water chestnuts, drained

1. Combine chicken breasts, water, onion, celery tops, salt, bay leaf and peppercorns in a large saucepan; heat to boiling; cover. Simmer 30 minutes, or until chicken is tender.
2. While chicken cooks, drain syrup from pineapple into a 1-cup measure; add water, if needed, to make ½ cup. Stir in gelatin to soften. Set pineapple aside.
3. Remove chicken from broth; strain broth into a 4-cup measure; add water, if needed, to make 3 cups. Return to same saucepan; stir in softened gelatin.
4. Heat slowly, stirring constantly, until gelatin dissolves; remove from heat. Blend in mayonnaise or salad dressing, lemon juice and mustard.
5. Pour into a shallow pan. Freeze 20 minutes, or just until firm about 1 inch from edges but still soft in middle.
6. While gelatin mixture chills, pull skin from chicken and take meat from bones; dice meat. (There should be about 1½ cups.) Dice ham and water chestnuts; combine with diced chicken and pineapple in a medium-size bowl.

7. Spoon partly frozen gelatin mixture into a chilled large bowl; beat until thick and fluffy. Fold in chicken-ham mixture; spoon into an 8-cup ring mold. Chill several hours, or until firm.

8. When ready to serve, loosen salad around edge and center ring with a knife; dip mold *very quickly* in and out of hot water. Cover with a large serving plate; turn upside down; gently lift off mold. Fill center of ring with salad greens, if you wish.

## SUMMER CHICKEN DIVAN

*A winter casserole turns cool for summer salad days.*

*Makes 6 servings.*

3 chicken breasts
(about 12 ounces
each)
1 small onion, peeled
and sliced
1 teaspoon salt
Dash of pepper
Water
2 packages (10 ounces
each) frozen
asparagus spears
1 envelope Parmesan
salad dressing mix

Vegetable oil
Cider vinegar
1 head Boston lettuce,
separated into leaves
2 cans (3 or 4 ounces
each) whole mush-
rooms, drained
½ cup mayonnaise or
salad dressing
2 hard-cooked egg
yolks

1. Combine chicken, onion, salt, pepper and 2 cups water in a large frying pan; cover. Simmer 30 minutes, or until chicken is tender. Remove from broth; cool until easy to handle, then pull off skin. Remove meat from each half of breast in one large piece; set aside. (Strain broth and chill for soup another day.)

2. While chicken cooks, cook asparagus, following label directions; drain; place in a shallow dish.

3. Prepare salad dresisng mix with vegetable oil, vinegar and water, following label directions; drizzle ½ cup over asparagus; let stand 30 minutes to season.

4. Line a large shallow serving dish with lettuce; arrange asparagus spears over lettuce, then place chicken breasts, overlapping, in a row on top of asparagus. Pile mushrooms at each end.

5. Blend mayonnaise or salad dressing into remaining dressing in asparagus dish; drizzle over chicken. Press egg yolks through a sieve on top.

## Sandwiches

### STUFFED SALAD ROLLS

*A tasty jumble of chopped chicken, cheese and celery, piled on frankfurter rolls.*

*Makes 4 servings, 2 rolls each.*

| | |
|---|---|
| 2 cups chopped lettuce | 2 tablespoons pickle relish |
| 1 cup diced cooked chicken | 1/4 teaspoon curry powder |
| 1/2 cup diced process American or Swiss cheese | 8 frankfurter rolls, split, toasted and buttered |
| 1/2 cup chopped celery | |
| 1/2 cup mayonnaise | |

1. Combine lettuce with chicken, cheese and celery in medium-size bowl.

2. Blend mayonnaise, pickle relish and curry powder in small bowl; stir into salad mixture to coat well; pile into prepared rolls.

# CHICKEN CHEESE CLUBS

*Chicken, bacon and Muenster—a flavory combo—spiked with tomatoes and cucumber.*

*Bake at 450° for 5 minutes.*
*Makes 4 sandwiches.*

12 slices bacon (½
  pound)
2 medium-size toma-
  toes, each cut in
  4 slices
½ small cucumber,
  sliced
12 slices whole-wheat
  bread, toasted and
  buttered

¼ cup prepared
  sandwich spread
8 slices cooked
  chicken
4 slices Muenster
  cheese (from an
  8-ounce package)
8 pitted ripe olives
8 small sweet pickles

1. Sauté bacon until crisp in a large frying pan; drain on paper toweling.
2. Place tomato and cucumber slices and bacon, dividing evenly, on 4 pieces of the toast; add another slice of the toast; spread with sandwich spread.
3. Top with chicken slices, then cheese and remaining toast, buttered side down. Place sandwiches on a cooky sheet.
4. Bake in a very hot oven (450°) 5 minutes, or until cheese melts slightly.
5. Press wooden picks into sandwiches to hold; cut each sandwich diagonally into quarters. Top picks with olives and pickles.

# CHICKEN LIVER BOUNTIES

*Here's a sandwich to please gourmets. Cook the livers gently, then combine with broiled tomatoes and crisp bacon.*

*Makes 6 sandwiches.*

6 slices bacon
1 pound chicken livers
2 tablespoons flour
¼ teaspoon seasoned salt

1 can (3 or 4 ounces) chopped mushrooms
3 large tomatoes, each cut in 6 slices
3 large hamburger buns, split

1. Sauté bacon just until crisp in a large frying pan; drain on paper toweling, then crumble. Drain off all drippings, then measure 2 tablespoons and return to pan. (Set bacon aside for Step 5.)

2. Halve chicken livers; snip out any veiny parts or skin with scissors. Shake livers with flour and seasoned salt in a paper bag to coat.

3. Brown slowly in drippings in frying pan; stir in mushrooms and liquid. Heat, stirring constantly, to boiling; cover. Simmer 3 minutes, or just until livers lose their pink color.

4. While livers cook, place tomato slices and bun halves in a single layer on rack in broiler pan. Broil 3 to 4 minutes, or until tomatoes are heated through and buns are toasted.

5. Place 2 tomato slices on each bun half; spoon hot liver mixture over, dividing evenly. Top each with another tomato slice; sprinkle with crumbled bacon. Garnish with parsley, if you wish.

## CHICKEN SALAD HEROES

*Carried to the picnic in an insulated bag, this delightful sandwich is really heroic in flavor and nutrition.*

*Makes 4 servings.*

¼ cup milk
1 package (3 ounces) cream cheese, softened
2½ cups diced cooked chicken
¼ cup chopped celery

¼ cup chopped pared carrot
⅓ cup chopped radishes
½ teaspoon onion salt
Dash pepper
4 hero rolls
Butter

1. Blend milk into cream cheese and beat until smooth. Add chicken, vegetables, onion salt and pepper; mix well.

2. Cut rolls in half and scoop out some of the bread to make a cavity. Spread with butter.

3. Fill each roll with ¼ of chicken salad mixture (about ⅔ cup); replace tops and wrap tightly in foil or plastic wrap. Chill before taking to picnic.

## PARTY CHICKEN BURGERS

*Open-faced sandwiches the whole crowd will relish.*

*Makes 12 servings.*

2 cups cubed cooked chicken
1 can (10½ ounces) condensed cream of celery soup
¼ cup finely chopped onion
¼ cup finely chopped green pepper
3 tablespoons chopped pimiento

1 can (4 ounces) sliced mushrooms, drained
1 tablespoon prepared mustard
½ teaspoon salt
½ teaspoon monosodium glutamate
6 hamburger buns, split

1. Preheat broiler. In large bowl, combine all ingredients except buns.

2. Spread an equal amount of mixture, about ¼ cup, on each bun half.

3. Broil 6 to 8 inches from heat for 7 to 10 minutes, until golden brown and bubbly. Serve immediately.

## CHICKEN JUMBOS

*White meat and pineapple in a creamy dressing on raisin bread make delicious stay-moist picnic sandwiches.*

*Makes 4 sandwiches.*

1 can (about 1 pound, 5 ounces) pineapple spears

16 thin slices cooked chicken breast

8 slices unfrosted cinnamon-raisin bread, buttered

¼ cup mayonnaise or salad dressing

2 tablespoons chopped pecans

1. Drain syrup from pineapple into a cup; set aside for Step 3.

2. Arrange chicken slices and pineapple spears, overlapping, on each of 4 slices.

3. Blend mayonnaise or salad dresssing, 1 tablespoon of the pineapple syrup, and pecans in a cup; spoon a generous teaspoonful over filling for each sandwich. Cover with remaining slices of bread. (Chill remaining syrup to add to a beverage.)

4. Place each sandwich in a plastic bag, or wrap in foil or transparent wrap.

## CHICKEN DOUBLE-DECKERS

*Fat sandwiches of Italian bread, filled with avocado spread and fruited meat salad.*

*Makes 16 sandwiches.*

| | |
|---|---|
| 1 **broiler-fryer (about 2½ pounds)** | 1 **cup mayonnaise or salad dressing** |
| 1 **cup water** | 1 **medium-size firm ripe avocado** |
| 1½ **teaspoons salt** | |
| Few **celery tops** | 6 **slices crisp bacon, crumbled** |
| 1 **can (about 9 ounces) pineapple tidbits** | Few **drops red-pepper seasoning** |
| ½ **cup halved green grapes** | 2 **loaves Italian bread** |

1. Combine chicken with water, 1 teaspoon salt and celery tops in a large saucepan; heat to boiling; cover. Simmer 1 hour.

2. Remove from broth and cool until easy to handle; strain broth and chill for soup or gravy. Pull skin from chicken and take meat from bones; dice. (There should be about 2 cups.) Place in a medium-size bowl.

3. Drain syrup from pineapple into a cup. Add pineapple and grapes to chicken. Blend 2 tablespoons of the syrup with ½ cup mayonnaise or salad dressing and remaining ½ teaspoon salt in a small bowl; fold into chicken mixture. Chill.

4. Halve avocado; pit and peel. Mash in a small bowl; stir in crumbled bacon, ¼ cup of the remaining mayonnaise or salad dressing and red-pepper seasoning. (Fix avocado mixture no longer than an hour ahead so that it keeps its bright color.)

5. Cut each loaf of bread lengthwise into 3 even slices; spread with remaining ¼ cup mayonnaise or salad dressing.

6. Spread avocado mixture on bottom slices and chicken salad on middle slices; stack loaves back in shape; cover with top slices. Cut loaf crosswise into 8 thick double-decker sandwiches.

# CHICKEN STROGANOFF ROUNDS

*To round out a light supper menu, just add raw relishes and a simple dessert.*

*Makes 6 servings.*

1 broiler-fryer (about 3 pounds), cut up
1 medium-size onion, chopped (½ cup)
½ cup chopped celery
2 tablespoons butter or margarine

1 package Stroganoff sauce mix
1 cup (8-ounce carton) dairy sour cream
6 split hamburger buns, toasted

1. Simmer chicken, covered, in 2 cups lightly salted boiling water in a large frying pan 40 minutes, or until tender. Remove chicken from bones; dice meat. Measure 1 cup of the broth and set aside.

2. Sauté onion and celery in butter or margarine until soft in same frying pan; stir in chicken.

3. Blend sauce mix with the 1 cup chicken broth in a small bowl; stir into chicken mixture. Heat to boiling; cover. Simmer 10 minutes.

4. Stir about 1 cup of the hot sauce mixture into sour cream in a small bowl; stir back into pan. Heat very slowly just until hot. Spoon over toasted buns to serve open-face style.

## CHICKEN-CHEESE PUFF

*A unique sandwich idea that's made with your own homemade puff.*

Bake at 375° for 55 minutes.
Makes 4 servings.

1 cup milk
4 tablespoons (½ stick) butter or margarine
1 teaspoon onion salt
¼ teaspoon pepper
1 cup sifted regular flour
4 eggs
1 package (6 ounces) sliced Swiss cheese, diced

2 cups diced cooked chicken
1 cup finely chopped celery
½ cup mayonnaise or salad dressing
1 can (4½ ounces) deviled ham
2 tablespoons lemon juice

1. Heat milk, butter or margarine, ½ teaspoon of the onion salt, and pepper just to boiling in a medium-size saucepan. Add flour all at once; stir vigorously with a wooden spoon 2 minutes, or until batter forms a thick smooth ball that follows spoon around pan. Remove from heat.

2. Beat in eggs, 1 at a time, until batter is shiny-smooth.

3. Set aside ¼ cup of the diced cheese; stir remainder into mixture in saucepan. Drop batter by heaping tablespoonfuls onto a large cooky sheet to form a rectangle about 12x5. (Batter will spread during baking to make a long loaf.) Sprinkle with the ¼ cup cheese.

4. Bake in moderate oven (375°) 45 minutes, or until puffed and golden.

5. While puff bakes, combine chicken and celery in a large bowl. Blend mayonnaise or salad dressing, deviled ham, lemon juice and remaining ½ teaspoon onion salt in a small bowl; fold into chicken mixture.

6. Cut a thin slice from top of puff; scoop out any bits of soft dough from bottom with a teaspoon. Spoon chicken mixture into bottom; set top back in place.

7. Bake 10 minutes longer, or until filling heats through. Carefully slide onto a large serving platter; cut crosswise into 4 thick slices.

## Chapter 14

# Dishes for One

How many times have you told yourself there's no incentive to cook dinner when you're the only one who's home? You'll open a can of stew, toss a tv dinner in the oven or make a sandwich. These are easy solutions. But we offer better ones with the recipes in this chapter. They'll help make lonesome hours a little more pleasant without a great deal of work. And because they can be made ahead of time and kept waiting in the refrigerator or oven, they're also ideally suited for nights when your husband is going to be late for dinner or when you're out and he's home alone.

For a week when you'll be alone for several nights we offer recipes that make enough for 2 or 3 solo dishes. A bonus with these multiple-serving recipes: If a friend calls at the last minute, you can invite her over for dinner!

# SUPERMARKET CHICKEN SUPPER

*A ready-barbecued chicken and prepared macaroni salad from the supermarket can make 2 dinners for a loner.*

*Makes 1 serving for 2 meals.*

1 container (1 pound) prepared macaroni salad
½ package (4 ounces) shredded Cheddar cheese
½ small can (7 to 8 ounces) lima beans, drained
¼ cup chopped celery
¼ teaspoon fines herbes

½ small head chicory, washed, dried and separated into leaves
1 medium-size tomato, cut in wedges
1 ready-to-eat barbe-cued chicken (about 2 pounds)
Sweet mixed pickles
Stuffed green olives

1. Combine macaroni salad, cheese, lima beans, celery and herbes in a large bowl; toss lightly to mix well. Chill at least an hour to season.

2. Line a platter with chicory leaves; break remaining into bite-size pieces in center; spoon half the macaroni salad on top. Tuck tomato wedges around salad. Put rest of salad in a covered refrigerator container for next meal.

3. Cut chicken in half with kitchen scissors; place one half, skin side up, on platter beside salad. Wrap other half in transparent wrap and place in meat keeper compartment of refrigerator for tomorrow's meal.

4. Garnish with pickles and olives, and serve with rye bread-and-butter sandwiches, if you wish.

# LONE RANGER CHICKEN

*The sauce will help keep this chicken from drying out—
either in the oven or the refrigerator—until it's needed
for a single dinner.*

*Bake at 400° about 1 hour.*
*Makes 1 serving for 2 meals.*

**2 large chicken breasts      Butter or margarine
   OR 2 legs with thighs      Savory Sauce**

1. Wash chicken pieces; pat dry; remove skin if
you wish.
2. Arrange chicken pieces in a single layer in a well-
buttered shallow baking pan.
3. Spoon Savory Sauce over so chicken pieces are
well coated.
4. Bake, uncovered, in hot oven (400°) about 1
hour, or until chicken is tender.
5. Remove one breast or leg with half the sauce,
and cool; then refrigerate in a covered jar for reheating
tomorrow (or perhaps the next day, but better not
keep it longer than that).
6. Leave other breast or leg tightly covered in the
oven (with the heat off) to be eaten within an hour
or two, or refrigerate in a small covered baking dish
for reheating the same night.

## SAVORY SAUCE

*Makes 1½ cups.*

**1 can (8 ounces)          2 tablespoons soy
   tomato sauce               sauce
1 small onion,            1 tablespoon sugar
   chopped                ½ teaspoon dry
½ teaspoon garlic            mustard
   powder              Dash cayenne pepper**

Mix all ingredients in a medium-size bowl.

# LONER'S SALAMI-CHICKEN DUO

*These spicy drumsticks taste delicious hot or cold.*

*Makes 1 serving for 2 meals.*

| | |
|---|---|
| 2 **chicken drumsticks** **with thighs** | ¼ **teaspoon paprika** ¼ **teaspoon leaf** **oregano, crumbled** |
| 1 **slice (1 ounce)** **salami** | **Dash pepper** |
| 2 **tablespoons flour** | 3 **tablespoons vege-** **table oil** |
| ½ **teaspoon salt** | |

1. Cut through chicken legs at joints to separate drumsticks and thighs, then cut an opening along bone of each drumstick and in meaty part of each thigh with a sharp knife to make a pocket for stuffing.

2. Cut salami into 4 strips; stuff 1 strip into each piece of chicken.

3. Shake pieces, a few at a time, in mixture of flour, salt, paprika, oregano and pepper in a bag to coat evenly.

4. Cook pieces slowly in vegetable oil in a medium-size frying pan 20 minutes; turn; cover loosely. Cook 20 minutes longer, or until tender and crisply golden. Remove from pan and drain on paper towel. Wrap tightly in foil and place in oven or refrigerator to keep.

## SINGLE SAM'S SALAD SANDWICH

*Delicious chicken salad makes 2 summer suppers (or 1 for a hungry husband).*

*Makes 1 serving for 1 or 2 meals.*

1 whole chicken breast (about 12 ounces), OR 1 can (5 or 6 ounces) boned chicken, diced
1 cup water
1 small onion, sliced
Handful of celery tops
½ plus ¼ teaspoon salt
Pepper
½ cup diced celery

¼ cup slivered almonds
4 tablespoons mayonnaise
1 tablespoon milk
⅛ teaspoon dry mustard
1 or 2 large Vienna rolls
Butter or margarine
Lettuce
Cherry tomatoes

1. If using chicken breast, place it in a medium-size saucepan with the water, onion, celery tops, ½ teaspoon salt, and a dash of pepper. Simmer, covered, 20 to 30 minutes, or until chicken is tender. Let stand until cool enough to handle, then skin chicken and take meat from bones. Dice chicken (you should have about 1 cup).

2. Combine chicken, celery and almonds in medium-size bowl. Mix mayonnaise, milk, ¼ teaspoon salt, mustard and a dash of pepper; stir into chicken mixture, tossing lightly to mix. If making 2 portions, chill 1 portion on a plate until serving time; place remainder in a covered refrigerator container in coldest part of refrigerator for tomorrow's meal.

3. At mealtime, split Vienna roll and butter it. Line buttered roll with lettuce; fill with salad. Garnish with cherry tomatoes.

# BOWLING-NIGHT SALAD

*Stash these cooling little salads in the refrigerator for someone's dinner tonight—and tomorrow night.*

*Makes 3 individual molds.*

1 broiler-fryer (about 2½ pounds), cut up
3 cups water
½ small onion, sliced
Few celery tops
1½ teaspoons salt
3 peppercorns
1 envelope unflavored gelatin
¼ cup apple juice

½ cup mayonnaise or salad dressing
¼ cup diced celery
2 tablespoons chopped toasted slivered almonds
2 tablespoons chopped stuffed green olives
Boston lettuce

1. Combine chicken, water, onion, celery tops, salt and peppercorns in a kettle; cover. Simmer 1 hour, or until chicken is very tender; remove from broth. Strain broth into a 2-cup measure.
2. Soften gelatin in apple juice in a medium-size saucepan; stir in 1½ cups of the broth. (Chill any remaining broth to add to soup for another meal.)
3. Heat gelatin mixture slowly, stirring constantly, until gelatin dissolves; remove from heat. Cool for Step 5.
4. Pull skin from chicken and take meat from bones; dice fine. (There should be about 2 cups.)
5. Blend mayonnaise or salad dressing into gelatin mixture in saucepan; pour into an ice-cube tray. Freeze 20 minutes, or until firm about 1 inch in from edges.
6. Spoon into a chilled large bowl; beat until fluffy thick. Fold in diced chicken, celery, almonds and olives. Spoon into 3 individual molds. Chill several hours or until firm.
7. Salad can be eaten from the mold, or unmolded onto a lettuce-lined plate and garnished with melon crescents.

## Chapter 15

# Chicken on a Diet

No one likes to diet. But, fortunately, today even the most stringent diets are more creative and palatable than ever before.

Take chicken. By itself it offers the dieter real flavor and high protein in exchange for very few calories and little fat. And with thought and planning, it becomes downright gourmet.

Because it's a short-fibered, easily-digested meat, chicken is also ideal for anyone on a geriatric or convalescent diet. The low- or no-salt dieter can enjoy chicken, too, because it responds so well to all other seasonings.

A 3-ounce portion of skinless, boneless broiled chicken breast has only 115 calories; with skin, it has only 185. Have a piece of chicken. You'll enjoy your diet as well as the results!

# SKINNY-GIRL PAELLA

*A low-calorie version of the favorite from sunny Valencia.*

*Bake at 350° for 1 hour.*
*Makes 6 servings.*

1 broiler-fryer (about 2 pounds), cut in serving-size pieces
1 large onion, chopped (1 cup)
1 clove garlic, minced
1 cup uncooked rice
6 small slices salami (about 2 ounces), diced
2 teaspoons salt
1 teaspoon sugar
¼ teaspoon pepper
⅛ teaspoon crushed saffron
1 can (about 1 pound) tomatoes

1½ cups water
1 envelope instant chicken broth OR 1 chicken bouillon cube
1 pound fresh shrimps, shelled and deveined, OR 1 package (12 ounces) frozen deveined shelled raw shrimps
1 can (4 ounces) pimientos, drained and cut in large pieces

1. Pull skin from chicken pieces, if you wish. Place chicken, meaty side down, in a single layer on rack of broiler pan.
2. Broil, 4 inches from heat, 10 minutes; turn; broil 10 minutes longer, or until lightly browned; set aside for Step 4.
3. Pour drippings from broiler pan into a medium-size frying pan. Stir in onion and garlic; sauté until soft; spoon into a 12-cup baking dish with rice, salami, salt, sugar, pepper and saffron.
4. Combine tomatoes with water and instant chicken broth or bouillon cube in same frying pan; heat to boiling, crushing bouillon cube, if used, with a spoon. Stir into rice mixture with shrimps. Arrange chicken and pimientos on top; cover.

5. Bake in moderate oven (350°) 1 hour, or until liquid is absorbed and chicken is tender. Garnish with parsley and serve with chopped green onions to sprinkle on top, if you wish.

**Dieter's Portion:** ½ breast, 5 shrimps, and 1 cup rice mixture—406 calories.

## CHICKEN SALAD PLATE

*Cottage cheese as you've never known it before.*

*Makes 6 servings.*

| | |
|---|---|
| 2 pounds chicken breasts | 3 tablespoons buttermilk |
| 2 cups water | 1 small onion, chopped (¼ cup) |
| 1 slice of onion | 1 cup pared and chopped cucumber |
| Few celery tops | |
| 2 teaspoons salt | 2 tablespoons chopped pimiento |
| 3 tablespoons vinegar | |
| 1 teaspoon paprika | 1 head Boston lettuce, washed, dried and separated into leaves |
| ¼ teaspoon seasoned pepper | |
| ¼ teaspoon garlic powder | 18 radishes, trimmed |
| ¾ cup low-fat cottage cheese (from an 8-ounce carton) | 3 hard-cooked eggs, quartered |

1. Combine chicken breasts with water, onion slice, celery tops and 1 teaspoon of the salt in a large saucepan; cover. Simmer 30 minutes, or just until tender.

2. Remove chicken from broth; cool until easy to handle but still warm, then pull off skin and take meat from bones; cut into cubes. Place in a medium-size bowl.

3. Combine vinegar, remaining 1 teaspoon salt, paprika, seasoned pepper and garlic powder in a small bowl. Add to chicken and toss lightly until well mixed. Chill in refrigerator at least 1 hour.

4. Combine cottage cheese, buttermilk and chopped onion in an electric-blender container; cover. Whirl until creamy-smooth. Spoon into a small bowl and refrigerate until serving time.

5. When ready to serve, combine chicken mixture with cucumber, pimiento and cottage cheese dressing. Toss lightly to mix.

6. Place lettuce leaves to form cups on 6 serving plates; place ⅔ cup of chicken salad in each lettuce cup. Arrange 3 radishes and 2 egg quarters attractively on each plate.

**Dieter's Portion:** The amount specified in Step 6—215 calories.

# BONELESS CHICKEN CACCIATORE

*Plump chunks of chicken and bright green strips of pepper in a spicy tomato sauce spiked with wine. How could this be diet fare?*

*Makes 6 servings.*

| | |
|---|---|
| 2 broiler-fryers (about 1½ pounds each) | 1 medium-size onion, chopped (½ cup) |
| 2 cups water | 1 large green pepper, halved, seeded and sliced |
| 2 cans (8 ounces each) tomato sauce | |
| 1 tablespoon leaf oregano, crumbled | 1 clove of garlic, minced |
| ½ cup dry white wine | ½ teaspoon salt |
| | ¼ teaspoon pepper |

1. Simmer chicken in water in a large covered saucepan for 30 minutes. Remove. Cool until easy to handle. Pour stock into a 4-cup measure. Refrigerate. Remove meat from chicken. Discard skin and bones. Skim any fat from chicken stock.

2. Put chicken, 2 cups of the stock and remaining ingredients in a saucepan, cover. Simmer 20 minutes.

Uncover. Allow to simmer, stirring occasionally, until sauce has thickened, about 10 minutes.

**Dieter's Portion: 1/6 of the chicken—248 calories.**

## LOW-CALORIE CHICKEN ORIENTALE

*A sweet-and-sour chicken dish that's off the "forbidden list," thanks to today's easy-to-use sugar substitutes.*

*Bake at 325° for 55 minutes.*
*Makes 6 servings.*

2 broiler-fryers (1½ pounds each), cut up
1 can (1 pound) unsweetened pineapple chunks in pineapple juice
3 tablespoons wine vinegar
1 tablespoon soy sauce
½ teaspoon dry mustard
1 teaspoon salt
¼ teaspoon pepper
2 green peppers, seeded and cut in strips
1 tablespoon cornstarch
2 tablespoons water

1. Place chicken pieces skin side up in a shallow baking dish and surround with pineapple chunks.
2. Mix juice with vinegar, soy sauce, mustard, salt and pepper and pour over chicken. Bake, uncovered, in moderate oven (325°) for 40 minutes, basting occasionally. Add pepper strips.
3. Combine cornstarch and water in a cup. Stir into liquid in baking dish and bake an additional 15 minutes, or until bubbly.

**Dieter's Portion: 1/6 of the chicken—248 calories.**

# CHICKEN-LIVER RAGOUT

*Your diet seems like something in the past when you try this dish.*

*Makes 4 servings.*

3 slices bacon, cut in 2-inch pieces
1 pound chicken livers, halved
2 medium-size onions, peeled and quartered
2 medium-size green peppers, quartered and seeded
1 tablespoon flour
½ teaspoon paprika

1 cup water
2 envelopes instant chicken broth OR 2 chicken-bouillon cubes
¼ teaspoon leaf thyme, crumbled
1 small bay leaf
2 cups hot cooked noodles

1. Sauté bacon until crisp in a medium-size frying pan; remove and drain on paper toweling. Pour off all drippings.
2. Sauté livers slowly in same pan 3 to 5 minutes, or just until they lose their pink color; remove and set aside for Step 4.
3. Stir onions and green peppers into frying pan. Sprinkle with flour and paprika, then stir in water, chicken broth, thyme and bay leaf; cover. Simmer 15 minutes, or until onions are tender; remove bay leaf.
4. Add chicken livers to sauce; heat 5 minutes, or until bubbly.
5. Spoon noodles onto serving plates; top with liver mixture; sprinkle with bacon.

**Dieter's Portion: ¼ of the chicken liver-noodle combination—323 calories.**

## DIETER'S DELIGHT

*A masterpiece, and fun to make: Chilled chicken breasts in a gelatin glaze decorated with vegetable flowers.*

*Makes 6 servings.*

| | |
|---|---|
| 3 chicken breasts (about 12 ounces each), halved | 1 tablespoon instant minced onion |
| 2 envelopes instant chicken broth OR 2 chicken bouillon cubes | Few sprigs of parsley |
| | 1 envelope unflavored gelatin |
| 1½ cups water | 6 carrot slices |
| 3 teaspoons leaf tarragon | 2 green onion tops, cut in strips |
| | Fresh spinach leaves |

1. Combine chicken breasts, instant broth or bouillon cubes, and water in a large saucepan. Tie tarragon, onion and parsley in a cheesecloth bag; add to saucepan; cover. Simmer 30 minutes, or until chicken is tender. Remove from broth and cool until easy to handle; pull off skin; chill. Chill broth until fat rises to top, then skim off.

2. Soften gelatin in ½ cup of the broth in a small saucepan; heat, stirring constantly, until gelatin dissolves; remove from heat. Stir in remaining broth.

3. Place chicken breasts in a single layer on a wire rack set in a shallow pan.

4. Measure ½ cup of the gelatin mixture; set cup in a small bowl of ice and water; chill just until as thick as unbeaten egg white. Brush over chicken breasts to coat. (Keep remaining gelatin at room temperature.)

5. Arrange a flower in gelatin on each chicken breast, using a carrot slice for blossom and a long strip of green onion top for stem and short pieces for leaves. Chill until firm.

6. Measure out another ½ cup of the gelatin mixture and chill until thickened; brush over decorations on chicken; chill until firm. Chill remaining gelatin

mixture; brush over chicken a third time to make a thick coating, then chill several hours.

7. When ready to serve, arrange chicken on a spinach-lined large platter. Garnish with cherry tomatoes cut to form flowers.

**Dieter's Portion: One-half chicken breast—196 calories.**

## WEIGHT-WORRIER'S FRICASSEE

*A happy combination of rich-tasting gravy and sensible calorie count.*

*Makes 6 servings.*

| | |
|---|---|
| 3 whole chicken breasts (about 12 ounces each), halved | 2 teaspoons salt |
| | ⅛ teaspoon pepper |
| | 1 cup water |
| 1 small onion, chopped (¼ cup) | 2 tablespoons instant-type flour |
| ½ cup finely chopped celery | ½ cup skim milk |

1. Simmer the chicken, covered, with onion, celery, salt, pepper and water in a medium-size frying pan 30 minutes, or until tender; remove to a heated serving platter.

2. Mix flour and skim milk in a cup; stir into hot broth in pan. Cook, stirring constantly, until gravy thickens and boils 1 minute. Serve in a separate bowl.

**Dieter's Portion: ½ chicken breast and ¼ cup gravy—200 calories.**

## POT AU FEU (Dinner in a Pot)

*A low-calorie version of a French classic.*

*Makes 4 servings.*

1 pound boneless
   round steak
3 cups water
1 can condensed beef
   broth
1 large onion, chopped
   (1 cup)
1 clove of garlic,
   minced
2 teaspoons salt
4 sprigs parsley

1 bay leaf
6 peppercorns
½ teaspoon leaf thyme
1 whole chicken breast,
   weighing about 12
   ounces
4 large carrots (about
   ½ pound)
2 zucchini
3 cups celery sticks

1. Trim all fat from beef. Place steak in a heavy kettle or Dutch oven. Add water, beef broth, onion and garlic. Place parsley, bay leaf, peppercorns and thyme on a small piece of cheesecloth; bring up corners to enclose herbs; tie securely; add to kettle.

2. Heat to boiling; lower heat; cover. Simmer 1 hour. Add chicken breast; simmer 30 minutes, or until meats are tender. Remove meats; keep warm.

3. While meats cook, pare carrots and cut in sticks; trim zucchini, cut in sticks.

4. Reheat broth in kettle to boiling; add carrots; cover. Cook 15 minutes. Add zucchini and celery sticks; cook 15 minutes longer, or until tender. Remove.

5. Strain broth into a large bowl, pressing onion and garlic through sieve into liquid; let stand about a minute, or until fat rises to top, then skim off.

6. Carve meats; combine with broth and vegetables in a heated tureen.

**Dieter's Portion:** ¼ of recipe—380 calories.

# STREAMLINED CHINESE CHICKEN

*Meal-in-one teams white meat with pineapple and vegetables.*

*Makes 6 servings.*

3 whole chicken breasts (about 2½ pounds)
3 tablespoons soy sauce
1 tablespoon salad oil or peanut oil
1 can (1 pint, 2 ounces) unsweetened pineapple juice
4 tablespoons cornstarch

1 can (8 ounces) diet-pack pineapple chunks
2 cans (3 or 4 ounces each) sliced mushrooms
½ teaspoon salt
1 package (10 ounces) frozen peas, thawed
6 cups shredded Chinese cabbage (about 1 head)
3 cups cooked hot rice

1. Remove skin and bones from chicken breasts; slice meat into long thin strips.
2. Place soy sauce in pie plate; dip chicken strips into sauce; brown quickly in salad oil or peanut oil in large frying pan.
3. Stir just enough unsweetened pineapple juice into cornstarch in cup to make a smooth paste; save for Step 5.
4. Stir remaining pineapple juice, and pineapple chunks and mushrooms with liquid into chicken in pan; heat to boiling.
5. Stir in cornstarch mixture and salt; cook, stirring constantly, until sauce boils 3 minutes. Cover; simmer 15 minutes.
6. Stir in peas; arrange cabbage on top. Cover; cook 8 minutes, or until peas and cabbage are tender. Serve over cooked hot rice.

**Dieter's Portion: 1 cup chicken mixture and ½ cup rice—398 calories.**

## SWEET-AND-SOUR CHICKEN

*The Oriental way to diet . . . delicious.*

*Makes 4 servings.*

2 **whole chicken
breasts (about 12
ounces each)**

3 **tablespoons teriyaki
sauce or soy sauce**

1 **tablespoon vegetable
oil**

2 **medium-size yellow
squash, trimmed and
sliced**

1 **package (9 ounces)
frozen cut green
beans, thawed**

2 **cups water**

2 **tablespoons lemon
juice**

1 **can (8½ ounces)
diet-pack pineapple
tidbits**

2 **tablespoons corn-
starch**

1 **can (6 ounces) water
chestnuts, sliced**

**Granulated or liquid
low-calorie sweetener**

1. Pull skin from chicken breasts, cut meat from bones; cut into thin strips.

2. Marinate chicken with teriyaki sauce or soy sauce in a bowl for 15 minutes.

3. Heat oil in a large skillet; remove chicken from sauce; brown quickly in hot oil. Add yellow squash and green beans. Sauté, stirring gently, 3 minutes, or just until shiny-moist. Add remaining teriyaki sauce or soy sauce, water, lemon juice; cover; steam 5 minutes.

4. While vegetables steam, drain liquid from pineapple into small cup; stir in cornstarch to make a smooth paste.

5. Add pineapple tidbits and sliced water chestnuts to skillet; heat just to boiling. Stir in cornstarch mixture; cook, stirring constantly, until mixture thickens and bubbles 3 minutes. Stir in your favorite low-calorie sweetener, using the equivalent of 1 tablespoon sugar. Serve with Chinese noodles, if you wish (70 calories per ⅓ cup).

**Dieter's Portion: ½ chicken breast and ¼ of all other ingredients—306 calories.**

# BARBECUE CHICKEN

*Broiled chicken with a flavorful basting sauce.*

*Makes 4 servings.*

1 broiler-fryer (2½ pounds), cut up

1 can (about 5 ounces) tomato juice (¾ cup)

1 small onion, grated (¼ cup)

2 tablespoons tarragon vinegar

1 tablespoon prepared mustard

1 tablespoon Worcestershire sauce

½ teaspoon salt

¼ teaspoon pepper

Granulated or liquid low-calorie sweetener

1. Preheat broiler.
2. Place chicken, skin side down, in a single layer on rack in broiler pan.
3. Combine tomato juice, onion, vinegar, mustard, Worcestershire sauce, salt, pepper and your favorite low-calorie sweetener, using the equivalent of 1 tablespoon sugar, in a small bowl. Brush some over chicken.
4. Place broiler pan about 8 inches from heat. Broil, basting often with sauce, 20 minutes; turn skin side up. Continue broiling, basting often with sauce, 20 minutes longer, or until chicken is richly browned and tender.
5. Serve with cooked rice, if you wish (92 calories per ½ cup serving).

**Dieter's Portion: ¼ of chicken—259 calories.**

# CALICO CHICKEN FRICASSEE

*Simmered chicken with a creamy gravy.*

*Makes 4 servings.*

| | |
|---|---|
| 1 broiler-fryer (2 pounds), cut up | 2 teaspoons salt |
| 1 pound carrots, diagonally cut (about 2 cups) | 1 teaspoon leaf sage, crumbled |
| 1 large onion, chopped (1 cup) | 1 cup frozen peas (from plastic bag) |
| 1 cup thin-sliced celery | 2 tablespoons flour |
| 1 cup hot water | ½ cup skim milk |
| 1 envelope instant chicken broth OR 1 teaspoon granulated chicken bouillon | 2 tablespoons chopped parsley |

1. Place chicken pieces skin side down in a large skillet over *very low* heat. (Do not add fat.) Cook until chicken is a rich brown on skin side, about 10 minutes; turn and brown on other side.

2. Add carrots, onion and celery to skillet; toss to coat with drippings from chicken. Cook and stir 10 minutes.

3. Add hot water, instant chicken broth, salt and sage; mix well; return chicken; cover; simmer 10 minutes; add peas, simmer another 10 minutes, or until chicken and vegetables are tender. Remove chicken; keep warm.

4. Mix flour and skim milk to a smooth paste in a small bowl; stir into vegetables; heat to bubbling, stirring constantly. Cook 1 minute, or until thickened and bubbly. Stir in parsley; spoon onto serving dish; top with chicken.

**Dieter's Portion:** ¼ of chicken—306 calories.

## SLIM-JIM HAWAIIAN CHICKEN

*Cooked to a turn in a zippy soy-and-onion sauce. No fat needed.*

*Bake at 350° for 1½ hours.*
*Makes 6 servings.*

3 small broiler-fryers (about 1½ pounds each)
1 small onion, chopped (¼ cup)
¼ cup soy sauce
1½ cups water
6 slices diet-pack pineapple (from a 1-pound, 4-ounce can)
2 tablespoons chopped parsley

1. Arrange split chickens, skin side down, in a large shallow baking pan. Mix onion, soy sauce and water in a small bowl; pour over chicken.
2. Bake in moderate oven (350°) 45 minutes; turn chicken; bake, basting several times with soy mixture in pan, 45 minutes longer, or until brown and tender.
3. Drain pineapple slices well on paper toweling; roll edge of each in chopped parsley. Serve with chicken.

**Dieter's Portion:** 1 chicken half with 1 pineapple slice—287 calories.

## DEVILED CHICKEN

*Onion and mustard make this a tangy way to diet.*

*Makes 4 servings.*

2 chicken breasts
   (about 14 ounces
   each), halved
½ teaspoon salt
¼ teaspoon paprika
1 medium-size onion,
   peeled and sliced

1 can (about 2 ounces)
   deviled ham
2 tablespoons dry
   white wine
½ teaspoon prepared
   mustard

1. Wash chicken; dry well. Place, skin side down, in a single layer in a large frying pan; sprinkle with salt and paprika. Place onion slices on top; cover tightly. (No need to add any water.)

2. Cook over low heat 30 minutes. Push onion to side of pan; turn chicken.

3. Blend deviled ham, wine and mustard in a cup; spoon over chicken; cover.

4. Cook 20 minutes longer, or until chicken is tender. Place on a heated serving platter; spoon onion and remaining liquid in pan over top.

**Dieter's Portion:** ½ chicken breast and ¼ of the sauce and onion—240 calories.

# ORANGE CHICKEN

*A taste of honey . . . and much more.*

*Bake at 375° for 50 minutes.*
*Makes 4 servings.*

4 chicken legs with thighs (about 8 ounces each)
1 teaspoon salt
1/4 teaspoon pepper
1/4 cup orange juice

1 tablespoon honey
1 teaspoon Worcestershire sauce
1/4 teaspoon dry mustard

1. Place chicken, skin side up, in a single layer in a shallow baking pan; sprinkle with salt and pepper.
2. Bake in moderate oven (375°) 30 minutes.
3. Blend orange juice, honey, Worcestershire sauce and mustard in a cup; brush part over chicken.
4. Continue baking, brushing again with remaining orange mixture, 20 minutes, or until chicken is tender and richly glazed.

**Dieter's Portion: 1 chicken leg with thigh—216 calories.**

# OVEN-BAKED "SOUTHERN FRIED" CHICKEN

*Crisp and crunchy-perfect chicken every time, thanks to an inexpensive easy-do "convenience mix" you make yourself and keep in the pantry to use as needed.*

*Makes 6 servings.*

1/2 cup "Skinny Shake" (recipe follows)

2 broiler-fryers (about 2 1/2 pounds each), cut up

1. Measure out 1/2 cup of "Skinny Shake" mix and put it in a heavy paper bag. Moisten the pieces of

chicken with water and shake them up in the bag, a few pieces at a time.

2. Arrange chicken, skin side up, in a single layer on a non-stick baking pan and bake in a moderate oven (375°) about 45 minutes, adding absolutely no other fats or oils. Don't be alarmed if the chicken seems dry for the first 20 minutes; then the "Skinny Shake" starts to work, and at the end of the baking period, it will be crisp and perfect.

## BASIC "SKINNY SHAKE"

(Recipe makes enough to coat about 20 cut-up chickens or about 30 servings of fish fillets): Empty one 16-ounce container (about 4 cupfuls, dry measure) of bread crumbs into a deep bowl and stir in ½ cupful of vegetable oil with a fork or pastry blender until evenly distributed. Add 1 tablespoon salt, 1 tablespoon paprika, 1 tablespoon celery salt and 1 teaspoon pepper. This is a good seasoning for chicken, fish or chops. Or season it to suit yourself: Onion or garlic powder, sesame or poppy seeds, dried herbs, lemon pepper . . . use your imagination!

**Dieter's Portion: 1/6 of the chicken—244 calories.**

# COQ AU VIN (Chicken With Wine)

*This is Family Circle's method of frying chicken without fat, and using the natural fat from the chicken (calories already counted) to sauté vegetables.*

*Bake at 350° for 30 minutes.*
*Makes 4 servings.*

1 broiler-fryer (2½ pounds), cut up
1 large onion, chopped (1 cup)
1 clove of garlic, minced
1¾ cups water
½ cup dry red wine
1 teaspoon salt
1 teaspoon leaf tarragon, crumbled
1 bay leaf
½ pound small white onions, peeled
2 envelopes instant beef broth or 2 teaspoons granulated beef bouillon
1 pound fresh mushrooms
2 tablespoons flour

1. Place chicken pieces, skin side down, in a large skillet over *very low* heat. (Do not add fat.) Cook slowly until skin side is a rich brown, about 10 minutes; turn and brown other side.

2. Remove chicken from skillet with tongs and place in an 8-cup casserole. Remove 2 tablespoons of the chicken drippings from skillet.

3. Sauté chopped onion and garlic slowly, until soft, in remaining drippings in skillet; stir in 1 cup of the water, red wine, salt, tarragon and bay leaf. Heat to boiling. Pour over chicken in casserole; cover.

4. Bake in a moderate oven (350°) for 30 minutes, or until the chicken is tender.

5. While chicken bakes, return reserved chicken drippings to skillet; brown peeled onions slowly. Leave 6 of the mushrooms whole, for garnish; halve remainder; add all to skillet. Toss to coat with pan drippings.

6. Add instant beef broth and ½ cup boiling water to skillet; cover. Simmer 5 minutes. Remove mush-

rooms with a slotted spoon and reserve. Continue cooking onions, 15 minutes, or until tender and broth has evaporated, leaving a rich brown residue. (Watch carefully lest they scorch.)

7. Place cooked chicken, mushrooms and onions in a heated serving dish. Remove bay leaf. Pour liquid from casserole into skillet. Heat to boiling. Blend flour with ¼ cup cold water to make a smooth paste. Stir flour mixture into boiling liquid in skillet. Continue cooking and stirring until mixture thickens and bubbles 1 minute. Pour over chicken and vegetables. Garnish chicken with whole mushrooms and chopped parsley, if you wish.

**Dieter's Portion:** ¼ of broiler-fryer—339 calories.

## SLICK CHICK

*Each dieter rates a half golden-glazed chicken plus spicy apple stuffing in this too-good-to-be-true roast.*

*Roast at 375° 1½ hours.*
*Makes 4 servings.*

2 small whole broiler-fryers (about 1½ pounds each)
1½ teaspoons salt
1 large onion, chopped (1 cup)
¼ cup water
¼ teaspoon ground coriander

¼ teaspoon curry powder
3 medium-size apples, pared, quartered, cored and chopped
Granulated or liquid no-calorie sweetener
1 teaspoon paprika
½ cup chicken broth

1. Rinse chickens inside and out with cold water; drain, then pat dry. Sprinkle insides with ½ teaspoon of the salt.

2. Simmer onion in water in a medium-size frying pan 5 minutes, or until soft; stir in coriander, curry powder, apples, another ½ teaspoon of the salt and

your favorite no-calorie sweetener, using the equivalent of 1 teaspoon sugar.

3. Cook, stirring often, over medium heat 10 minutes, or until apples are slightly soft. Remove from heat.

4. Stuff neck and body cavities of chickens lightly with apple mixture. Smooth neck skin over stuffing and skewer to back; tie legs to tail with string. Place chickens, side by side, in a roasting pan.

5. Mix remaining ½ teaspoon salt and paprika in cup; sprinkle over chickens.

6. Roast in moderate oven (375°), basting several times with chicken broth, 1½ hours or until drumsticks move easily and meaty part of a thigh feels soft. (If you want to garnish chickens with onions, thread wedges of peeled onion onto dampened wooden picks and insert into chickens for last half hour of cooking time.)

7. Remove chickens to a heated serving platter; cut away strings and remove skewers. Garnish platter with parsley and a few thin apple slices, if you wish. Cut chickens in half, divide stuffing evenly.

**Dieter's Portion: ½ chicken plus half of stuffing from 1 chicken—421 calories. (Crash dieters can omit the stuffing.)**

## NO-FAT FRY WITH ONIONS

*This magic chicken cooks golden brown with no fat, no turning.*

*Makes 4 servings.*

| | |
|---|---|
| 1 broiler-fryer (about 2 pounds), cut in serving-size pieces | ⅛ teaspoon pepper |
| | 2 large onions, sliced |
| 1 teaspoon salt | ½ cup water |

1. Place chicken, skin side down, in a single layer in a large frying pan.

2. Sprinkle with salt and pepper; place onion slices on top; cover tightly. (No need to add any fat.)

3. Cook over low heat 30 minutes. Tilt lid slightly so liquid will evaporate; continue cooking 20 minutes longer, or until chicken is tender and golden.

4. Place chicken on a heated serving platter, pushing onions back into pan; stir in water, mixing with browned bits from bottom of pan; cook until liquid evaporates. Spoon over chicken.

**Dieter's Portion:** ¼ of the chicken and about ¼ cup onions—221 calories.

## PEACHY LOW-CALORIE CHICKEN

*Chicken pieces baked with fruit and a seasoned glaze that add almost no calories.*

*Bake at 400° about 1 hour.*
*Makes 6 servings.*

3 whole chicken breasts, split
3 chicken drumsticks
3 chicken thighs
1 can (about 1 pound) diet-pack cling peach halves
2 tablespoons lemon juice
1 teaspoon soy sauce

1. Arrange chicken pieces in a single layer in shallow baking dish, 12x8x2.

2. Drain peach syrup into a cup (save halves for Step 3). Add lemon juice and soy sauce to syrup; brush about half over chicken.

3. Bake in hot oven (400°), brushing every 15 minutes with remaining peach syrup mixture and pan juices, 1 hour, or until chicken is tender and richly browned. Place peach halves around chicken; brush with pan juices; bake 5 minutes longer to heat peaches.

**Dieter's Portion:** ½ chicken breast, 1 drumstick or thigh, and ½ peach—210 calories.

# CHICKEN TERIYAKI

*An inexpensive calorie-counter's delight.*

*Makes 6 servings.*

6 chicken breasts
(about 6 ounces
each), split
½ cup lemon juice
¼ cup water

3 tablespoons soy sauce
¼ teaspoon ground
ginger
1 teaspoon garlic salt

1. Marinate chicken breasts in sauce made by combining all other ingredients. After several hours, remove chicken from marinade; reserve marinade.
2. Barbecue chicken about 30 minutes, or until tender, on the hibachi or under your broiler; baste frequently with marinade.

**Dieter's Portion: 1 breast—159 calories.**

## Chapter 16

# Leftovers: Planned
# and Unplanned

Your intentions were good when you carefully wrapped that leftover chicken and placed it in the refrigerator 2 days ago. You had planned to use it, but when it came right down to it, you couldn't think how. Now, here you are again, throwing it out for lack of a good recipe. Stop! Before you discard one more piece of chicken, read this chapter. It has those recipes you've been looking for—plus some that will have you planning leftovers on purpose. These planned leftovers show you how to cook two chickens at one time. Use one at once and save the other for one of the recipes in this chapter. By preparing chicken in this way, you'll save on shopping trips, cut down on the use of your stove, and on the time you spend in the kitchen.

Now, go back to the refrigerator and start all over again!

# CHICKEN RISOTTO

*Cooked chicken on hand? Dice the meat and combine with rice in a soy-soup sauce.*

*Bake at 375° for 30 minutes.*
*Makes 4 servings.*

2 tablespoons thinly
    sliced green onion
1 tablespoon butter or
    margarine
1 cup chopped celery
1¼ cups packaged
    precooked rice
1 can condensed cream
    of chicken soup
1½ cups milk
2 tablespoons soy sauce

1½ cups diced cooked
    chicken
1 can (3 or 4 ounces)
    chopped mushrooms,
    drained
1 can or jar (2 ounces)
    pimientos, drained
    and sliced
1 can (3 ounces)
    chow-mein noodles

1. Sauté onion in butter or margarine until soft in a large frying pan; stir in celery and rice; cook 1 minute longer.
2. Stir in the soup, milk, soy sauce, chicken, mushrooms and pimientos; heat to boiling. Spoon into a 7-cup baking dish; cover.
3. Bake in moderate oven (375°) 20 minutes; uncover. Sprinkle noodles over top. Bake 10 minutes longer, or until noodles are hot.

## CHICKEN AMANDINE WITH RICE RING

*A creamy chicken dish topped with almonds.*

*Makes 12 servings.*

3 cups chicken broth (reserved from Simmered Chicken)
3 cups light cream
½ cup butter or margarine
1½ pounds mushrooms, sliced
⅔ cup flour

1½ teaspoons salt
¾ teaspoon liquid red-pepper seasoning
6 cups diced cooked chicken (from Simmered Chicken)
½ cup toasted slivered almonds

1. Combine chicken broth and cream; reserve. Melt butter or margarine over low heat. Add mushrooms and cook, stirring occasionally, 10 minutes. Add flour; stir to a paste.

2. Add chicken broth mixture. Cook, stirring constantly, until mixture thickens and comes to a boil.

3. Stir in salt, red-pepper seasoning, chicken; heat to serving temperature. Turn into Rice Ring; sprinkle with almonds.

## SIMMERED CHICKEN

3 broiler-fryers (2½ pounds each), whole or cut in serving-size pieces
4 cups water
3 small onions

6 celery tops
3 bay leaves
2 teaspoons monosodium glutamate
2 teaspoons salt

1. Put chicken in large kettle with tight-fitting lid. Add water and remaining ingredients; cover. Bring to a boil; reduce heat and simmer 1 hour, or until tender.

2. Remove from heat; strain stock and reserve. Remove meat from bones in as large pieces as possible.

## RICE RING

Press 12 cups hot cooked rice into 12-cup ring mold.
Turn out on large platter.

## PAGODA CHICKEN BOWL

*Here is a delightful cold version of popular chicken and
noodles.*

*Makes 4 servings.*

1 package (6 ounces)
noodles with chicken
sauce mix and
almonds

1 can (about 9 ounces)
pineapple tidbits,
drained

1 cup sliced celery

2 cups cubed, cooked
chicken OR 2 cans
(5 or 6 ounces)
diced cooked chicken

⅓ cup mayonnaise or
salad dressing

¼ cup milk

¼ teaspoon curry
powder

Boston lettuce

Radish slices

1. Prepare noodles with chicken sauce mix, following label directions for top-range method; set almonds aside for Step 3. Spoon noodle mixture into a medium-size bowl; stirring lightly several times at room temperature.

2. Set aside several pineapple tidbits and celery slices for a garnish; stir remaining with chicken into noodle mixture. Blend mayonnaise or salad dressing, milk and curry powder in a cup; fold into noodle mixture. Chill at least 30 minutes to season.

3. When ready to serve, spoon into a lettuce-lined salad bowl; sprinkle with saved almonds on top. Garnish with rows of radish slices, and saved pineapple and celery threaded onto a wooden pick.

## CHICKEN CROQUETTES

*When you go to a little trouble with leftover meat, it becomes a whole new dish.*

*Makes 8 croquettes.*

2 cups coarsely ground cooked chicken
1 cup (about 2 slices) soft bread crumbs
2 eggs, well beaten
2 tablespoons plus ½ cup milk
1 tablespoon minced onion
1 tablespoon minced green pepper
½ teaspoon salt
¼ teaspoon savory
Dash of pepper
¼ cup finely chopped, blanched, toasted almonds
½ cup fine dry bread crumbs
Melted shortening, lard or salad oil to make a 3-inch depth in kettle
Velouté Sauce

1. Combine chicken, soft bread crumbs, eggs, 2 tablespoons milk, onion, green pepper, salt, savory, pepper and almonds in medium-size bowl; chill about 2 hours.
2. Shape into 8 cylindrical croquettes, each 1 inch in diameter; roll in fine dry bread crumbs; dip in ½ cup milk; roll again in crumbs; brush off loose crumbs.
3. Heat fat in deep heavy kettle to 365° or 375° (a 1-inch cube of bread will brown in about 1 minute).
4. Fry croquettes, 2 or 3 at a time, 2 minutes, or until golden-brown; drain on absorbent paper.
5. Serve on a heated platter with Velouté Sauce.

## VELOUTE SAUCE

*Makes 2 cups sauce.*

¼ cup (½ stick) butter or margarine
¼ cup sifted flour
⅛ teaspoon pepper
1 can chicken consommé
¼ cup water
1 teaspoon lemon juice

1. Melt butter or margarine in small saucepan; remove from heat.

2. Blend in flour and pepper; gradually stir in consommé and water.

3. Cook over low heat, stirring constantly, until sauce thickens and boils 1 minute; stir in lemon juice. Serve hot.

# CHICKEN HASH IN RAMEKINS

*The next time you cook chicken, cook 2—serve 1 immediately and save the other to make this oven treat.*

*Bake in 375° oven for 20 minutes.*
*Makes 4 servings.*

| | |
|---|---|
| 2 tablespoons butter or margarine | 2 tablespoons dry sherry (optional) |
| 4 teaspoons flour | 1 tablespoon chopped chives |
| ½ teaspoon salt | |
| 1 teaspoon monosodium glutamate | 2 cups cooked potatoes, diced |
| Dash pepper | 2 cups cooked chicken, cut up |
| Dash paprika | |
| 1 cup light cream | ½ cup buttered soft bread crumbs |

1. Melt butter or margarine in a saucepan; blend in flour, salt, monosodium glutamate, pepper and paprika.

2. Gradually add cream and cook, stirring constantly, until mixture thickens and comes to a boil. Remove from heat; stir in sherry and chives.

3. Add potatoes and chicken; mix well. Spoon into 4 ramekins. Top with buttered crumbs. Bake in moderate oven (375°) 20 minutes, or until heated through.

# CHICKEN SLICES WITH SUPREME SAUCE

*Tasty sauce goes over slices of cooked chicken in two layers; then you can pop the whole thing under the broiler to puff and brown.*

*Makes 4 servings.*

**4 servings of sliced
    cooked chicken
Supreme Sauce**

1. Arrange chicken slices on broilerproof platter.
2. Spoon Supreme Sauce over in two layers as directed in sauce recipe.
3. Broil, about 4 inches from flame, for 3 to 5 minutes, or until sauce puffs and browns. Serve at once.

## SUPREME SAUCE

*Makes about 2½ cups.*

| | |
|---|---|
| 1 tablespoon finely chopped onion | 1 chicken bouillon cube |
| 5 tablespoons butter or margarine | 2 cups milk |
| 5 tablespoons flour | 4 tablespoons grated Parmesan cheese |
| ½ teaspoon salt | 2 tablespoons cream for whipping |
| ⅛ teaspoon pepper | |

1. Sauté onion in butter or margarine just until soft in a small heavy saucepan; stir in flour, salt and pepper; cook, stirring all the time, over low heat, just until mixture bubbles; add bouillon cube.
2. Stir in milk slowly; continue cooking and stirring until bouillon cube dissolves and sauce thickens and boils 1 minute. Stir in 2 tablespoons of the cheese. (Set remaining cheese aside for Step 4.)
3. Measure out ½ cup sauce and set aside for next step; spoon remaining over chicken slices on platter.

4. Beat cream until stiff in a small bowl; fold into saved ½ cup sauce; spoon over first layer of sauce on chicken slices. Sprinkle with the saved 2 tablespoons of Parmesan cheese.

# CHICKEN-FRANKFURTER JAMBALAYA

*This version of a Southern specialty goes from skillet to table in about 40 minutes.*

*Makes 6 servings.*

8 frankfurters, sliced ¼ inch thick
1½ cups uncooked rice
2 tablespoons butter or margarine
2 cans (about 1 pound each) stewed tomatoes

1½ cups water
1½ teaspoons garlic salt
2 cups diced cooked chicken OR 2 cans (5 or 6 ounces each) boned chicken, diced
¼ cup diced green pepper

1. Sauté frankfurters and rice in butter or margarine in a large frying pan, stirring often, until rice is golden.
2. Stir in tomatoes, water and the garlic salt; place chicken on top; cover.
3. Simmer, stirring once, 30 minutes, or until rice is tender and liquid is absorbed.
4. Spoon into a serving bowl; sprinkle with green pepper.

## CURRIED CHICKEN LEFTOVER

*This one is a whole meal in itself. Almonds and apple add texture.*

*Makes 4 servings.*

¾ cup precooked rice
½ cup chopped red apple
1 cup diced cooked chicken OR 1 can (5 or 6 ounces) boned chicken. diced
¼ cup toasted slivered almonds
1½ teaspoons grated onion

⅓ cup mayonnaise or salad dressing
2 tablespoons cream
1 tablespoon lemon juice
½ teaspoon curry powder
¼ teaspoon salt
¼ teaspoon sugar

1. Cook rice in a small saucepan, following label directions; cool to room temperature. Combine with apple, chicken, almonds and onion in a medium-size bowl.
2. Blend remaining ingredients in a cup; stir into rice mixture: chill. Just before serving, garnish with red apple slices, if you wish.

## ALL-IN-ONE CHICKEN DINNER

*An economical way to feed a family well with only a few cups of cooked chicken on hand.*

*Makes 6 servings.*

2  cups chicken stock, broth or bouillon
12  small white onions (½ pound)
6  medium-size carrots, cut in 2-inch pieces
1  package frozen lima beans
½  cup chicken fat, butter or margarine
½  cup flour
1  teaspoon thyme
1  teaspoon salt
⅛  teaspoon pepper
1  teaspoon Worcestershire sauce
2  cups milk
3  cups cooked chicken (boiled, broiled or roasted), cut into large pieces
Cranberry Biscuits

1. Put chicken stock in a kettle and bring to boiling; add the onions, carrots and lima beans; reheat to boiling, cook 15 minutes, or until vegetables are tender.

2. Heat chicken fat, butter or margarine in large saucepan while vegetables cook; remove from heat.

3. Blend in flour, thyme, salt, pepper and Worcestershire sauce.

4. Drain vegetables, saving stock; save vegetables for Step 6; blend stock into flour mixture; stir in milk.

5. Cook over low heat, stirring constantly, until gravy thickens and boils 1 minute; remove from heat.

6. Stir in chicken and cooked vegetables; set aside while you make Cranberry Biscuits.

7. Reheat chicken mixture over low heat, stirring often to avoid scorching, while biscuits bake.

8. Pour hot chicken mixture into heated serving dish as soon as biscuits are done; top with biscuits; serve at once.

## CRANBERRY BISCUITS

*Bake at 450° for 10 to 15 minutes.*
*Makes 6 large biscuits.*

2 cups biscuit mix
⅔ cup milk

About 6 tablespoons
    canned whole-cran-
    berry sauce

1. Blend biscuit mix and milk with fork in medium-size bowl just until dry ingredients are dampened.
2. Drop in 6 mounds onto buttered cooky sheet; make a depression on top of each mound of dough with back of teaspoon.
3. Bake in hot oven (450°) 10 to 15 minutes, or until biscuits are golden-brown.
4. Fill depressions in biscuits with cranberry sauce just before serving.

## DOUBLE SALAD JUMBO

*Luscious for luncheon: Seasoned asparagus, carrots and crunchy chicken salad, perched on golden waffles.*

*Makes 6 servings.*

2 cups diced cooked
    chicken OR 2 cans
    (5 or 6 ounces each)
    boned chicken, diced
1½ cups diced celery
1 tablespoon chopped
    parsley
½ teaspoon seasoned
    salt
¼ cup mayonnaise or
    salad dressing

1 can (1 pound) sliced
    carrots, drained
1 can (about 15
    ounces) asparagus
    spears, drained
3 tablespoons bottled
    thin French dressing
12 frozen waffles
Boston lettuce
Pretzel sticks

1. Combine chicken with celery, parsley and seasoned salt in a medium-size bowl; fold in mayonnaise

or salad dressing. Chill at least 30 minutes to blend flavors.

2. Place carrots and asparagus in separate piles in a shallow dish; drizzle French dressing over all. Chill at least 30 minutes to season.

3. Just before serving, toast waffles, following label directions; place 2 on each of 6 serving plates; top each with several leaves of lettuce.

4. Spoon ½ cup chicken salad on one waffle on each plate; arrange carrots and asparagus in bundles on remaining waffles. Garnish each plate generously with pretzel sticks.

*Chapter 17*

# Gravies, Sauces, Glazes

In previous chapters we offer you recipes for some great chicken dishes. Some include recipes for special gravies, sauces and glazes. Others ask you to turn to this chapter for a particular recipe. However, don't be misled. The recipes here are not designed to complement only one chicken dish from another chapter. They're also meant to be used inventively anytime you bake or roast a chicken. As you'll see, they're easy to make . . . contrary to what many people think when it comes to gravies, sauces and glazes. The next time you're thinking chicken, take a look at the recipes in this chapter first. They may change your mind about serving that chicken plain.

## BROWN GRAVY

*Makes 1 cup.*

|  | Thick | Thin |
|---|---|---|
| Fat (from pan meat was cooked in) | 2 tbls. | 1 tbls. |
| Flour | 2 tbls. | 1 tbls. |
| Liquid from cooked meat plus water or stock, if needed | 1 cup | 1 cup |
| Salt and pepper | to taste | to taste |

1. Pour all liquid from pan into measuring cup; skim off fat; return to pan measured amount of fat needed; save liquid.
2. Blend flour and fat in pan.

3. Place pan over low heat; stir, scraping bottom of pan to loosen meat pieces, until fat-flour mixture is richly browned.

4. Remove from heat; stir in liquid.

5. Cook over low heat, stirring constantly, until gravy thickens and boils 1 minute.

6. Season to taste; color with bottled gravy coloring, if you wish; strain.

# CREAM GRAVY

*Makes 2 cups.*

Melt 2 tablespoons chicken fat, butter or margarine in small saucepan; remove from heat. Blend in 2 tablespoons flour; stir in 1 cup light cream and 1 cup chicken broth. Cook until gravy thickens and boils 1 minute.

# MILK GRAVY

*Makes 2 cups.*

| | |
|---|---|
| 2 **tablespoons butter or margarine** | 1 **teaspoon meat-extract paste dissolved in 1 cup hot water** |
| 2 **tablespoons flour** | **Salt and pepper** |
| 1 **cup milk** | |

1. Melt butter or margarine in small saucepan; remove from heat.

2. Blend in flour; stir in milk and meat-extract paste dissolved in hot water.

3. Cook, stirring constantly, until mixture thickens and boils 1 minute; season to taste.

# PAN GRAVY

*Makes 1¼ cups.*

Blend 2 tablespoons drippings from chicken with 2 tablespoons flour, 1 tablespoon brown sugar, and ½ teaspoon salt; stir in 1¼ cups water. Cook until gravy boils 1 minute.

# QUICK CREAM GRAVY

*Makes about 1½ cups.*

Blend ¼ cup evaporated milk into 1 can (10 ounces) chicken gravy in small saucepan. Heat slowly, until bubbly-hot and smooth.

# CREAM GIBLET GRAVY

*Makes about 2½ cups.*

| | |
|---|---|
| Chicken giblets, back and neck | 1 small onion, sliced |
| 1½ cups plus 2 tablespoons water | 2 tablespoons flour |
| | 1 cup evaporated milk |
| | Salt and pepper |

1. Combine giblets (except liver), back, neck, 1½ cups water and onion in pan; cover.
2. Simmer 1 hour. Add liver last 20 minutes.
3. Remove giblets and chicken pieces (reserve broth); cool; dice; save for Step 5.
4. Strain broth, adding water if needed to make 1 cup. Remove broth to saucepan; stir in flour blended with 2 tablespoons water.
5. Cook over low heat, until gravy boils 1 minute; stir in milk and chopped giblets and chicken; season with salt and pepper.

# BARBECUE SAUCE

*Makes 2½ cups.*

2 cans (8 ounces each)
  tomato sauce
1 medium-size onion,
  chopped (½ cup)
1 clove garlic, minced
¼ cup soy sauce

2 tablespoons sugar
1 teaspoon dry
  mustard
⅛ teaspoon cayenne
  pepper

Mix all ingredients in a medium-size bowl.

# PLUM SAUCE

*Makes about 1 cup.*

1 cup plum jam
1 tablespoon cider
  vinegar
1 teaspoon grated
  onion

½ teaspoon ground
  allspice
¼ teaspoon ground
  ginger

Combine all ingredients in a saucepan; heat slowly,
stirring constantly, to boiling. Cool.

# HAWAIIAN BARBECUE SAUCE

*Makes 1¾ cups.*

1 cup pineapple juice
¼ cup soy sauce
¼ cup vinegar
¼ cup salad oil

½ teaspoon ground
  ginger
1 tablespoon sugar

1. Combine ingredients well.
2. Brush on broiler-fryer halves or quarters frequently until they are done.

## MORNAY SAUCE

*Makes about 1¼ cups.*

| | |
|---|---|
| 2 tablespoons butter or margarine | ¾ cup grated sharp Cheddar cheese |
| 2 tablespoons flour | ½ teaspoon prepared mustard |
| ½ teaspoon salt | |
| ⅛ teaspoon pepper | ½ teaspoon Worcestershire sauce |
| ½ cup milk | |
| ½ cup chicken stock | 1 tablespoon chopped parsley |

1. Melt butter or margarine in small saucepan; remove from heat.
2. Blend in flour, salt and pepper; stir in milk and chicken stock.
3. Cook over low heat, stirring constantly, until sauce thickens and boils 1 minute.
4. Add cheese, mustard and Worcestershire sauce; continue cooking, stirring occasionally, until cheese melts; remove from heat.
5. Stir in parsley. Serve hot.

## DARK CHERRY SAUCE

*Makes about 2 cups.*

| | |
|---|---|
| 1 can (1 pound) pitted dark sweet cherries | 1 tablespoon molasses |
| 2 tablespoons cornstarch | Few drops red-pepper seasoning |
| 1 tablespoon prepared mustard | Dash of salt |
| | 3 tablespoons lemon juice |

1. Drain syrup from cherries into a 2-cup measure; add water to make 1½ cups.
2. Blend a few tablespoons syrup into cornstarch until smooth in a small saucepan; stir in remaining syrup, mustard, molasses, red-pepper seasoning and

salt. Cook over low heat, stirring constantly, until mixture thickens and boils 3 minutes.

3. Stir in cherries and lemon juice; heat slowly just until bubbly. Serve hot.

## DOUBLE ORANGE GLAZE

*Makes about ¾ cup.*

Combine ½ cup thawed frozen concentrated orange juice (from a 6-ounce can), ¼ cup orange marmalade and 2 tablespoons bottled meat sauce in a small saucepan. Heat slowly, stirring constantly, until marmalade melts and mixture is blended; remove from heat.

## GOLDEN PINEAPPLE GLAZE

*Makes about ¾ cup.*

Combine ¼ cup pineapple syrup, ¼ cup orange juice, 2 tablespoons bottled meat sauce, 1 tablespoon melted butter.

## GINGER-HONEY GLAZE

*Makes about ¾ cup.*

Combine ½ cup soy sauce, 6 tablespoons honey and 2 teaspoons ground ginger in small saucepan. Heat, stirring constantly, just to boiling.

# Index

285

# The MS READ-a-thon needs young readers!

Boys and girls between 6 and 14 can join the MS READ-a-thon and help find a cure for Multiple Sclerosis by reading books. And they get two rewards — the enjoyment of reading, and the great feeling that comes from helping others.

For complete information call your local MS chapter, or call toll-free (800) 243-6000. Or mail the coupon below.

# Kids can help, too!

# BALLANTINE
# HAS YOU IN MIND

# Bestsellers from BALLANTINE